Cover Image is a photo that shows an x-ray of the Lara Easting's right lower leg after the surgeon stabilized the bone fragments but before reconstructing her leg.

INTO THE
F O G

THIS CAN'T BE GOD'S PLAN!

Lara Easting, RN

iUniverse®

INTO THE FOG
THIS CAN'T BE GOD'S PLAN!

iUniverse books may be ordered through booksellers or by contacting:

iUniverse
1663 Liberty Drive
Bloomington, IN 47403
www.iuniverse.com
1-800-Authors (1-800-288-4677)

ISBN: 978-1-5320-3462-6 (sc)
ISBN: 978-1-5320-3463-3 (e)

Library of Congress Control Number: 2017915305

Print information available on the last page.

iUniverse rev. date: 10/12/2017

To Dave and Phillip, Ann and Jeannette,
To my extraordinary surgeons, physicians,
nurses, technicians, physical therapists, and healers.
To Tamara and all the rest of my angels.

FOREWORD

When the call came from the Emergency Room that fateful September evening, it seemed at first ridiculous. Impossible. Even comical. "What?!? Hit by a tree? It just fell right on top of her? You've got to be joking!" But as the hours progressed into days, months, and years – the event passed from unbelievable to unforgettable to undeniably divine. "How could such a freak thing happen?" became "Why did God allow this to happen?" became "Praise God."

As orthopedic surgeons, we see the entire spectrum of human existence. Rich, poor, old, young, sick, healthy – they all usually have some sort of musculoskeletal issue at some point. Sometimes they suffer from the arthritis that plagues joints after decades of overuse, coming to us for joint replacements. Sometimes they enter into this world with the challenges of a congenital limb deformity. Sometimes they reap the consequences of poor decisions, arriving in our trauma bay with injuries that never should have happened. Indeed, trauma is not a random disease. Alcohol, drug use, risk-taking behavior – they all seem to play in to the "accidents" that bring us to work in the wee hours of the morning. Trauma becomes predictable, even if not preventable.

And then there are the cases that break our hearts. Horrible things that occur for no reason. With no pattern. With no warning. To people who did nothing wrong – other than to stand in the wrong spot in the forest, where a dead tree would change their life forever.

As we care for patients like Lara, we often find ourselves struggling with existential questions – even though all the while we keep up an objective, professional facade. We hide behind big "doctor words" while we rage against God internally. "Why her, Lord? She did nothing to deserve this!" We can justify in our minds the drunk driver who breaks his leg in a car crash. We can accept the gunshot wound to the arm of the gang-banger. But the world-altering injuries that explode into an innocent situation give us pause. Fear whispers quietly, "This could happen to YOU."

Many times, I find myself wondering how anyone could function in the world of trauma care without following one of two roads. One road leads to a disconnectedness, wherein we shed our souls to become robotic automatons, isolating ourselves from the questions that underlie the events we see. We view trauma in animalistic terms, removing the humanity – and certainly the divinity-- of the situation. We say "oh well," and move on to the next patient, the next injury. We become callous. Bitter. Dead.

For me, the other road leads to the Cross, where I fall on my knees. I submit to the will of a God who is bigger than me. Than my medical knowledge. Than my trained surgical hands. Than anything that can roll through the doors of my emergency room. This other road leads to the understanding that our Lord does indeed have a higher purpose for the horrible things that happen in our lives. He alone can turn evil into good, injury into healing, and despair into hope.

As you read *Into the Fog*, I hope you will see that it is more than Lara's story. It is more than Dave and Pierce's story. It is more than my story and that of my team.

It is God's story.

For those of us in health care, this book is a sobering reminder that the smallest comments or actions can either lift or crush a patient's spirit. That the simplest gesture – requiring no effort on our part–becomes the ray of hope in the darkness to which a patient so desperately clings. We are reminded that we are not just doing our jobs. No. We are wielding the power of much greater things.

I consider it one of the great honors of my career to have been involved in Lara's care. Her injuries were some of the worst I have ever seen, and her recovery has been nothing short of miraculous. But it is not her bones and her body that inspire. It is her soul. Watching the transformation of her attitude and her spirit was like watching the morning sun rise over the ocean. From a great depth, a blinding light emerges.

Enjoy the sunshine.

Dr. Marlin Bolling, MD

PREFACE

"What are you doing?" my doctor asked, a quizzical look crossing his face as he watched me struggling to scrawl letters with a dull pencil on a small scrap of paper.

"I'm making notes," I replied, squinting up at him from my hospital bed. "I'm thinking of writing about this strange experience when I go home, and I don't want to forget anything."

"You definitely should write a book," he said. "I've never known another patient who lived after injuries like yours. You need to tell all of us in the medical field what it's like to be a critically injured patient in the Trauma Unit, especially since you're one of us. We really don't know."

From what I'd experienced, he was right. Often my nurses and doctors didn't seem to have a clue. Before the tree fell on me, I didn't either. A few didn't get that sometimes we "unconscious" patients could hear them. That we desperately craved their comfort and reassurance and needed hope. In my early days in the ICUs, I remember only a handful of nurses giving it to me. In fairness, the rest probably thought I was just too out of it to benefit much from their words.

But that wasn't true. When my nurses didn't talk to me, I filled in their silence with fear, sometimes imagining they didn't care or, worse, thought I was too far gone to bother with.

Weeks later after they sent me home, despite my doctor prodding me to write, all I wanted to do was forget. I couldn't wait to get strong enough to get out of the wheelchair and back to my old life again. Yet something I couldn't fully comprehend kept nudging me to record what had happened. Even when I could barely hold a pencil, the motivation to do so had been strong. Why?

Would writing be God's way of purging my demons? Would it help me make sense of all the strange and powerful things I'd witnessed in the hospitals? Would it keep me sane during my long months of recovery at home?

Would telling my story convince nurses, technicians, and doctors everywhere just how important a few reassuring words could be for their patients? Would it persuade them that even the smallest loving gesture held the power to make their patients fight when they'd been tempted to give up?

In the hospital, I'd witnessed firsthand the amazing power of Jesus' love. I saw that without hope, absolutely nothing could heal, and with it, everything became possible. Once home, I wanted to share that hope with everyone who'd suffered something so painful that they, too, just wanted to forget. Maybe I could, by writing my story.

As I sat remembering the gift of hope and so many others God had given me, I made a promise to sit for a couple of hours each morning at my computer. After that I'd see what happened.

Lara Easting, RN

January, 2010

ACKNOWLEDGEMENTS

This book is dedicated to all those suffering from loss and needing hope.

From the deepest places in my heart, thank you to everyone who answered God's call to share love, support, time, medical skills, prayers, and laughter. You gave me exactly what I needed to heal. I will be forever grateful and always love you.

To everyone who prayed for me, held me in the light, and guided me on my spiritual path.

To all those in my writer's critique group for their relentless and valuable feedback.

To Martha who read my first draft and told me I was "a writer."

To Ken, who, after reading my manuscript and offering suggestions, encouraged me, saying, "Don't worry, it's good."

To Barbara, who patiently and meticulously proofread my story and provided invaluable feedback.

To Phillip, who always knew what to say to encourage and make me laugh.

And to Dave, without whom none of this would have been possible.

To Jesus and the Holy Spirit for showing me in no uncertain terms They are real.

INTRODUCTION

I'd been a nurse for thirty years and never really knew what it was like to be a patient who had to depend on the kindness and care of other nurses.

I'd been a seeker all my life and had never knowingly experienced the presence of God's Spirit.

I'd loved my family and friends deeply, yet hadn't truly known how deeply they loved me.

Then a tree fell. My body and life were shattered and I was driven into the fog. This is the story of that experience, and of all that followed.

PROLOGUE

August 2009

I sat at my desk in the factory nursing clinic and felt it in my bones. A big change was coming. I smiled. But what kind of change would it be?

There was little indication, yet something told me it was going to be good. A greater sense of purpose. A bigger opportunity to help others. A stronger faith in God. These were the kinds of things I hoped for. I did an internal check and felt ready for whatever would come.

TABLE OF CONTENTS

PART ONE

Part One

DISASTER STRIKES

I will never know what possessed me to go into the forest that September afternoon. Rain had stopped falling in the foothills and my feet squished in the wet earth as I ventured into the woods with my family and friends. Sun peeked through the branches as clouds cleared to the west and water dripped from the trees. The first chill of fall filled the air.

It was still light as the five of us gathered down the hill below our log house. There, in the center of the woods, a natural tunnel occurred between the rows of big pine trees, creating a perfect setting for a shooting range. At the end of the tunnel in the side of the hill, Pierce, my son and Dave, my husband had built a target. The pines had grown large in that area with generous spacing between them and the forest floor clear of underbrush. A light haze shrouded the trees. "A spooky old pine forest" was how Dave's mother had once described that section of our property. Though it wasn't cold, I shivered.

Perry, my son Pierce's instructor from the police academy, offered me his twenty-two pistol. With little fanfare, I pushed in my ear plugs, walked to the firing line, and took aim. My arms shook as I tried to line up the sights. I emptied the magazine into the target with average results and trudged over to the side of the clearing, standing well under the trees to watch. I kept my ear plugs in for good measure. As I leaned against a big tree for support, I noted the stark outline of a dead pine thirty or forty feet away in the woods. I studied it for only a moment, before shifting my gaze back to the others.

Frances, Perry's wife, lined up her sights and fired. I noticed that while I tended to flinch, Frances didn't. Her cluster of holes formed a nice neat group in the middle of the target. She wandered over to join me, stopping only a few feet away to put up her pistol.

Perry took his position on the shooting line next. He had the practiced look of someone who'd done it a thousand times and it didn't surprise me when his first shots found their mark. I was making a mental note to emulate him, when something caught my eye. I glanced up. What looked like two massive bone colored wings were plummeting toward me. The "wings" struck me in the forehead so hard, the sound and lights went out.

I awoke on my side. The smell of dirt and blood filled my nostrils. The woods, so silent a moment before, hummed with sound. A huge tree trunk lay before me. Through blood, I could just make out the tangle of bare branches overhead. I tried to make sense of what happened. *Something knocked me out. A tree?*

I lay awkwardly, but in little pain. A pleasant numbness enveloped me. Light filtered through the trees in muted patterns, and shadows etched the ground. I looked toward my feet. My breath caught. Below the knee, my leg bent sideways and twisted horribly, so the grey sole of my shoe faced me. Shivering violently, I tried not to vomit.

With great effort I raised my head. The world lurched off kilter and righted itself. I blinked to make certain what I saw was real. My lower limb was still there, but barely. It looked mostly severed from my leg, yet the sight of it didn't bother me nearly as much as I knew it should.

I must be in shock.

No narcotic could have killed the pain so well. I looked back down at my leg, and my stomach gave a sickening lurch.

"This isn't good," I muttered, as if I were assessing an injury at the factory.

People were shouting. I heard Dave, Pierce, and Perry. I struggled to sit up, but couldn't. Someone was grabbing me from behind and pinning me down.

Why won't they help me?

Pierce darted into view and squatted on the ground facing me.

His gaze locked on mine. "You're going to be okay, Mom. I'm going to get you some help."

As I glanced down at the mangled leg, I couldn't see how anything would ever be *okay* again. "But, how will I go to work?" I stammered, thinking about the factory workers I'd scheduled to give flu shots and hearing tests on Monday.

"Don't worry about work right now. We'll deal with it later." Pierce's sentences came out in little bursts between gasps, like gun fire. Then he shouted to someone behind me and sprinted off. Despite his encouraging tone, I sensed fear.

I tried to pull myself together. *If I can just get up, I'll be all right.*

Having a plan made me feel better. I couldn't stand on the crooked leg, so I'd have to balance on the other. I struggled to pull that foot from under the branches. It seemed to be stuck. I tried to yank it free with little jerking motions. "I've got to get it loose. I've got to get it loose," I repeated, growing agitated.

Pierce reappeared. "Help me stand up," I pleaded.

Pierce didn't return my gaze. He seemed to be listening to the person behind me. Panic took hold of me. "This can't be happening," I mumbled, shaking my head.

My body trembled. I willed myself to control its shaking, but couldn't. For the first time I noticed the ground felt cold and soggy through my clothes. I tasted blood and felt sick.

"Mom, don't worry, the paramedics will be here soon." Pierce spoke each word with exaggerated calm. As a nurse, I knew what he was trying to do. We'd often talked about how important it was to keep an injured person from going into shock. Yet despite seeing through his ploy, the words soothed me.

Thank goodness someone's taking charge. My own thoughts felt slow and jumbled.

I heard Dave behind me. "Lara, just lie still. Don't move. The EMTs are coming." His voice sounded tense.

The light in the woods had faded into shades of grey when the unmistakable sound of ambulance sirens pierced the twilight. Lights pulsed through the trees. The shrieking grew louder until it stopped below us on the road. In seconds, voices I didn't recognize filled the quiet woods. They moved closer until they stopped over my head. I didn't bother to look up.

Without warning, chain saws screamed in the dim light. Vague forms moved around me and bent over the dead pine. Clouds of sawdust engulfed my face. Dave kneeled in close beside me. He threw a towel over our heads to protect us from the dust that swirled through the air. I could feel his breath on my face. His nearness comforted me. In an instant, I felt the tree move. Frances yelled.

Oh, my God, Frances is under the tree. In a flash, I understood the terrible truth. But what happened to Frances after that, I didn't know.

Pain slammed me with the force of a freight train. I heard myself screaming. I screamed till I ran out of air. "Stop," I wanted to shout. "What are you doing?"

"Hang on, Mom." Pierce held my hands and was squeezing them tightly.

The agony stopped. My body went limp. A paramedic moved toward me with a stiff neck-collar. He tried to fasten it around my neck. I felt the hard plastic against my larynx. *I'm going to vomit.*

"I'm an RN and my neck's fine." I asserted as forcefully as I could.

"Then you know why I've got to put this on." His tone was emphatic.

I knew he was right.

He finished securing the brace and strapped me onto a stretcher.

"One, two, three," he shouted as he and another man hoisted my gurney into the back of the ambulance. Once inside, I glanced toward my feet. My right leg was now straight and lying parallel to the left.

How on earth did he do that?

As a nurse I knew I would never have attempted to straighten a limb so obviously fractured. Nonetheless, relief flooded me to see my legs side by side, back where they belonged.

"Mom, I'm up here." Pierce spoke from the front seat of the ambulance. "Dad's going with Perry in the truck."

"Okay," I tried to say, but my jaw had stopped working. I nodded as best I could in the general direction of his voice to show him I was all right. My body felt weighted to the stretcher.

"How do you feel?" the paramedic asked.

"Good," I mumbled, fading.

The g force hit me as the ambulance zoomed down the road. Lights pulsed and sirens shrieked in the darkness.

"Take her to Regional Medical as fast as you can. It's the closest trauma center," the paramedic shouted to the driver from his seat next to my stretcher. His were the last words I heard.

Dead Pine Tree that fell on the author in late 2009.

PIERCE TELLS HIS VERSION

Crack! The unmistakable sound of a tree splintering jolted me. The dead tree cracked just a foot from the ground and as it fell, it split again midway up. I lunged forward just as the big trunk shook the ground and wind gusted in its wake. Two heavy top sections landed on either side of me. I stood, riveted to the spot. *I'm okay.* Cold beads of sweat dripped from my brow.

Through the branches I could just make out what remained of a dead pine. It was pale in color and jagged spikes three feet in length jutted all along its trunk.

"Oh God, Oh God, Oh God!" I heard my father yelling. A chill ran down my spine.

I bolted in the direction of his voice to where I found him squatting on the ground. There, beside the trunk of the tree, was Mom. Her gaze was fixed at the sky as she lay without moving. Was she alive?

I scanned down her body and saw the right leg first. It jutted sideways at the knee. Ragged pieces of muscle, ligament, and bone stuck out in all directions. On her left ankle, the rounded end of a bone poked through her ankle and her foot dangled by a few pieces of tissue. I strained to breathe, but my chest felt tight.

A moment later Mom came to, mumbling and thrashing around on her side. I felt sick at the sight of her. Dad held her head in his hands and strained to apply pressure to slow the river of blood that flooded her face. I tried not to recoil when I saw that one eye had no lid.

"Call 911!" Dad yelled.

"Give me your cell," I shouted back, my heart pounding. My father threw his phone at me.

Calm down, Pierce. I needed to compose my thoughts to communicate our location to the dispatcher.

"Yes, what is your emergency?" she asked in a calm voice.

"My mother's been hit by a tree and she's badly hurt," I said as clearly as I could.

"Where's her car located?"

"There's no car. She wasn't in a car. She was in the woods and a tree fell on her."

"A tree?"

"That's right. She was hit by a tree." My heart raced.

I continued to answer questions and explain what I could see of Mom's injuries. I hung up and knelt down to support her left leg and foot in my lap. I felt stupid but didn't know what else to do.

As I looked at her pitiful form, she turned her face toward mine, her brow drawn into a deep furrow. "How am I going to work like this?" she murmured, searching my face.

It was ironic that despite her horrendous injuries all she was worrying about was not being able to go to work. *She doesn't have a clue how bad off she is.*

"Mom, don't think about that right now." I forced my face to assume a relaxed expression.

Perry rounded the tree. He stared down at Mom in disbelief before looking up at me. Our eyes met. It was a few seconds before he spoke. "Lara, your injuries don't look all that bad." I forced myself not to look at my mother. I didn't want her to see the truth in my eyes.

Perry grabbed my elbow and pulled me aside. "Frances' foot is pinned under the tree," he whispered. It was the first time I'd realized that she was hurt. I followed him back to the other side of the trunk where his wife slumped sideways against it. "My ankle's stuck," she said in a dreamy voice.

Perry and I tried to dig around her foot to take some pressure off it, but the ground was too hard and rocky under the pine straw. "This isn't working." Perry said, breathing hard. "Maybe we could use a board to lift the trunk." We rested a moment to catch our breaths.

"Or a jack," I said. A silent understanding passed between us.

"I'll be right back. Don't move." Perry shouted at Frances, who nodded.

Perry was jogging up the hill to get a board from Dad's workshop when I passed him on the drive. We panted in time to our steps.

"I saw a lot of terrible injuries in Vietnam and on the police force, but none of that prepared me for what I've seen today. How in *hell* did this happen?" Perry gasped.

"I don't know," I said shaking my head. Once in the house, I snatched a couple of towels off the rack in the bathroom and ran into the workshop to locate Dad's heavy automotive jack. I dragged it out the door and lumbered down the drive, pulling it behind me.

As I turned into the woods, the jack plowed a deep trench in the dirt. My heart pounded. Already back at the tree ahead of me, Perry grunted as he strained to pry the heavy trunk off Frances's ankle, using the board as a lever. The tree wouldn't budge. "Here, Perry, try the jack," I shouted and lugged it over to him.

"How on earth did you haul this heavy thing?" Perry asked, looking incredulous.

I parked the jack with Perry, pondering his question, and hurried around the tree. Dad reached out grabbing the towels from my hand.

I stood and stared at the places where Mom's bones poked through her skin. It struck me that her leg wounds weren't bleeding much, when compared with the cuts I could see on her forehead and scalp. I mulled that over for a minute before coming back to my senses. Dad was struggling to wrap the towels around Mom's head when we heard sirens scream.

I jumped up and sprinted through the forest and out onto the road. There I waved my arms over my head until two ambulances stopped right in front of me, lights flashing. In a moment a fire truck and rescue vehicle joined them. I waved the fire truck and one of the ambulances into our driveway, while the rescue vehicle and second ambulance parked on the street. When the men got out, I led all four EMTs and two paramedics, huffing and puffing, through the woods, aided by the wavering beams from their flashlights.

The taller paramedic came to a stop over Mom and quickly sized up the situation. He barked orders at the others. "We need chain saws, stretchers, and back boards. Don't forget the neck collars," he shouted in a voice that boomed.

The EMTs took off at a trot back through the dim woods to the trucks. When they returned, their arms full of equipment, I heard one fellow groan as he dropped his back boards to the ground. Another fired up a chain saw. He began cutting through the tree trunk next to Frances's ankle. I bent my knees and got into position on her other side.

The moment I felt the segment shift as it separated from the rest of the tree, I hoisted my end of the log off Frances. An EMT grabbed her under the arms and pulled her out. I let the log thud to the ground.

"God almighty, that was heavy," I exclaimed, trying to stretch a cramp out of my back.

I hurried around some branches to where a paramedic assessed Mom. *Please, God, let her be okay.*

With help from an EMT, the paramedic rolled her onto her side and cut her jacket and pants legs off with shears for a better look.

Mom, an RN, spoke right up to him. "How bad are they?" Her voice quavered.

"You know your legs are broken, but we're going to get you fixed up." I recognized his feeble attempt to reassure her.

Without another word, he took hold of the twisted part of her right leg with both hands and moved in to straighten it. I squatted and held her hands, squeezing them tightly. "It's okay, Mom." I moved in closer.

She screamed. The reverberation of that sound went right through me and I broke out in a cold sweat. Up until that moment I'd been okay, but with that scream, my legs buckled.

The paramedic and his partner, an EMT, rolled Mom carefully onto a back board and placed foam blocks to stabilize her legs. As the paramedic pushed a neck collar toward her, Mom put up a fight, tucking in her chin. "That'll make me throw up," she said in a hoarse voice.

Mom had always had an irrational fear of vomiting. The paramedic continued to secure the neck brace and bandage her head. "Who do you want to ride with you?" he asked her.

She looked around and spotted me. "Pierce," she said.

"You've got five minutes before we pull out," the EMT hollered at me.

I gathered my strength and ran back up the long drive to the house to get my cell and wallet. I was thoroughly out of breath by the time I walked in the door. Dad was already in the bathroom trying to wash the blood off that covered his arms. His hands trembled. Would he be okay to drive so far alone?

"Be careful, Dad. Take it slow," I shouted as I ran for the door. "I'm going with Mom."

I dashed back down the hill. When I got to the ambulance, the paramedic looked up from Mom. "I've given her some morphine." I nodded at him.

She was quiet now. The EMT motioned me into the front seat. "Mom, I'm up here," I called over my shoulder, wanting to hear her voice.

"Okay," she murmured weakly.

The paramedic, who was riding in the back with Mom, shouted to the driver, "Take her to Regional Med. Go as fast as you can safely go!" The driver stomped hard on the gas and we roared down the road.

"There are a lot of sharp turns around here. If you go too fast, you might go into a ditch or hit a deer," I warned, my heart racing.

"Give me a heads up about the bad curves. But if a deer runs out, I'm not gonna swerve to miss it," he shouted over the roar of the engine.

"Have you ever hit one?"

"A few."

I let that sink in for a minute. "I just went through the police academy," I said, wanting to change the subject.

"Is this the first time you've run with lights and sirens?"

"Yeah," I took a deep breath and leaned back in my seat. Mom wasn't the only one in shock. My legs felt wobbly and my hands trembled. I hoped I wouldn't be sick. Odd thoughts kept popping into my head. I saw Mom wearing her favorite pink nursing scrubs and working in the clinic at the factory. She was deftly wrapping an ace wrap around an injured worker's ankle.

"I'm like a school nurse for big people," she'd told me. "I dress wounds, test hearing, and teach CPR. But more important than all that, I motivate the workers to take better care of themselves." Wincing, I thought of how much she loved her job and how the employees there all trusted and liked her. They'd told me as much when I'd spent my summers during college working in the factories. Now it looked like Mom might never walk again.

My thoughts shifted. Mom's preacher friend, Gerald Ford, was dunking her in a tank full of water and baptizing her.

"Why, Mom?" I'd asked when she came home with her hair still dripping.

"I haven't gone crazy. Just needed to feel closer to God, to know He's really with me."

I thought about what she said and wondered what kind of God would let this happen.

As we rocketed through the darkness, I shut my eyes and tried not to think.

INTO THE FOG

Months later, when I tried to recall my first five days in the ICU at Regional Medical, I felt oddly happy to reflect on them. But when I fast forwarded to the weeks that followed in the much larger hospital a couple hours from us, I wept.

Why did I have such pleasant memories from the first hospital and so many painful ones from the second? I had to know.

But first, I needed to sort reality from delusion. That would be no easy task.

My memories carried me back to the Regional Medical ICU, the first place they took me after the tree collapsed. As a nurse who'd worked hard to educate patients and their families all over that hospital, I'd never liked the feeling I got when I walked into the ICU. The patients there lay still in their cubicles. *Too still.* I forced myself not to look at them as I passed by.

But something fascinated me. *What was it like to be a patient there? Did they feel helpless? Were they scared? Did they think they might die?*

When the tree fell, I got a chance to find out. For the first five days after the accident, I lingered, mostly unconscious, in the same ICU I'd visited as a nurse.

"She probably won't remember much of what happens here," Dr. Bolling, the orthopedic surgeon on call that night had told Dave and Pierce.

In the ICU, I struggled to hold onto life. The doctors and nurses kept me so sedated from narcotics and anesthesia that my husband and son rarely saw me awake. Yet, I did have a few recollections from that place and a profound sense of peace when I thought of them later.

I remembered the hazy forms of Dave, Pierce, and my sister, Hillary, hovering over and comforting me. As I listened to their voices, I was aware of their love as well as their fear.

From what Dave later told me, friends and coworkers flooded in to see me, too, though I seldom remembered. "The nurses at Regional Med often looked the other way to accommodate your many visitors," he said.

I guess they bent the rules because I was a registered nurse and because many who came to visit were nurses, too.

The few visitors I did recall looked like they were trying hard to smile and sounded more cheerful than they probably felt. I suspected that was because I must have looked pretty awful and that they weren't sure I'd make it.

By contrast, I believed I'd be fine. *Why can't they see I'm okay?*

Weeks later, Dave told me my face and body were swollen to twice their normal size and the rest of me looked so black and blue, it appeared as if someone had used me for a punching bag. The right eyelid wouldn't close and stared disturbingly at him from the mangled eye socket. Sutures and scabs decorated my head and ears. No wonder my husband said my appearance shocked all those who came to see me.

I lay in the tiny cubicle, unable to move, drifting in and out of consciousness. I didn't know it then, but the tree had not only shattered my right leg, but torn off my left foot, crushed my spine, and mangled my eyelid, scalp, ear, nose, and face.

A friend at the factory later told me that his daughter, a respiratory therapist on staff at the hospital, had called him after seeing me that first night. "Get everyone at church to pray for her," she'd told him. "Otherwise, your nurse is not going to make it."

Back in my ICU bed for one brief conscious moment, I considered I might just be stuck in some strange, but lucid dream. *Maybe if I try hard enough, I can wake myself up.*

Straining with everything I had, I struggled to extract myself from the nightmare. Nothing happened. I remained stuck, immobile, broken. I gave up trying to wake up.

In the hospital, I hovered in that twilight state between life and death, floating weightless and cushioned on a cloud of morphine. Despite my compromised mental status I understood that I'd been badly hurt, that I was a patient in the ICU at Regional Med, and that my sister, Hillary, a physician's assistant, was with me. The thought of her being there filled me with peace. I pictured her orchestrating my care with the doctors and nurses and lending loving support to Dave and Pierce.

Though I lay close to death, thoughts of God were all but forgotten. If I considered Him at all, it was only during the one visit I remembered having with friends. That day I awoke to see the hazy outlines of a dozen people lined up in the corridor across from my bed.

I must be the guest of honor at a party.

As if in confirmation, each person crossed the floor in turn to greet me.

"I'm so glad to see you, Lara," Jake, a friend from work leaned in and whispered. 'We all miss you and we're praying for you. You're going to be just fine." A broad smile stretched across his face and I felt his big hand pressing gently on my shoulder.

As he moved in closer, a soft beam, suggesting candle light, illuminated his face. It gave him a celestial quality and shone on the others standing behind him. *They look like angels.* I could just make out Ren, Gerald, MJ, and Jenny from Great Foods Manufacturing, the factory where I worked, and several of the nurses from Regional Med.

Some of the visitors, like Jake, beamed at me. Others dabbed tears from their eyes. But whether they cried or smiled, all emanated a palpable sense of love. Calm washed over me as I gazed at them. Surely it was God's love I saw reflected in their eyes? Had He brought them to comfort me, to remind me He was near?

"Don't worry, I'm okay," I told the ones who cried, falling back into my nursing role to soothe them.

"You really do care about us," whispered MJ, in a rare serious moment.

"Well of course I do," I murmured, surprised she hadn't known.

The scene faded.

One morning that same week, for a brief moment I awoke again and saw Dave standing beside me.

"How're you feeling, Lara? They're getting you ready for surgery."

"I'm okay. I'm over here in Ireland sitting in a pub."

"You're in Ireland, huh?"

"Uh huh, and I'm having such great time I'm not coming back any time soon." That prompted smiles from my husband and son. I still remember how good it felt to sit in that cozy pub. I'd never been to Ireland, but it must have sounded like a lot more fun than having another surgery.

My memories of the nurses who cared for me in the ICU were a little less vivid, but I distinctly remembered one big male nurse named Larry. He was loud and boisterous and acted like he was used to being in charge.

"You need to eat if you're going to heal," he boomed, striding back and forth like a TV evangelist.

Eating a healthy diet was a topic that ordinarily would have spoken to me, given my line of work, but now, even the thought of food made me sick.

From then on, Larry and I locked horns. "I'm going to have to order you a liquid meal in a can if you don't start eating," he barked.

His pronouncement filled me with dread. I knew from experience with hospital patients how sickeningly sweet those concoctions tasted and how they reeked of synthetic vitamins. I panicked, thinking that in his effort to get me to eat, Larry might try to pour the nasty stuff down my throat or insert a nasogastric tube into my nose.

"They have too much sugar. It'll make me throw up." I gave Larry a fierce look.

"Well, you've got to eat something. I tell you what, if you tell me what you like, I'll get it for you."

"I don't know. Maybe some yogurt," I said in a dull tone. Nothing I could think of sounded good. Larry brought in yogurt, an enormous fruit plate, and a big bowl of chicken soup, all things Dave had told him I liked.

I lay there staring at them when they arrived.

Larry looked put out. "How about a cheeseburger from the fast food place down the street?" he offered, looking hopeful. At that moment, as disoriented as I felt, I knew Larry cared.

One evening the big nurse must have grown tired of arguing. He turned his back and marched out of my room. *He's abandoning me.* I yelled after him. "Larry, please come back. Don't leave."

Larry ignored me, but later came back.

"You're gonna make it," he said, giving me a hard look. "You're strong and you're gonna make it."

By the end of that week, after Hillary had flown back to Maine, Dave later told me that Dr. Bolling had given him a choice. "There are only two surgeons I know of who can work with those legs. If she stays here, we'll have to amputate both."

"Whatever we need to do to save her legs," Dave had replied, "let's do it."

Dr. Bolling arranged my transfer to County Hospital. A medical center with a class one trauma unit, County Hospital boasted a higher level of care. Ironically, once I left Regional Medical, my mood turned darker, my thoughts more fearful.

Just five days after the tree fell, two EMTs loaded me into the back of their ambulance to make the three hour long journey to County Hospital. A nurse rode in the back with me. As we bumped along the three of them chatted.

"I'm going to a big party out in the country," one EMT said. "There should be plenty of people there. You guys want to come?"

The EMTs and the nurse proceeded to discuss their plans as if I didn't exist.

Where are they taking me? To a party? Oh my God, they must be kidnapping me.

I pictured a scene from *Deliverance* and panic seized me.

What if I never see my family again?

It didn't occur to me that such a notion was completely absurd;

that no one in their right mind would want to take a critically injured patient to their beer party.

By the time we pulled into the covered entrance to the ER at County Hospital, my heart was pounding in my chest. The paramedics pushed my stretcher into a small room where an Admission Nurse with curly hair like mine hastened over to talk to me. Dave and Pierce sat down to join us. I liked the nurse right away, especially since her style of gathering information involved including me in the conversation. In hindsight I'm sure the only reason she did was to assess my level of consciousness, but, oblivious to her motivation, I joined in the fun.

"Have you had any illnesses over the past several years?" she said, speaking slowly and looking me directly in the eye.

There was little to tell, but I wanted to stay in the conversation, so I searched my memory for something to say. "I had a couple bladder infections a few years ago," I offered.

"Really?" She looked concerned.

"Uh huh, but no serious problems with my urinary tract, just an active sex life," I volunteered. *There, now she'll understand.*

The nurse's eyes widened, while Dave and Pierce fell silent. I turned to my son whose face registered dismay.

"Don't look so surprised," I said, giving him a defiant stare.

"Well, let's just chalk that one up to the meds," the Admission Nurse interjected, without missing a beat. She shifted her attention back to questioning Dave and Pierce.

Some of my thoughts must have passed through a drug induced filter, while others apparently traveled through no filter at all. Dave later told me he'd been terribly worried I might have brain damage. When he also mentioned what I'd said to the Admission Nurse, we both laughed. But back in the hospital, once the Admission Nurse had finished interrogating me and two orderlies wheeled me into the Trauma ICU, parked me in a small room across from the nurse's station, and swung me on a draw sheet into my bed, there was little reason to smile.

Not knowing my days from my nights, I drifted, feeling as if I were trapped in a deep, dark pit. From there, I surfaced only long enough to hear Dave and Pierce calling my name. Bone fragments in my legs were bolted together with massive external fixators, metal spikes that stuck out in all directions, making it impossible for me to move.

During brief moments when I did manage to open my eyes, the world looked dim and fuzzy. I struggled to think. Where exactly was I? Far above me, shadowy figures busied themselves and talked with each other.

Their voices filled the air, yet those who spoke always seemed just out of reach.

Why don't they tell me what's going on? Don't they know I can hear them? Don't they realize I can still understand?

Despite a severely compromised mental status, I could hear them quite well. I listened as my nurses assigned chores to their aides and shared plans for the weekend.

Sometimes they let me know when they were going to roll me onto my side, but more often than not, they said nothing to me. As a veteran nurse, not keeping me posted made me feel out of the loop, out of control, and unimportant to them. My mind filled in their silence with fearful thoughts. *Do they think I'm too far gone? Don't they care? Will they let me die?*

More than one night, I drifted uneasily through the gloom and listened as my nurse talked to her assistant.

At first, her words sounded pleasant.

Then, slowly, they turned sinister.

They're plotting to kidnap me.

Just like that, before I could stop them, they'd loaded me onto a gurney and carted me off to a foreign country.

Now, I'll never get back to Dave and Pierce.

Later, I concluded that the medication, anesthesia, and head injury must have fueled my paranoia and fears, but what struck me the most was that I couldn't remember a single person in that ICU reassuring me. At least not in words that might have calmed my fears, and not in the way Pierce and Dave did when they visited.

"Don't worry, Mom. We're going to come every night," Pierce said, patting my arm. His touch comforted me and gave me courage.

"Lara, you have a wonderful surgeon, and he's doing a great job," Dave said.

How I longed to hear words like those from the silent nurses who hung my IV bags, infused my meds, and took readings off digital displays. Instead, I lay there feeling more alone, frightened, and lost than I ever thought possible.

Through the haze, my room looked crowded with equipment. Each piece attached to one part of my body or another. Altogether, their alarms beeped and screamed at me twenty-four seven, disturbing my sleep and jarring my nerves. Higher and higher the volume rose, until one night, I couldn't stand it.

"Turn them off!" I shouted at the top of my lungs, not caring if anyone thought me rude or deranged.

I particularly hated the sound the cuffs made that attached to my feet. Every fourteen seconds they choked and hissed and sputtered as they squeezed and released each foot in turn. The image they conjured was like two Pac-man mouths, chomping away at me.

"What are those things? They sound like coughing dogs," I asked Dave when he visited one night.

"They're taking your blood pressure. I know you don't like them, but they're monitoring the circulation in your legs."

"They never stop," I muttered, wearily, slipping back into unconsciousness.

My nurses at County Hospital administered a long list of medications through my IV. There was an anti-nausea drug, an anticoagulant to prevent blood clots, five or six antibiotics, and hydromorphone, the narcotic injected every three hours for pain. Looking up I could see the fuzzy outlines of half dozen little bags of hanging over my head. *Ornaments on a Christmas tree.* The nurses infused them through what they called my "central line." It was the catheter one of my surgeons had implanted into the subclavian vein on the right side of my chest.

It was also a godsend.

The central line provided a painless route for nurses and doctors to administer drugs and IV fluids and allowed others to draw blood from me. Without it, I would have had to endure the constant poke of needles. Veins in my hands, arms, and feet had long since collapsed from too many IVs at Regional Medical. It would be months before they healed.

Though some of my early memories at County Hospital were unpleasant, receiving hydromorphone through my central line was anything but. The instant my nurse injected the narcotic into the *line*, I felt the liquid warmth spread throughout my body. The pain relief was immediate and absolute. During those early days at County Hospital, what little happiness I experienced came from the hydromorphone and visits from my family.

Most of the time, I lay in a stupor, but when Pierce and Dave showed up, I struggled to open my eyes to let them know I was okay. Then, I let them close. That was all I could do. At Regional Medical, the nurses had let Dave and Pierce visit most anytime they wanted, but in the County Hospital Trauma Unit, things were different. The staff unlocked the doors to the ICU only thirty minutes twice each day, allowing my husband and son to enter. They were like bright lights in a storm.

"We're here, Mom," Pierce said, patting my arm.

"Are you doing okay, Lara?" Dave asked and stroked my hair.

I tried to raise my head to nod at them, but couldn't.

Ann, Dave's mom, lived only twenty minutes away from the hospital and accompanied them now. Her presence cheered me. "You already look better than you did yesterday," she drawled and petted the top of my head.

I wasn't sure what she meant, but she sounded happy. The three of them functioned as my lifelines. They were the only ones at County Hospital who knew the person I'd been before the accident, and their visits the only times I felt remotely safe and loved.

While my body waged invisible battles to fight infection, there were times when I fought more interpersonal ones. I had only been at County Hospital a day or two when I must have started asking a lot of questions. That didn't make me very popular with my ICU nurses.

HOLDING MY LIFE IN THEIR HANDS

I awoke the second night at County Hospital sensing something was wrong. "Ouch," the night nurse groaned as she bumped into the corner of my bed, jarring it in the dim light.

"Are you okay?" I asked.

No response.

"Is everything all right?"

Silence.

Then I felt it. *Resentment*

"Is something wrong?"

A nurse who looked around Pierce's age looked down and scowled at me. "I've had to work hard at liking you," she fumed. "You question everything I say and do."

Her comment stung.

"I'm sorry, but have we spoken before?" I squinted to bring her face into focus. She looked familiar.

"I was your nurse last night and you asked me what minerals the pharmacy had put in your IV. When I told you it was just D5W, you said that wasn't enough. You kept talking about magnesium."

The conversation was starting to come back. I'd been trying to explain how important magnesium would be for healing my fractures and keeping me alive. And how D5W would never be enough when it was little more than sugar water.

She left and I tried to make sense of her attitude, but it was so hard to think. *Why am I having so much trouble remembering? Judging from her reaction, I must have come across pretty arrogant. I'm at her mercy* so *I better apologize.* I lay there going over what I should say.

When my nurse returned, I said. "I'm really sorry if I offended you. I'm a nurse, myself, but certainly no expert on nursing in a trauma unit."

Without answering, she busied herself with something overhead.

Why won't she say something? Why does she care if a patient questions her?

I tried again, "I'm not at my best, so please try not to judge me too harshly."

Silence.

Tears stung my eyes. I closed them. It was the best I could do. I drifted back into the fog. And my fear grew.

During that first week at County Hospital, my surgeons performed several more surgeries. The chief of surgery implanted a vena cava filter into my largest vein to prevent clots from traveling from my fractured legs to points north in my body. The filter, about an inch long, looked like a small jellyfish with filaments. It was designed to catch clots before they stopped the flow of blood and triggered a cardiac arrest or stroke.

On the fourth day at County Hospital, a young male nursing assistant named Andrew rolled my bed from the Trauma ICU to a room just a few doors down the hall in an area they called the Intermediate Care Unit. From what I could make out, the new space looked identical to the previous one.

In the new room, my gut began cramping.

"I must be constipated," I said in a weak voice to a nurse I didn't recognize with pale skin. I tried hard to bring her face into focus. "Would you give me an enema?"

"Just a minute," she said, not meeting my eyes.

When she left and didn't come back, I pushed the buzzer.

A few minutes later, the same nurse flung open the door. "What do you want now?"

"I need an enema," I repeated, more forcefully. "I'm pretty sure it's been over a week since…"

"The doctors on this unit don't get concerned unless it's been at least ten days," she interrupted.

Did I hear her right? Or is my mind playing tricks on me again? It was hard to imagine any nurse or doctor saying such a ludicrous thing. I knew from experience that even after a few days a patient could develop an impaction when stool became too hard to pass.

"First, we'll have to try a stool softener and give it a few days to work," she said, her face blank. "Then we'll consider an enema." She turned toward the door.

I've got to convince her.

"I can't wait that long. My gut hurts."

In the dim light, I saw her eyes narrow. "Well, all right," she snapped.

Obviously perturbed, she rummaged through her supply cart. Then she was back. Pushing me onto my side, she rammed the enema applicator tip toward my rectum.

It missed, hitting tender tissue near the opening.

"Ow!" I yelled.

She pushed harder. When it hit the tender spot again, I cried out even louder. Not wanting her to hurt me a third time, I reached back to guide the tip in myself. She placed the bed pan against my bottom, rolled me onto my back, and hustled out of the room, leaving me alone with Andrew, her young male assistant.

In a few moments, the enema began to work. In my confusion, I imagined I was squatting over the dirt floor of a thatched hut. Utterly mortified, I apologized to Andrew. "I'm so sorry."

"That sort of thing doesn't bother me much," he replied gently.

His kind words touched me deeply. They contrasted sharply with those of the nurse. I replayed them over and over in my mind. I remembered something else. The loving friends who'd come to visit me in the ICU at Regional Med. Their smiling faces hovered lovingly in my mind, comforting me. Then it hit me. *God must have given me that memory, knowing how much I'd need it later.*

I tried hard to hold onto their beautiful faces and the solace they gave me, but another thought pushed them away. My new nurse didn't seem to like me any more than her predecessor. She'd been rough and even hurt me. A growing sense of misery threatened to swallow me whole. A sob forced its way from my chest and into my throat.

God, why have you left me alone with another nurse who doesn't seem to care?

A long time after Andrew left, my room echoed with shrill alarms and the racket the Pac-Man monsters made. I slipped deeper into my pit of despair.

DAVE TELLS HIS VERSION

I saw the tree hit Lara in the head and crumple her to the ground. I ran to where I'd seen her fall. There in the dirt, she lay on her side. "Lara, can you hear me," I shouted down at her. She didn't move. *Is she dead?* That thought sucked the life out of me.

I knelt on the ground beside her. Fearing her neck and back might be broken, I cradled her in my arms to hold her as still as possible. Blood streamed down her face, obscuring everything except a lidless eye that protruded from the red background. A baseball sized lump jutted from her forehead. Scanning down to her legs, I gasped in horror. Her left foot dangled limply from the ankle and hung by a thread, while the right leg was mostly torn off at the knee.

I wanted so badly to hold her head up out of the dirt. With extreme care, I slipped my fingers under her head, trying hard not to jostle her neck. She started to move and muttered something I couldn't understand. The fact that she spoke at all reassured me, but I couldn't shake the notion that she might die at any moment. A wave of nausea passed over me. There were so many injuries that demanded my attention. What could I do?

Then in the midst of my panic and confusion, I knew. *Just keep her still.* It was a moment of complete clarity. I held her as still as possible as she continued trying to sit up.

I took some deep breaths trying to resist the urge to panic. Blood now covered her entire head, face, and chest. A lidless eye protruded from the red background. I had no idea what to do to stop the flood of blood that poured from under her mat of curly hair. I held her head with one arm and her body with the other, working to keep her spine as straight as possible. Lara kept squirming. We struggled that way for what must have been a half an hour before the paramedics came. That was the only time in my life I felt overjoyed to hear sirens.

The paramedic who shouted orders to the others went to work on Lara. "I'm going to have to straighten her leg to get it splinted," he whispered to me. "It's going to hurt."

I looked away and held her firmly. She screamed bloody murder. This was a nightmare.

He finished immobilizing her legs and looked up at me. "Is any of that yours?" he asked indicating the blood covering my arms and entire shirt.

"I don't think so," I said, not sure.

Sweat and blood drenched me by the time they loaded Lara and Frances into the ambulances. Up at the house, Perry and I washed up in the bathroom sink and got ready to drive to Regional Medical in separate cars. I noticed his face was uncharacteristically pale and devoid of expression.

"Perry, are you okay?" Was he going to have a heart attack?

"Yeah, I'm all right." He sighed heavily. I felt a deep ache in my own chest as I labored to breathe.

An hour later, we both pulled into the parking lot in front of the Regional Medical ER. Pierce met us in the lobby, and someone funneled the three of us into a bizarre little room to wait. The look of that place disturbed me, given its asymmetrical shape and one curved wall. It made me feel even more off kilter than I already felt. After an hour of financial and insurance questions, a woman poked her head into the room. "Come with me." She motioned.

In the middle of a tiled room that echoed with our footsteps, Lara lay like a mannequin on a treatment table. Tool boxes and glass cabinets lined the walls. Blood still covered her face and chest. In the places where the bruises didn't show, her skin looked the color of porcelain. The nurse had piled big plastic heater blankets on top of her, and warm air blew in through hoses to heat up her cold body.

Was she going to make it? What would I do if she didn't? The full weight of those questions drained what little energy I had left.

While in that room, we met Dr. W. Marlin Bolling, the young

orthopedic surgeon who happened to be on call that night. That turned out to be our amazing great fortune.

"I plan to take charge of your wife's care." His voice was solemn, but kind. "As you know she's in very critical condition. I'm going to do everything I can to keep her alive."

Truthfully, I remember little of what he said after that.

While he spoke to Pierce and me, the nurse inserted another IV and prepared Lara for surgery. Someone herded us into a larger, more open waiting area where a vent blew so cold that Perry, Pierce, and I, still damp from the woods, shivered miserably.

"How about some warm blankets and hot drinks?" a nice patient advocate greeted us.

We huddled together in our blankets for what seemed like hours without saying much. "Waiting is hard," Pierce sighed. "I hope Mom and Frances are going to be okay."

A little later, a doctor wheeled Frances out in a wheelchair. She smiled weakly. "She has a fractured sternum and a badly sprained ankle," he said. "Luckily, she won't need surgery, so you can take her home."

"That's a relief," Perry said, shaking the doctor's hand.

"How are you feeling, Frances?" I asked, studying her face.

"My chest hurts, but other than that, I'm okay. How's Lara?" She joined our little group to wait on any news.

"We don't know anything yet," I said, tired.

When Frances's doctor left, another hour went by before Dr. Bolling came out to report on the surgery. "I cleaned and debrided the wounds," he began.

"What do you mean by debrided," I asked.

"I've removed all the pieces of tissue and bone fragments that can't be repaired or saved."

"Have you set the fractures?" I asked, trying to process what he'd said.

"Oh no. That's way down the road. Her right leg is in about fifty pieces and her knee is essentially gone. The bone fragments are so small they're like gravel. There's a whole lot more work to do before anyone can even think about setting them. First I've got to try and keep her alive. Her body's dealing with the systemic effects of her trauma. We're going to see things like shock, rapid heart rate, blood loss, and swelling of her entire body. I secured the bone fragments with external metal fixators to keep them from moving. I've had to remove so many there isn't enough bone left in her right leg to hold up the knee joint. One option might be to allow her right leg to heal in a straight position. That would give it time to grow more bone. Eventually we'd have enough to attach an artificial knee. If we choose that option, the whole process could take a year or more."

"What are you going to do next?"

"I can't attempt anything else until I've done all that is humanly possible to prevent infection in her legs. That concerns me more than anything. Her open wounds were ground into the dirt. They're horribly contaminated with leaves, pine straw, and soil. Infection is the greatest threat to her recovery of all." He paused, to let all he'd said soak in.

His last comment scared me. I knew from reading that an infection could cause her to lose her legs or worse.

"On the plus side, the CT scans and MRIs of her head have miraculously failed to show any signs of brain damage. That's amazing considering she was hit in the head by a tree."

When Dr. Bolling left, we sat there awhile longer before Perry and Frances drove home. It was around four or five in the morning by then. An hour later, Dr. Baker, an Ear, Nose, and Throat Surgeon, emerged from doing a second surgery on Lara's head and face. The doctor, a petite woman, who, like Dr. Bolling, appeared to be in her early thirties, quickly described how difficult it had been to reattach Lara's severed eye lid. "I had to use all the tricks in my bag on that one, but I think it'll work fine." Her voice sounded tired, but positive. "I also reattached her ear, set her broken nose, and sutured the deep gashes on her face and scalp. There were close to a hundred staples and stitches in all."

For the second time that morning I felt lucky Lara had a wonderful surgeon. But by the time she left, Pierce and I were so bone tired we'd given up trying to converse. In the early hours of the morning on Sunday, Dr. Bolling admitted Lara to the ICU. Someone escorted us to a new waiting area just outside its door. It looked even less inviting than the previous ones. The only recliners were already occupied by a group of women who, it turned out, were to be camped there all week. The remaining chairs felt hard and uncomfortable. Worse, a TV blared twenty-four seven, jarring our frayed nerves and making it impossible to sleep. To keep ourselves sane, we turned our attention to the fish that swam in an aquarium at the opposite end of the room. "Just keep focusing on the fish," I encouraged Pierce. His face looked pale and haunted.

At around eight Sunday morning, Dr. Court, a young neurosurgeon, came in to report on Lara's back. "Four of her vertebrae are crushed, but amazingly there is no spinal cord damage. I'll watch her closely over the next few days and do surgery to fuse her spine once her blood pressure and pulse are stable. Dr. Bolling and I don't feel comfortable transferring her until her back can be done."

Later that morning the ICU nurse took us in to see Lara. I shuddered when I saw her. She looked even worse than before. Dr. Bolling had told us to expect swelling, but Lara's face was now so swollen and purple that I didn't recognize her. He'd said swelling would result from the dramatic inflammatory response that happened with severe injuries when fluid literally seeped out of the blood vessels and into all the surrounding tissues where it didn't belong.

"Why hasn't anyone thought to clean the blood off her face?" I mumbled to Pierce, as I stared at my wife.

"I guess cleaning her up just hasn't been a priority, given everything else they've had to do," he said. My son's rational response jolted me to my senses.

Pierce was right. They'd had to insert IVs into new sites as her veins collapsed. When the IVs in her hands, arms, and elbows had all failed for the second time, the nurses attempted to start new ones in her feet. I noticed the new IVs didn't last any longer than their predecessors. The nurses had also hung dozens of bags of fluid and medications over her bed.

For the first time, we saw the two metal external fixators Dr. Bolling had screwed into her leg bones to hold the fragments in place. "Hideous metal sculptures" was how Lara would later describe them. One of the fixators extended all the way from the bottom of her right shin to the middle of her thigh, while the other encased her lower left leg and foot.

Pierce and I were trying to take it all in when, without warning, the alarms sounded. A big display flashed, "50/20." "Her blood pressure is crashing," I shouted to Pierce.

The ER doctor and nurse flew into the cubicle. "Order three more units of whole blood, stat, and call a code!" the doctor shouted at the nurse. He elbowed us out of the way.

"You'll need to go to the waiting room," the nurse yelled at us. My heart raced.

Is this it?

It would be over an hour before we knew. Dr. Bolling came rushing into the waiting area and pulled us aside. "A huge volume of fluid in your wife's blood stream backed up into her lungs and resulted in congestive heart failure," he said, looking weary. "I considered airlifting her to the County Hospital north of here, but honestly, I didn't think she'd make it."

Around ten o'clock Sunday evening, Pierce and I drove home. Before we could rest, our three cats and Marley, our dog, all had to be fed. I called Hillary, Lara's sister in Maine. Without eating, Pierce and I both collapsed into our beds for a few hours' sleep before driving back to Regional Medical.

By Monday, Hillary arrived at our house. The three of us drove to a fast food restaurant to get a bite to eat and then on to the hospital. Those chicken sandwiches were the first food Pierce and I had tried to get down since the accident.

It felt good to have Hillary with us. Her presence calmed and reassured us. Despite her years as a physician's assistant, though, she wasn't prepared for what she saw when she entered the ICU. Lara lay absolutely still with tubes inserted from head to foot. IV fluids ran into both hands and elbows. Equipment surrounded her bed, making it difficult for any of us to get close to her.

Worse, she continued to be completely out of it. She slept all of the time and even for the brief moments when she woke up, she didn't seem to have any idea we were with her. When she did speak, her words made little sense. "I have a shiftless life," she muttered one night.

"What do you mean?" I asked.

"I'm just not getting anything done."

Hearing comments like that, I felt more concerned than ever that my beautiful wife might have brain damage.

"What do you think?" I asked Dr. Bolling. "She's like a different person."

"I'm not sure. The MRIs didn't show any bleeding in her brain." He frowned.

Given her strange behavior and inability to stay awake, I wasn't convinced. Lara's pulse rate always registered a hundred and thirty or higher and her blood pressure continued to go up, then crashed without warning. Hillary wondered if she might have increased pressure in her head. *Increased intracranial pressure*, she called it.

Regardless of what happened, Dr. Bolling always made us feel he cared. He took great pains to explain everything he did or planned to do in detail. In keeping us up to date, he never minced words.

"It will take an incredible level of expertise and skill to reconstruct her legs. I'm going to consult with the other bone doctors in this area to see if any of them feel capable of taking her case."

By Monday afternoon, he came back with an answer. "None of the other orthopedic surgeons feel comfortable taking on your wife's injuries, so I've made a decision. I'm planning to transfer her to County Hospital as soon as she's stable. They have a Trauma ICU and an Intermediate Care Unit. She'll need that kind of staged care. I know of an amazing surgeon up there. Dr. Norton is considered to be one of the best in the field. If anyone can save her legs, he can."

In the meantime, we waited.

On Monday evening at least a dozen visitors poured into the hall in front of Lara's cubicle and waited to see her, agitating the nurse who worked with her. I was surprised that the staff allowed so many to come in at once. *They must think she won't make it. They're letting all of us tell her good-by.*

Up until that time, Pierce looked numb in response to everything that had gone on. Then Jake, his dear friend from Great Foods Manufacturing, showed up with the group.

"Hey Man," Jake said and pulled Pierce into a hug. With that, Pierce started to sob. That tore everyone up and some of us cried right along with him.

"Dave, how're you holding up?" Lara's nursing friend, Liz, asked me and looked concerned.

"Not too well," I said, feeling sick.

"Let me know if I can do anything to help," she said earnestly. "You know you and Pierce are always welcome to stay at our house overnight when you come to see Lara. That would save you a long drive home."

"That's really nice of you, but we have pets to feed." Her kind words comforted me.

On Tuesday morning, the nurse prepared Lara for a second leg surgery with Dr. Bolling. As we waited, she writhed on the bed as if she were coming out of her skin and muttered things we couldn't understand.

"Are you in pain?" I leaned over her. She seemed to struggle to find the right words. In her frustration, she blurted out something that made little sense.

"I need to, to, to *yodel,*" she stammered. I felt sure that wasn't what she meant to say.

"You just go right ahead, Lara," Hillary said, as Pierce managed a weak smile for the first time in days. But Lara had already lost consciousness again.

Later that afternoon, back in the ICU after surgery, Lara shocked us all when she reached up and grabbed the nasal prongs out of her nose. An alarm sounded as her oxygen level plummeted. Next she ripped the cast off the bridge of her nose and pulled at her IVs.

Pierce took hold of her arms. "Mom, you're okay. I'm right here," he shouted, looking distressed.

Lara didn't seem to know him. The nurse restrained her arms to the bed rails. That was how we found her when we came for a visit later that night. She looked so pitiful I wanted to cry.

Meanwhile, other patients were dying around her in the ICU. The police brought in one woman who was hand-cuffed to her gurney. The side of her head was caved in. Twelve hours later, the next time we came to visit, that woman's bed was empty. Several other patients breathed only with the help of ventilators.

"At least Mom doesn't need one of those," Pierce gulped.

More than once we heard someone call a code and saw nurses run to get the red crash cart from the nurse's station in the center of the ICU. Twice we witnessed them wheeling a patient out the door covered from head to toe with a sheet.

By her fifth morning, Lara opened her eyes and acknowledged us for the first time. She greeted Hillary and smiled at her. Then she nodded off again. It was such a relief to see her respond to her sister.

That same day Dr. Court performed a back surgery to insert screws, rods, and connectors into her thoracic spine to keep her back from folding in two. "The fractures were far worse than I originally thought from the x-rays. It's a good thing we waited to transfer her to County Hospital. The ride might have paralyzed her," he said.

With her back stable, Dr. Bolling moved forward with plans to transfer Lara. As it turned out, I wasn't available for her trip. I'd been struggling with some stress related medical symptoms of my own. At Hillary's urging I went to see our family doctor. When I received the call from Dr. Bolling, I was right in the middle of an EKG to assess the chest pains I'd had since Saturday. Thankfully, I checked out okay. Pierce and I loaded our clothes and personal items, and took off for County Hospital.

We finally pulled into the hospital about midnight and met with the Trauma ICU Admission Nurse just as she was questioning Lara. "We've had quite a time trying to decipher the paperwork that came with your wife." She sounded frustrated.

I did my best to help her sort out the correct details. "Well, I can tell you *this* is wrong," I said, scrutinizing one of the papers. "Someone wrote here that she's a two pack a day smoker when she doesn't smoke at all."

I was making sure the nurse knew Lara had become increasingly confused since the accident when out of the blue, my wife spoke up. "The EMTs who brought me here tried to kidnap me. So did the nurse." Her eyes grew wide.

The Admission Nurse glanced over at me as if to say, "I see what you mean."

Once admitted, Lara continued to come out with things that were ever more out of character, causing Pierce and me to worry even more.

In the Trauma ICU the staff only allowed us to visit her half an hour once or twice a day and, sometimes, not at all. Given that she often underwent surgeries and had hyperbaric oxygen treatments in the mornings and afternoons, we normally just saw her in the evening. Meanwhile, Pierce refused to set one foot in the new ICU waiting room, preferring to stand outside in the hallway to wait for news. "I just can't watch the other visitors wait for their family members to die." He shook his head.

Most days we hung out at the hospital in hopes that one of Lara's doctors would show up to tell us something, anything hopeful, on her condition. That was particularly true on surgery days, when we were even afraid to leave the area for a moment to eat.

On one of our first visits to see Lara at County Hospital, my mom, Pierce, and I arrived to find the ICU doors locked. "Three of our patients are having trouble and no one can come in right now," a nurse told the large crowd of anxious looking visitors who'd congregated with us outside the door.

"What about Lara?" I asked, but she'd turned and disappeared back inside. There was a certain moral dilemma to my question.

"I feel guilty hoping and praying that Mom isn't one of the patients who are in trouble," Pierce said, echoing my thoughts.

We waited, crammed in that hall with the other visitors. No one came out to offer any further explanation. An hour and a half later, we all looked exhausted from worry. I imagined all kinds of horrible things. On top of that, I worried that my mother, Ann, in her late eighties and joining us for the first time, might collapse from the stress.

People hung out everywhere in that narrow hallway. There was a young youth director with a large bunch of teenagers, who waited to visit someone in the ICU. He was working hard to impress his group with loud jokes.

"Have you heard the one about the preacher?" he boomed, while the kids cut up and laughed raucously. All at once a couple of nurses came rushing through from the other end of the hall, pushing someone on a stretcher *into* the ICU. It was Lara. She looked pale and lifeless. Now, I really felt confused. Had she had some sort of emergency procedure?

Before I could give it any further thought, a teenager shouted, "Whoa, look at that," and pointed at Lara.

"I'll bet her husband beat her up," the woman next to us announced in a loud voice.

"Yeah," another woman nodded in agreement.

I could see the color rising in Pierce's face at her crass remarks. "I'll give them a taste of this, if they don't shut up!" he snapped, waving his fist in the air and shaking with rage.

All the while, the kids laughed, partied, and joked, and we still didn't know if Lara was okay.

A few minutes later an aide opened the door and let the three of us in. We walked over to my wife's cubicle and peaked around the curtain. "Lara, it's Dave," I announced in a trembling voice, fearing she wouldn't respond.

Amazingly, she opened her eyes, focused on my face, and smiled weakly. "Hi Dave. Are you okay?"

"Just tired," I said, taking her hand and shaking with relief.

"She had a very late session in the hyperbaric oxygen center," the nurse explained as she strode in to check Lara's IVs.

"Hi Ann," Lara murmured, catching sight of my mother.

"How're you feeling?" Mom leaned over her.

"Don't worry. I'm okay," she mumbled, a little color coming back into her cheeks.

I continued to hold her hand while Pierce patted her shoulder. "We're all here, Mom," he reassured her.

Ann moved around to the other side of the bed and gently combed Lara's hair with her fingers when I heard my wife speak. "Ann, you'd be interested to know, I got baptized recently. My friend Gerald Ford baptized me." She sounded perfectly normal and looked pleased.

Mom smiled at her, but was clearly puzzled.

When Lara nodded off again, Mom exclaimed, "Oh my goodness, she thinks she's been baptized by the former president."

"Oh, no," Pierce corrected. "Gerald Ford is actually a work friend of hers and he really did baptize her."

I'd felt reassured to hear Lara sounding more like herself, but I was still worried. What had started as mild concern on my part at her odd remarks at Regional Medical had escalated into true alarm by the time they admitted her to County Hospital. At the new medical center she'd come out with even stranger statements that left Pierce and me shaking our heads.

Had I lost the woman I loved?

At my prodding, and two days after they admitted her, the doctor in charge of Lara's medical care took her off all her pain meds to check for evidence of brain damage again. To Pierce's and my great relief, the tests came back normal.

The third day at County Hospital, a transporter, a hospital worker whose job it was to move patients around the hospital, took Lara down for her fifth surgery. Dr. Norton was to perform the operation. The renowned trauma surgeon and professor specialized in the reconstruction of impossibly damaged legs.

Once done with the surgery, Dr. Norton came out to speak with us. "I've reworked your wife's external fixators and continued the process of debriding her leg wounds. I might be able to rebuild the bones eventually, though right now the soft tissue damage and possibility of infection are a lot more worrisome. Her admitting lab work shows the presence of some infection in her left ankle, so I'm planning to implant antibiotic bone beads around her bone fragments and continue her on an aggressive regimen of hyperbaric oxygen treatments. All of those things should help get rid of the infection and promote healing."

As with Dr. Bolling, I felt confident in Dr. Norton's abilities to tackle those challenges.

"What about the future?" I asked.

"We won't know for quite a while," he said, looking me in the eye.

"Oh, I see." Now, I understood it would be a long, uncertain process.

The next couple of weeks, Lara was in surgery every few days. Soon Dr. Norton had reconstructed her left ankle, reassembling the bone fragments with the help of several long screws. The problem still remained with what to do about the deep wound cavity left in that joint.

"I had to remove an awful lot of the soft tissue in the ankle," Dr. Norton explained patiently when I asked him about it. "I'm going to call Dr. Wexler. He's an excellent plastic surgeon. Maybe he can help."

On surgery day, Dr. Wexler took out an enormous chunk of muscle from Lara's thigh and implanted it into her deep ankle crater, hoping to see it take hold there. Meanwhile, out in the waiting area, my mom prayed. I sat next to her and forced my mind to concentrate on what task I needed to do next. It was all I could do. My endless list echoed through my head. *Be available to talk to the doctor, read and sign the latest consent form, call the insurance company, visit Lara, drive the ninety miles home, answer calls from nervous family members, friends, and bosses, feed the pets, sleep a few hours, shower, change clothes, try to eat, get gas, pay the bills, and drive back to the hospital.*

That routine went on day after day for weeks as Lara continued her glacial process toward recovery. As I buttoned my pants each morning, I realized my wife was not the only one losing weight. Pierce told me his clothes were getting loose, too.

By October twelfth, a little over two weeks after the accident and twelve days at County Hospital, Dr. Norton told us it was time to try to rebuild Lara's right leg and knee. I remembered what Dr. Bolling had told us about the number of bone fragments in that leg. Pierce, Mom, and I sat saying little as we waited.

After nine hours, Dr. Norton came out to see us. "Everything went well," he said, deep, tired lines showing around his eyes. "It took all my energy and then some to assemble the metal struts and screws I needed to support so many pieces of bone."

"That's good news," I said, relieved. He nodded wearily.

When he left I turned to Pierce. "He didn't mention whether she would walk again, did he?"

"No," he replied.

A feeling of dread and sorrow took up residence in my chest and didn't leave. How would Lara come back from so much damage? Would I ever see her walk again?

I wrote to Lara's close friend, Barbara:

I'm sorry, but I have a long and terrible story to tell you; Lara asked me to write and relate it since you are her best friend and she thought you should know. On Sept. 26, we were having a party in the front yard of the house, and a large dead tree snapped off for no apparent reason and smashed Lara. She is alive, her brain, organs & central nervous system are all OK. She sustained a concussion and severe lacerations to her head and eye, crushed several vertebras in her back, and had severe compound fractures in her left ankle and right tibia. She has been in Intensive Care since then, first four days at Regional Medical Center, and then was transferred to the Trauma ICU at County Hospital. She is still there in the Intermediate Care Unit at present. I wish she could call you, but she can't manage the phone yet. Lara has had eleven surgeries in the past three weeks, the last one this morning. All day and night they give her heavy doses of hydromorphone, a strong narcotic, for pain, plus the anesthetic from the surgeries keeps her pretty out of it.

MONSTERS IN THE DARK

After the long surgery to rebuild my right leg, I languished in a state of unconsciousness for another week in County Hospital's Intermediate Care Unit. I lay there just as disoriented and paranoid as I'd been in the previous ICUs. Later I understood that I'd suffered a syndrome not uncommon to intensive care patients, called *ICU Psychosis*. It resulted from the constant disruption of sleep as well as the untoward effects of so many drugs and anesthesia.

During my stay, Dr. Norton continued to structure my days with surgeries, long sessions in pressurized oxygen chambers, and consultations with teams of doctors. At night, though, I lay alone.

Around seven each evening, Dave, Pierce, and Ann came to visit. What seemed like a short time later, they left. I didn't know my days from nights, but after about two and a half weeks in the hospital, I began to understand that when the three of them left, the night was not far behind.

About that time, something changed. All at once, someone turned off the sound. My room grew quiet, so quiet, it unnerved me.

In the ICUs, I'd grown accustomed to the clamor of equipment and alarms blaring twenty-four/seven. Now the silence was deafening. Once visitors left and the nurses turned the lights down low and settled us in for the night, the ambiance shifted. Odd sounds and voices emanated from the hall and were amplified in the silence of my room. For hours, without sleeping, I listened. *Are the people in the corridors out to get me?*

For some reason only known to the workers who frequented those halls at night, an awful lot of racket was reverberating through them. Not the conversations of nurses making their rounds, but what sounded more like a party. People talked and laughed, while someone played guitar. The melodies and rhythms that wafted through my door, though lovely, made me question whether those involved had found a preferable diversion to caring for trauma patients. *What if my nurse forgets I'm in here?*

Despite my worries, more than once that night my nurse showed up to check on me.

The next night two men were shouting from the street below my window.

"You better pay me what you owe," one yelled. His voice rose with anger.

"I'm not paying you nothin'," the other man countered. Despite the bravado, his voice sounded high pitched with fear.

Their cries grew louder.

What if the scared man climbs up the wall and into my window to get away from the angry one?

The shouting went on and faded into the night.

"Last night, two men were fighting right below my window in the street," I said when Pierce came to visit the next evening.

"Mom, you're a patient in the Trauma Unit and it's on the fifth floor of the hospital. The street's a long way down." He chuckled.

"Really, I'm on the fifth floor? But I heard them."

Pierce continued talking as if he spoke to a small child. "It's not very likely that the voices you heard came from the street. They probably came from the hall outside your door."

His words served as a reality check and made me question my perception. For the first time since the accident, I sensed how mixed up my thoughts had become.

Sometime later in the week, I awoke in the middle of the night in the basement of the hospital. Cobwebs hung from the rafters and gargoyles perched on the IV poles at the end of my bed. All around me, old, dusty relics littered the floor and covered the bedside table. Some looked oddly familiar. One resembled a paint encrusted version of my water pitcher.

Just like those objects, they've discarded me.

On the opposite wall, a narrow, stone staircase wound its way up to the place where the nurses presumably cared for their more promising patients. My leg pulsed with pain. I forced my mind not to panic. *Find the call box. How can I in this mess?*

I drew in a deep breath and tried to focus. *Look for something rectangular with a button.*

I felt around the covers. Sure enough, there was a small box attached to a cord lying next to me. I picked it up and punched the round button in the center. A voice burst from the speaker. "Yes, may I help you?"

"Thank heavens you answered," I said, relief pouring over me.

I must have sounded frightened because a moment later a male nursing assistant sprinted through the door. "Are you okay?"

"Yes, but somebody moved my bed and parked me in the cellar. I want to go back to my room?"

He gave me a quizzical look.

"I don't belong here," I said, motioning past him to the cellar, but the stone walls were already fading. So were the stairs and dusty artifacts that had covered the floor. I stared into the dark space in front of me. Just beyond the foot of my bed, a new wall emerged out of the darkness and came sharply into view in the faint light. An alcove and outline of a door appeared just beyond. I was back in my room.

"Never mind. Just please ask my nurse to bring me some hydromorphone."

"Sure, I'll tell her."

The very next night, I woke up in the cellar again. This time, I knew what to do. I stared at the stone walls until they faded and my hospital room reappeared. Then I pushed the button on my call box.

When a kitchen worker awoke me in the morning with my breakfast tray, I looked around to see if the gargoyles still perched on the IV poles at the foot of my bed. They were gone.

Had I dreamt about the cellar? Was I losing my mind?

DRIFTING THROUGH THE FOG

Nights in the Trauma Unit terrified and confused me, but during the days I drifted through the fog, barely conscious of the people who came and went from my room. As I lay, my thoughts ebbed and flowed between the past and present...I drifted back to a memory from three years before.

Clang Clang Screech. A production line lurched into operation at Great Foods Manufacturing. I walked on to the plant floor to check on the workers. Some waved and smiled at me as I strode by. I waved back. *Good, they're all wearing their hearing protectors and gloves today and everyone looks pretty happy.* Just past the first line, I spotted a big puddle. *The eyewash station's leaking again.* I grabbed some paper towels and tried to soak up the puddle. Then I pulled out a pad and made a note to call maintenance to fix it.

"Be careful. There's water on the floor," I shouted over the noise.

Several workers nodded they'd heard me.

On the second line, I found a big man and pulled him aside. "Ed, how's your back doing today?"

"I think it's getting better, just sore."

"Why don't you stop by this afternoon, so I can make sure you're okay."

He nodded. "I'll be there after lunch."

I gave him a thumbs up.

Further down the line, I spoke to another worker before doubling back to the nurse's clinic. Pulling open the heavy metal door, I strolled over to my desk and plopped down in the big leather chair, already tired. It was my third month on the job.

By mid-morning, a steady stream of workers had filed in to get me to review their lab results and check their blood pressures. When the last one cleared out, I breathed a sigh of relief.

"Are you okay?" a familiar voice called from the door.

I looked up. It was Leah, my new friend at the plant. She walked over to my desk and dropped into the seat across from me.

"Leah, you already know me too well. I'm feeling out of practice after taking a break from nursing to start a business. When my husband lost his job I had to give it up and get back to nursing. Sometimes I ask myself if I've got what it takes to organize and run these two new clinics, not to mention the hearing conservation and wellness programs. *And* do it all working part-time. Is that even possible?" I laughed, shooting her a halfhearted smile. "Hey, but where else would I get the chance to build all this from the ground up?"

I took a deep breath and leaned back in my chair. "The truth is I'm scared. With Dave out of work, my family's counting on me. Failure's not an option."

"Lara, everyone here thinks you're doing a great job. You've already succeeded in motivating a lot of us to lose weight and start exercising. No one would ever suspect you're feeling unsure of yourself."

"It's comforting to know they can't see me shaking in my nursing shoes."

Leah hesitated only a moment before offering a piece of advice. "Just turn your worries over to Jesus," she said, pointedly.

"To Jesus?" I stared at my friend to see if she was kidding. "You're serious?"

"I sure am. You should try it. You might be surprised."

"I would be. Don't get me wrong, I've always loved Jesus. I just never expected Him to show up when I called."

"Well, maybe you should try calling Him more often." She smiled.

Leah's advice sounded naïve. Yet noting her calm demeanor, I envied her. As hard as it was to admit, I'd always been a worrier. I took after my mother who took after her mother before her. But though I'd come by it honestly, worrying wasn't the way I wanted to live.

After Leah had gone to lunch, I settled back into my chair, lost in thought. I'd been lucky to grow up in a close knit family, and later marry a kind, intelligent man like Dave. I had two degrees and over six years of college. So why did I sometimes feel so uneasy? So insecure?

I sat up and took a deep breath. Was there any truth to what Leah suggested? Would turning my worries over to Jesus actually help? And what was it about Jesus that made so many trust and adore him, and now stirred deep longing within me?

But I thought I knew. It was his love. The same selfless and unconditional love that leapt off the pages in the Sermon on the Mount, and the same I'd lately seen mirrored in the faces of workers like Leah who were fast becoming my friends.

For some time, I sat picturing the Jesus part of God smiling down on me, infusing me with love, and asked myself if he really got involved. Listening to friends like Leah, it sounded like he did. While I worried, they prayed. While I clung to people, they turned to Jesus. But what could I, a woman of such limited faith, really expect from Him? Would He be there in a crisis, or had He simply set my life in motion, just to watch it play out?

Logic told me it was the latter. But despite my doubts over the next few weeks, Jesus' love beckoned like a beam of light in a dark room, offering the one thing I wanted, relief from anxiety and solace in the midst of my storm. I had no choice but to follow.

Something jarred my bed and knocked me out of the fog. I looked up to see a nurse hanging an IV bag over my head. I floated back into the mist again...

Tired of stressing over my job, I began talking to Jesus. Every morning as I drove the forty-odd miles to work over lonely country roads, I talked and hoped He was listening. As I prayed, sometimes

I felt a warm sensation spreading throughout my chest. Was it confirmation that he was near?

"Thank you, Jesus," I said, "for letting me feel your presence and for showing me something to love in everyone who comes to the clinic today... especially the hypochondriacs," I chuckled. "And thanks for guiding me to make the right choices for their healing."

That was how I often prayed. It was what Dave would later call my "thank you for not smoking" variety of praying.

Whether he was listening or not, talking with Jesus made me feel better. Was it because the connection I sensed in those moments was real? A nagging voice chided that I was surely more rational than that. Whose voice was it? My mother's, my aunt's? When I was young they'd talked about Jesus, the wonderful teacher and man, but never Jesus, the supernatural being.

But though the idea of trusting in Jesus was new for me, it appeared as natural as breathing for people like Leah, Jenny, and Gerald. While I offered advice on losing weight and lowering cholesterol, they taught me about leaning on Jesus.

It was a stressful day at Great Foods Manufacturing, when Gerald, who I often called Gerry, hurried into the clinic, sat down next to my desk, and held out his arm. "Whew! Do you have time to check one more blood pressure? I'll bet it's sky high."

"Gerry, you know I always have time for you. You been busy?"

He nodded, his blue eyes twinkling. "Sure am, but I'm not worried. Jesus always makes good out of the chaos." His serenity and obvious faith in the middle of so much turmoil astonished me.

Gerry had suffered some serious personal problems in his life, but after asking Jesus to heal him, against all odds had overcome them. Now he worked a full time job at the plant and pastored a small but growing church. He was a lay minister and the sort of guy who always seemed to put his spiritual beliefs into practice. As an example: just a few weeks after I'd started working, he'd offered to move all the medical equipment and office furniture from my old clinic into the new. On top of that, he helped me teach first aid classes. It was impossible not to love Gerry.

"It sounds good when you say it, but I have absolutely no idea how to trust in Jesus the way you do," I protested as I wrapped the blood pressure cuff firmly around his arm. "No idea even where to begin. I was raised by loving parents who rarely spoke of God. My mother was an agnostic while my dad a lukewarm Christian. It wasn't that my parents discouraged a belief in God; rather they rarely mentioned him. As a small child, my father was the only person I even remembered saying the word and then only when he was showing off a new flower from his garden. 'This has got to be one of God's finest miracles,' he would say, beaming and holding it out for approval."

I pumped up the blood pressure cuff and let the air out slowly, watching the needle on the gauge. "But I really don't blame them. My parents loved me. They taught me that helping others was the most important thing we could do and showed me through their own examples that a life without service was meaningless. They encouraged me to think for myself, work hard, and believe that whatever I had to accomplish came down to me. Neither suggested that God might be willing to help." I gave Gerry a wry smile. "Still, I've been searching for a relationship with God, though probably not in the same way you have. I've meditated. I've even visited the occasional church and synagogue." I laughed and he joined in. His robust laughter echoed merrily through the big room.

A loud voice pulled me back to the hospital room. "Mrs. Easting, are you awake? I brought you your lunch." A familiar looking man in hospital scrubs loomed over me. "Do you want me to take the lid off the lunch tray for you and raise the head of your bed so you can eat?"

"Uh, what? Oh, no thanks. I'm not hungry. You can take it back."

"Are you sure? You need to try to eat. You're getting way too thin. I can leave it and pick it up later."

"Okay." There were too many options. I tried to open my eyes, but the lids were too heavy. I slipped back into the shadows again…

It was the summer of 2009. I'd been working at GFM for three years when Gerry stopped by for a visit and sat down to chat. "You look happy. Did you get a promotion?" He laughed heartily.

"No." I chuckled. "Even better. I'm feeling on top of my job. Whatever comes through that door, I know I can handle it. I've decided I'm going to keep on working another seven or eight years and let Dave retire early. He'll be so happy."

"You've come a long way," Gerry said, and I knew he wasn't just talking about the job.

As often happened, our conversation turned to Jesus.

"I have come a long way, but I need to go further. I've been talking to Jesus for months, but despite how well things are going at work, it's still hard for me to have faith in him." I paused and looked at my friend. "So what I'm about to say may sound crazy, but I've decided I want you to baptize me. I want to show Jesus I'm ready to take our relationship to the next level, to develop some real trust in Him." I paused. "Will you do it?"

"Do you love Him?"

"I do. I've never struggled with loving Jesus, just believing he'd answer my prayers."

"Then, it would be my pleasure. Just tell me when."

"Is next week good? If I wait too long, I might not do it."

"Next week is fine. And it's okay to be nervous. I'd be surprised if you weren't. It's a big step." Gerry proceeded to explain all the details and answer my questions, and we set the date for the end of August at the Wednesday night service.

When that night came and I drove to his church, Gerry took my hand and together we climbed the stairs in the sanctuary that led up to the stage. Then carefully, we walked down some smaller steps and into a large tank of water.

He turned to the congregation. "We have a new sister in Christ who is taking a big step in proclaiming her faith. She wants to demonstrate that her old self is gone and a new woman in Christ is being born. Jesus lay in the earth for three days before He arose as a savior to the world. This water is symbolic of that watery grave." Gerry turned back to me. "When you come up out of the water, you will be a new person full of grace and mercy, saved, cleansed, and renewed."

Gerry laid his hand on my head. "I baptize you in the name of the Father, the Son, and the Holy Ghost." He tilted me backward and into the water for just a few moments before pulling me out. "Arise, new woman in Christ." He beamed at me.

The water streamed off me and with it, so would my worries and fears. I smiled back. Still wet, I drove myself home.

Dave and Pierce looked up when I walked in the door.

"I admit I'm surprised," my son said when I told him what I'd done. "I always thought you were more philosophical than religious. More of a *doubting Thomas.*"

Dave raised his right eyebrow and gave me a questioning look.

"I'm not religious," I countered, trying not to sound defensive. "Religions divide people. I want to bring people together."

"Then, why?" Pierce asked

"Baptism suggested a new beginning," I began. "It's hard to explain, but I wanted to feel closer, more connected to Jesus. I trusted, not reasoned, that baptism was what I needed to do to make that happen."

He scrutinized me. "Do you feel any different?"

"I'm not sure. I still haven't made that magical leap to faith if that's what you're asking. But you can bet I'll be keeping the lines of communication open."

Suddenly, I came back to my hospital room to find Andrew, my nursing assistant, tucking new sheets into the foot of the bed. The light had faded in my room.

"You must have been dreaming," he said. "You were muttering something about baptism."

"I was remembering being baptized."

"When was that?"

"I don't know. I've lost all track of time. In August, I think."

"What? That was only a month ago. It must have been a couple of weeks before the tree fell on you. What's the chance of that? That's just crazy." Andrew stared wide-eyed.

"I guess it is."

"Call me if you need anything." He picked up the dirty sheets and carried them out the door.

I lay there puzzled. Had there been some connection between my desire to be baptized and the tree falling on me? It did seem ironic. Was that what Andrew meant? I couldn't process his meaning. Gerry would have said there was always a reason for whatever happened, that there were no accidents. But what that reason was escaped me as I lay all but unconscious in the Intermediate Care Unit at County Hospital.

PANIC IN THE HYPERBARIC UNIT

From my earliest days in the County Hospital Trauma Unit, I underwent a therapy that turned out to be both indispensable and traumatic. Twice a day a transporter pushed me on a stretcher to the department that housed the pressurized oxygen chambers, commonly referred to at County Hospital as *Hyperbaric*. There, I underwent a two hour session every morning and another in the afternoon. The idea, relatively new to orthopedic trauma, was to drive oxygen into my tissues to help them heal.

During my first visits to Hyperbaric, I lay unconscious. Dave later informed me that a surgeon had inserted tubes into my ear drums to equalize pressure in my ears. In much the same way that a passenger on an airplane swallowed or yawned to clear his ears as the plane descended, the ear tubes provided that service for unconscious patients like me.

On the morning of my first hyperbaric treatment, though I was still unaware, I'm sure the routine unfolded much like the ones I remembered a few weeks later. My nurse and assistant came into my room after breakfast just in time to get me ready. Ordinarily my legs were weighted down with their attached metal fixators and connected to wound vacuums and blood pressure monitors. The nurse had to detach my legs from the machinery. A transporter pulled a stretcher in through my doorway while the nurse lowered the head of my bed from its usual half-raised position, until I lay perfectly flat. She grabbed hold of my draw sheet, a regular sheet folded and positioned sideways underneath me. Then she used it to pull me to the side of the bed closest to the stretcher.

"Make sure her IV tubes and vacuum hose don't get hung up. The wound vacuum needs to go with her, too," she directed the assistant, who hurried around the back side of my bed to help.

He untangled the IV tubes and vacuum lines and hastened to join her on the front side of the bed, where all three took hold of the corners of my draw sheet.

"One, two, three," the nurse directed in a loud voice.

In a moment I felt airborne as they swung me over to the waiting gurney. The nurse arranged me, along with my equipment and a cover sheet, on top of the narrow stretcher. The transporter raised the safety rails, snapping them into place, and wheeled me out the door. We sped through the labyrinth of corridors and onto an elevator, already crowded with staff. Some stared down at me. Their faces suggested they wanted to know more. When the door opened to the basement level of the hospital, the transporter pushed me along the final hallway. Ceiling tiles flashed past over my head. Finally he rolled me through the big doors that marked the entrance to the Hyperbaric Unit. There, four enormous, transparent, torpedo-shaped tanks awaited my arrival.

It took several workers to swing me over to a narrower stretcher. One of them pushed me feet first into the open end of one of the glass chambers. He slammed the hatch behind my head. Soon oxygen flowed around me until it reached the designated pressure.

I don't recall exactly how long I'd been going to Hyperbaric before I recognized it, but one morning after about three weeks in the hospital, I awoke to find myself flat on my back, unable to move, and ensconced in one of the big glass tanks. Air hissed in my ears, and a television blared outside the transparent wall presumably for my benefit. I stared at it for a moment before shutting my eyes.

Where am I? Is this a hyperbaric chamber?

As a former certified wound nurse, I thought I remembered how one looked.

Where is everyone? How long will I be in here? What if I need help? Who's going to hear me?

It was getting hotter. The smell of fear filled my nostrils.

Focus on your breath. I heard the message in my head. *Inhale, two, three, four, five. Exhale, slower, two, three, four, five.* I forced my breathing to slow. It was the nurse inside me talking another anxious patient down, but this time the anxious patient was me. *You're okay. Someone will show up soon.*

I strained to focus on what I knew. *A tree hit me in the head and fractured my leg, ankle, and back. That's why I can't move. Paramedics transported me to Regional Medical and later to County Hospital Trauma Unit. I imagined some of my nurses and paramedics were kidnapping me. Now, I'm in a hyperbaric chamber. Dave, Pierce, and Ann come visit me every night. My nurses give me narcotics for the pain. That must be why it's so hard to think clearly or remember what I've said. Dave says I have a wonderful surgeon. He has a funny name I can't remember.*

Pleased with everything I could remember, I kept talking to myself that way for a few minutes more, before I felt calmer.

Something caught my eye. I peered to my left through the glass wall that encircled me. Not fifteen feet away, an elderly patient shuffled slowly over to a chamber that was smaller than my own. His looked less like a torpedo and more like a glass box with a door on the side. He ducked his head to clear the doorway and sat down on a seat inside to wait. He pulled out a newspaper and began to read.

That lucky man can walk. He can get up and leave any time he wants. Longing swept over me.

I closed my eyes, but something was wrong. Devils and demons were now dancing wildly behind my eyelids, their crimson bodies outlined in black. Contorted faces leered at me. I blinked to make them go away.

It didn't work. I opened my eyes and concentrated hard on the television screen. *Focus on the TV.* Instead of providing a pleasant diversion, the images on the TV twisted into ever more sinister shapes.

Then it hit me. *I must be hallucinating.*

My ability to reason caught me completely off guard. Meanwhile, the devils writhed and sneered.

I remembered someone once telling me where demons appeared,

to call on Jesus. I willed my voice to sound strong. "In Jesus' name, devils, be gone," I shouted.

The demons faded.

"Thank you, Jesus." I relaxed and closed my eyes, slipping into the shadow world again.

A couple of hours later and back in my room, the nurse and transporter awoke me as they swung me into bed. "I think I'm hallucinating," I told my nurse. "I'm seeing devils."

Remembering to tell her represented another sign that my brain was recovering.

"I'm pretty sure it's your anti-nausea medication," she responded, looking over my medication record.

She gave Dr. Short, my medical doctor, a call from my room.

"He discontinued it," she said, glancing over at me.

The next time I awoke, the bizarre hallucinations had gone.

"Thank you," I said, smiling when the nurse wandered back into my room at the end of the shift to check on me. "I'm really impressed you knew which drug it was."

"I'm so glad it helped," she replied.

The tree had splintered and crushed my bones, but its effect on my skin and internal soft tissue was no less severe. Every night when Dave, Pierce and Ann came to visit, they commented on my appearance.

"Dad, Mom looks a lot better. The bruises are almost gone," Pierce said.

"Lara, the oxygen's doing a great job," Dave added. "You're starting to look a little more like yourself."

What are they talking about? I'd felt crusty scabs and sutures on my face as I lay mostly asleep and touched them with my fingers. Yet I refused to think about how I looked. It would be another two weeks before I had the courage to look in the mirror. I guess I wasn't too sure I wanted to face what the tree had done to my appearance.

A transporter had just rolled me into my room from a morning session in the Hyperbaric Unit when a kitchen worker carried in my lunch tray and placed it on the table over my bed. I lifted a corner of the lid, peeked inside, and lowered it. The thought of food still sickened me. I settled back into my mattress and slept for a few more hours before another transporter called my name. "I'm here to take you to Hyperbaric," he said. It was the last place I wanted to go.

With the first faint hint of awareness, came increased pain. One morning as I dozed in the oxygen chamber, an intense throbbing in my lower leg awakened me. Had someone propped my calf on the sharp edge of a cardboard box? Flat on my back and unable to move in the confined space, I couldn't look down to see.

The pain grew worse. I rapped on the glass wall. A nurse walked over.

"My leg hurts. Can you give me something for pain?" I asked.

She squirted something into my central line through a port in the chamber wall. "Here's a milligram of morphine," she said.

The pain raged unabated. I rapped again.

"Could you call my nurse on the Trauma Unit to bring some hydromorphone?" I'd begun to sweat.

"We aren't allowed to give anything that strong down here." She gave me a sympathetic look.

"Then you must not get many patients from the Trauma Floor."

Later a nurse on the Trauma Floor informed me that a milligram of morphine was comparable to only a tenth of my usual dose of hydromorphone.

During that same hyperbaric session, I first encountered the disagreeable Mr. Layton. Though I never really understood exactly what his role was in that department, he always seemed to be hovering somewhere nearby. Over the next week, I learned that Mr. Layton lacked anything remotely resembling a bedside manner. His style of communicating felt more brusque and detached than any person I'd ever witnessed working with patients. When he helped the others swing me over from my gurney to the narrow stretcher used in Hyperbaric to load patients into the pressurized oxygen chambers, more than once, the heavy metal rods that screwed into my leg bones hit the steel frame on his side, jarring me with pain. He never once apologized.

That day when the morphine didn't relieve the pain, I knocked for a third time on the glass wall of my chamber. This time, Mr. Layton looked up and strolled over with what seemed like exaggerated slowness. He donned a pair of head phones that hung outside my tank and waited for me to speak.

"The morphine didn't help. I need to go back to my room?" I did my best not to cry.

"Don't you know this is saving your legs?" he scoffed. "If we stop now, it'll be twenty minutes before the pressure in the chamber comes down enough to even open the hatch. Then we'll have to start the whole thing over again. Anyway, you only have thirty minutes left."

Only thirty minutes? That's an eternity. But I can't face doing it all over again. "Never mind." I clenched my teeth and stifled a sob.

Once back in my room and waiting for the hydromorphone to kick in, I struggled to figure out what had gone wrong. I couldn't suffer that much agony trapped in the hyperbaric chamber again. But what could I do?

"I hate Hyperbaric," I railed at Dave that night. "That awful man doesn't care one bit that I'm in pain and can't move."

"I know it's really hard, but I don't think there's anything more important for your legs right now than the hyperbaric oxygen. I wish I could go with you, but I have to work. I've already been out three weeks. Why don't you try to talk to him?" He gave me a sad, weary look.

"I'll try," I said. The idea filled me with dread.

The next morning, back in Hyperbaric my leg ached. After Mr. Layton helped swing me onto the narrow stretcher, I summoned the courage to bring it up. "Could you try putting a pillow under my right leg? I think that might help it hurt less?"

Mr. Layton avoided my eyes. If anything he appeared to be in a bigger rush than usual. He crammed a pillow under my right leg, and before asking if it helped, he shoved my stretcher into the big tube.

Clunk. He slammed the door behind me. My leg was on fire.

Determined not to lie in there for over two hours in pain, I rapped desperately on the thick glass. Mr. Layton trudged over and put on a head set. He wasn't smiling.

"What is it?" he growled, not bothering to conceal his irritation. He mumbled something else. With static on the line and the oxygen hissing in my ears, I couldn't make it out.

"Could you adjust the pillow before we start? My leg still really hurts," I asked.

But whether he understood me or not, he turned his back and walked away.

AN ANGEL IN THE HALLWAY

By the time they pulled me out of the chamber, I was limp with pain. The room swirled around me. *I'm trapped and at the mercy of that awful man. How will Dave and* Pierce *ever find me down here? And if they do, what can they do to help?*

I looked down at my stick thin legs with the spikes sticking out. *No one can help me. I'm beyond help.* For the first time since the tree hit me, I thought about giving up.

I barely noticed the tired looking woman, a hospital transporter, pushing my stretcher out the door and into the corridor.

"God, please help me. Help me or take me with you." I burst into tears. Dying didn't sound bad.

If the transporter was either annoyed or uncomfortable with her actively weeping patient, she gave no indication. She steered my gurney over to the side of the hallway and walked up to where I could see her. As she leaned in, her gaze locked on mine. High cheekbones etched a thin, dark face.

"You're going to be okay. *God* is going to heal you," she announced in a voice so full of power and conviction, I stopped crying to listen. She reached out to touch my arm, giving me a look that told me she knew far more than what she was saying. "You don't have to be afraid."

How long she stood there holding me in her gaze, I didn't know. When she finally walked back to the foot of the gurney and resumed pushing it slowly up the hall, all my pain had vanished. In its place, a warmth as comforting and uplifting as the sun on your face on a cool day filled my chest.

Stunned, I asked her, "Are you an angel? Jesus, is that you?"

The woman just kept smiling at me as if she knew a secret she wasn't sharing.

The weight that had suffocated me, lifted. My heart swelled with joy. I stared at the transporter believing with every fiber of my being that Jesus had spoken through her and taken up residence within me. Then it came to me.

God answered my prayer.

Nothing like that had ever happened to me before. My situation hadn't changed, but in that instant, I changed. God had transformed me.

I'm not alone. Jesus is real. He's right here with me. For someone who'd lacked faith, that was no small revelation.

I laughed out loud for joy. The presence I felt had to be Jesus. Clearly, Jesus was not the impersonal god of my youth, but rather the God my friends at the factory had talked about. He'd shown up in the hour of my greatest need and transformed my despair into hope.

I soon learned that when I called to Jesus for help, trusting perhaps for the first time that it would come, help showed up. Peace filled me as I lay motionless in the pressurized oxygen chamber and afterward when I confided what I'd witnessed to whoever wheeled me the long way back to my room. As close as I can remember, in the days that followed, all of my transporters sounded excited when they heard my news. In return, they shared what they knew about Jesus, too.

"He takes whatever bad happens to us and always works it out for our good. He loves us, no matter what we've done," one said as he propelled me through the corridor.

On more than one trip back from Hyperbaric an attractive woman named Delores, with distinctive hoop earrings, pushed me. Just like those before her, she proclaimed that Jesus had my life in His hands and planned to heal me. It never occurred to me to question how she knew.

One morning as she wheeled me into my room, Delores shared a problem of her own. "I'm stuck in a bad relationship," she said, "but I'm ready to get out. I just need a new place to live."

She can walk, but she feels just as trapped as I do.

"Pray for me," she said suddenly, her eyes imploring.

Her request startled me. No one had asked me to pray for them in a long time.

"I'd be glad to," I said, flattered by her request. Most of the people I'd encountered in the hospital hadn't acted as if they thought I was capable of much.

When she left my room, I bowed my head and clasped my hands, feeling useful for the first time since the tree had fallen. Then I drifted off to sleep.

Several days later, Delores stopped by my room to give me an update. "I moved," she said smiling. "I found just the right place. I couldn't believe how many showed up to help."

"That's wonderful." I sent a silent *thank you* to Jesus. Apparently God wanted Delores to make a change, too.

The next afternoon a physical therapist strode into my room.

"Take hold of the trapeze bar and pull your body up off the bed," he began.

I grasped the bar. As I pulled up, I found my arms were still strong, but my back ached.

This won't hurt my back will it?"

"Your back?" He looked puzzled.

"You know it's fractured, right?" He looked more perplexed than before.

"I better check with Dr. Norton," he said, grabbing his clipboard and hustling out the door. With all the focus on my legs, apparently everyone had forgotten my back.

The next day, right out of surgery and a lengthy stay in the Recovery Room, a transporter rolled me back through my door. No sooner had he helped swing me into bed when a second man with a stretcher came in behind him. "I need to take her to Radiology. Her doctor's ordered x-rays of her back," he said.

"Do I really have to go?" I moaned to my nurse, feeling groggy and utterly miserable. Pictures of a crowded x-ray department filled my head.

"I'm afraid you do. Dr. Norton ordered it." I'd recently learned that whatever Dr. Norton ordered was not open to debate.

Once in Radiology, the transporter parked my gurney against a wall across from a long counter where two women in scrubs sat talking. Otherwise the department was totally deserted. No sooner had I arrived when they hurried over.

"Hi there, how are you doing?" the first asked. She looked like she'd found an old friend.

"I just came from surgery and my back's broken. I'm not sure I can sit up."

"Don't you worry. We're going to help you." The corners of her mouth curled into a beautiful smile.

The two women wheeled my stretcher into the x-ray room. They stood on either side of me, grabbing me under my arms, and lifting me gently into a sitting position. With their support, I could sit without pain.

"I can't believe it doesn't hurt," I said, elated.

"Take a deep breath. Let it out…and you're done."

They lowered my head, rolled me out into the hall and parked me in front of the counter. But rather than leaving me to wait alone, the two women lingered.

It felt good to have their company. "How did this happen?" one asked, nodding at my legs, her eyes opened wide.

"A tree fell on me."

"It's a miracle you're even here, talking with us. God must have some important plans for you."

"I guess He does." I let her words settle in.

Back in my room, I reflected in awe and gratitude on the loving people who kept showing up. "This has got to be God's doing," I said to Ann when Dave's mother visited that night.

"I think you're right. It's amazing. I've never seen anything like it."

The next morning, I even found something to be happy about in Hyperbaric. While Mr. Layton's presence had filled me with dread, Kenneth's brought me love. He was a stocky man with a warm demeanor and a pin on his vest that read, "Semper Fidelis." I remembered that "Always Faithful" was the motto of the Marine

Corps. On the days when Kenneth worked in Hyperbaric, he made sure he transferred me to the stretcher with care.

One morning after an especially uncomfortable session in the torpedo-shaped chamber and another rebuke from Mr. Layton, I started to weep before the transporter could take me away. Kenneth hurried over.

"What's wrong?" His eyes filled with concern.

"I can't do this anymore," I sobbed. "I can't take the pain or that awful Mr. Layton."

"No, no, you can't quit now. Dr. Norton says this is really important for you. I'm going to make sure you're okay."

Kenneth worked part-time as an assistant in Hyperbaric, but the next morning when Mr. Layton shoved my stretcher into the chamber, true to his word, Kenneth was there. As I lay in the big tube, he came over to the glass. "Are you all right?" he mouthed.

I nodded, feeling safe. I let my body relax and breathed the warm oxygen into my lungs, enjoying how it felt for the first time. With Jesus and Kenneth looking out for me, I would make it through the rest of my sessions.

By the beginning of the third week at County Hospital, the transporters took me to Hyperbaric only once a day. Still, at two and a half hours a session, legs aching and unable to move, it felt like an eternity. I was just clear enough by then to remember to ask for a dose of hydromorphone right before they whisked me from my room to Hyperbaric to lie in the pressurized oxygen chamber.

"What's it like in there?" my nurse asked one day as she injected hydromorphone into my central line. "You're the first patient we've ever had on Trauma that goes to Hyperbaric every day."

"It's claustrophobic," I said. "Once they slide you in, close the hatch, and let the oxygen pressure build up, you can't move or get out for over two hours even if you're in pain."

"No wonder you ask for hydromorphone." She stared, wide eyed.

GOD SENDS ANOTHER ANGEL

The transporter had just wheeled me back to my room after surgery when a young woman leaned over me and introduced herself. "I'm Sara and I'm going to be your nurse today." Her voice sounded calm.

Just like Kenneth, I felt drawn to her the moment we met. I could just open my eyes and she spoke few words, but those she murmured soothed me. "I'm going to stay right here with you while you rest." She settled in the chair next to the bed with a chart and pen. "I've got to keep a close watch on your vital signs, and luckily I don't have any other patients right now. I might as well keep an eye on you." She gave me a wink.

My head felt too heavy to nod. I blinked and tried to smile instead. How did she know how much I needed to hear her comforting words? Something in her voice told me Sara would take good care of me.

I drifted off to sleep and dreamt I convalesced on a blue velvet sofa in a spacious Italian villa. Pink marble floors shone around me, and a pale pink light permeated the space with a feeling of tranquility. In that place too, Sara sat and wrote by my side as I slept.

It seemed like hours passed before I awoke. When I did, Sara was still sitting by my bed writing. I gazed at her, mesmerized by how serene she looked.

Was all of it a dream?

Since the accident, I'd grown accustomed to sleep disrupted by nightmares that often appeared real. For the first time in the three weeks I'd languished in the hospital, I felt completely refreshed.

Sara looked up and seeing my eyes open, greeted me with a warm smile. She stood and hovered over me, touching my shoulder. "How're you feeling?"

"Wonderful, now that you're here. I had a dream. You were my nurse and we were living together in a beautiful palace in Italy." Sara looked pleased but not surprised.

Over the next few days, I enjoyed the happy perception that my dream and the perfect peace it imparted had been real. It was another clear message I would be fine.

As the days passed, I didn't see Sara. Had she been real?

It wasn't until my last day at County Hospital that she strolled in. "I stopped by to let you know I've been thinking about you. I wanted to tell you goodbye and wish you the best." Her presence gave me the same feeling as before. One of peace.

I started to wonder about all the *angels* and was convinced that God had spoken through each and every one to lift my spirit.

A friend later told me, "Sometimes God whispers in someone's ear and encourages them to help us." He was now speaking through one person after another and always with the message I most needed to hear. That of hope.

"Love your neighbor as yourself," I reminded myself.

"You sure are looking a lot happier tonight," Dave said, a quizzical look crossing his face.

"I am," I said and meant it.

THE NURSE THE TREE FELL ON

By this time I'd lain in the hospital three full weeks and was continuing to slowly come back to myself. Sara and the other *angels* had awakened in me a new, far more hopeful state of mind. Though my thoughts still felt jumbled, my body heavy, and life, surreal, I smiled at my growing state of contentment.

I have a distinct memory of looking down at the huge metal fixators and at the network of incision lines, staples, and open wounds on my legs and having one clear thought.

My body's in a terrible mess, but I'm happy, really happy. How can that be?

But I already knew. It was Jesus. At the thought of Him, a warm sensation spread throughout my chest, followed by the most incredible feeling of love, peace, and joy I had ever known. It was as if some part of heaven now resided within me. Each moment shimmered with a transcendent glow. Months later someone would give what I described a different name. *The Holy Spirit*. But whatever they called it, I couldn't have been happier to have Jesus' Spirit with me.

The fog in my mind was lifting. I began to recognize my doctors and surgeons and realize just how fortunate I was to have Dr. Norton, in particular. Most everyone at the hospital spoke of him in reverent tones.

"Oh, you have *Dr. Norton*. You're *really* lucky," my nurse exclaimed one morning as she got me ready for Hyperbaric. Dave and Pierce hadn't exaggerated when they'd told me, at County Hospital and in the world of trauma medicine, Dr. Norton was something of a celebrity.

"How're you feeling today?" he asked one morning, as he strode into my room to check on me. He searched my face momentarily for feedback, in a way that let me know he valued my opinion. His caring allayed my fear and gave me hope.

"Okay," I replied, feeling exhausted.

"I reconstructed your right lower leg yesterday. I had to piece together your tibia. It was in dozens of pieces and missing several inches of bone. I reconnected the bone fragments using two struts and fifteen screws to stabilize them. It was a nine and a half hour surgery, so I'm surprised to see you awake today." He smiled. "I'm going to take a look at your leg. As you can see I also removed the big metal fixators that have been holding all the fragments in place. That's why we put this cast on."

I looked down at my leg and saw the long black cast that stretched from the top of my thigh to my ankle with hinges at the knee.

Dr. Norton unfastened the Velcro straps that held the cast firmly together and pulled the sides apart to expose my shin. "Tell me what you can feel and let me know if anything hurts." He felt for the pulses in my feet and checked sensation in my right foot and lower leg.

"I can feel you stroking my foot, but my leg's numb like it's made of wood. None of what you're doing hurts."

I looked down at my leg as he pushed on the tissue on either side of the fresh incision line that ran the length of my shin.

He's looking for infection. No fluid or pus is coming out. That's good.

"You've got good circulation in your legs and feet and I don't see any sign of infection." His eyes twinkled at me. "Let me try to bend your knee a little. I want to check its range of motion." I must have looked worried, because he added, "I'll go slowly."

He cradled my thigh with his right arm and grasped my foot with the left hand. Gently he moved my foot till the knee bent slightly. That was all he could do before I stopped him.

"That hurts."

"Okay, now just relax while I see how far I can flex your foot." He supported my right heal and pressed the foot toward my head.

"Ow!"

He frowned "Keep flexing your foot while you're in bed." It was obvious my ankle wasn't bending enough to suit him. "Since you're a nurse, you know what concerns me."

I felt sure he was referring to a problem called *foot drop*. It could prevent any bedridden patient from lifting the front of their foot, causing them to drag it once they started to walk.

Dr. Norton turned to my nurse. "Order a splint to hold her foot in a flexed position. I don't want this getting any worse." She hastened out the door. When Dr. Norton asked for something, people jumped.

One evening during visiting hours, seeing that I was a little more alert, Dave tried to fill me in. "Lara, I know you haven't been aware of it, but Dr. Norton's already been working hard for over two weeks to repair your legs. He's done five surgeries himself and recruited several specialists to do a few more. If you count the ones you had at Regional Medical, you've had eleven so far."

"Wow. I had no idea. Who operated on me at Regional Med?"

"Dr. Baker repaired your face and an Orthopedic Surgeon named Dr. Bolling worked on your legs. We were so lucky he just happened to be the one on call your first night in the hospital. He spent hours cleaning the dirt out of your wounds and stabilizing your bone fragments. In fact, he didn't go home for three solid days."

"One of the nurses told me he was a theology major before going to medical school," Pierce chimed in, raising his eyebrows.

My eyes widened at Pierce's remark.

As the days passed in the Intermediate Care Unit, I continued to become more conscious, and as I did I also began to know each time they wheeled me downstairs for surgery. While the atmosphere on the Trauma Units felt perpetually chaotic, from what I could tell, the Surgery Department ran like a Swiss clock.

On the first surgery day that I remembered, my transporter pushed me into that busy department and parked my stretcher inside a small stall. I looked out to face the nurse's station. Fortified with my new sense of hope, I wasn't afraid. I felt excited to be there. I had always been plagued with an assortment of fears and phobias. Now in the worst situation of my life, I felt calm.

I soon found that being Dr. Norton's patient afforded me some additional benefits. A big dry erase board clearly listed dozens of patient names and the times they were scheduled to have surgery. That morning and on all the surgery days that followed, my name was listed first.

The moment I arrived in that department, members of my surgical team approached me. They needed to make sure they had all the correct information prior to my surgery. In the Trauma Unit not many of my caregivers ever let on they knew I was an RN, but in the Surgery Department, everyone seemed to know. The Intake Nurse, a friendly fellow who looked about fifty, greeted me.

"So, *you're* the nurse the tree fell on." His face lit up. "You've always been asleep when they brought you in before. How did it happen?"

He didn't wait for a response before he launched into a few more questions. "I mean, was there a bad storm? Was it windy? Did you see it coming?"

I could tell he wanted details. For the first time I let myself think back to that terrible day in the woods. As muddled as my thoughts had felt, what I remembered now was crystal clear. I took in a deep breath to steady myself.

"It had just stopped raining. We went out to do some target shooting in our woods. I'd just finished taking my turn and gone over to stand under the trees."

I knew what was coming next. My stomach started to tremble. Then my whole body shook. *Fear.*

I focused on the loving presence inside me before I continued.

When I finished my story, the man stared at me, his eyes opened wide.

"Oh my heavens. I can't believe you're alive. The next time I go camping, I'm going to make sure there aren't any trees near the tent."

The circulating and scrub nurses hurried over next. "You're awake," one said and looked expectant. "We want to hear what happened, too."

I labored through my story again, feeling a little stronger than before. The two nurses looked stunned.

When two medical residents made the same request, I launched in without hesitation. I felt my stomach flutter again, but that time, it didn't bother me. I pressed on to the end. As a former mental health nurse, I told myself it was good to *get it out*. I understood the value in re-telling my story. Every time I remembered and talked about the details, I made peace with them a little more.

So many people in the Surgery Department seemed to know me, had I, like Dr. Norton, become something of a celebrity? Maybe they were interested in my story because like them I was a medical person, a peer who'd survived something unimaginable. I could almost hear their thoughts as they scrutinized me. "If this happened to her, it could happen to me." I didn't know for sure what they were thinking, but I knew it felt good to have something of interest to share. It felt good to be included in their conversation. Good to belong.

A young woman in a vibrantly colored uniform and cap caught my eye. "I like your cap," I said when she came over to question me.

"Thanks, I'm Bailey. I'm in my last semester of the Nurse Anesthesia Program. I'll be assisting the anesthesiologist today."

"I'm impressed. I have a couple of friends who've worked in that field. I know from talking to them putting patients to sleep can be a real challenge. Are you finished with your studies yet?"

"Almost. I have my last exam tomorrow. I hope I've studied enough." She chewed on her lip and talked about what she'd done to prepare.

"It sounds like you've studied quite a bit. I used to get pre-test jitters in nursing school. A long jog and a good night's sleep usually helped."

"I pray a lot," Bailey chuckled.

"Now that I think about it, praying might have been better. Hey, it's certainly been working for me lately." I laughed.

A few days later and back in my room, Bailey surprised me with a visit. She handed me two of the uniform caps in turquoise, pink, and coral, my favorite colors. She sat down next to my bed and began to eat her lunch.

"How'd your test turn out?" I asked.

"Good. I got the results this morning. I'm glad it's over. Hey, I don't mean to eat in front of you. Are you sure you don't want me to help you with your lunch? You look like you could use a few pounds." She nodded in the direction of my tray.

"I'm sure," I said, not feeling hungry.

Bailey was a pretty young woman, probably somewhere in her twenties, but her generous and considerate spirit made her seem older, more mature. Her friendship brought me another gift.

For years I'd dreaded the mention of surgery. Now, I found I preferred those days to the more routine ones at County Hospital. I enjoyed the camaraderie with the people who worked there. I also felt happy that on surgery days Dr. Norton never sent me to Hyperbaric. But most of all, I was grateful that after surgery, no one ever badgered me to eat.

STARVING

While the nurses back in the Regional Medical ICU had relentlessly nagged me to eat, few at County Hospital did. I guessed they were far more focused on my injuries. With Dave and Pierce, my poor eating habits had become a sore subject. The only meal I could make myself eat was breakfast. Every morning I had just enough of an appetite to eat a few bites of my scrambled eggs and the three strips of crispy bacon that arrived on my tray. The bacon's salty taste was appealing next to the bland powdered eggs. I had never been a bacon eater before, but at County Hospital it turned out to be the only thing that tasted good. Maybe the hydromorphone and five antibiotics that hung over my head had something to do with it. Maybe it was the stress of being trapped in a hospital bed and hyperbaric tank. But once I finished breakfast, my appetite went away and didn't return until the next morning.

As an employee health nurse who truly believed in the power of using the right foods to heal, and who'd been a tireless advocate in spreading that message (just ask the workers at the plant), I understood only too well how important it was for me to eat. At first, I really tried to make an effort. But after a couple of weeks of pushing myself, I just gave up the ordeal. When my body needed me most, I was failing it. Before the accident I'd taken in at least two thousand calories a day to maintain my hundred and twenty five pound frame. Now, I was eating less than five hundred. Something had to give.

Though my nurses at County Hospital didn't push me to eat, my dietician did. Francesca, an attractive blond in her early thirties, wandered in most afternoons.

"How's your appetite today?"

"Nonexistent."

"Tell me everything you ate for breakfast and lunch?"

"Half the eggs and all the bacon. For lunch, a carton of milk and a few bites of cottage cheese."

"And for dinner?"

"Nothing." *She's not going to be pleased.*

"Are you drinking the protein shakes I ordered?"

"Trying, but they're way too sweet. Funny, but I can only stand the taste of salty things."

"You know how important those shakes are," she said, ignoring me.

"I do but I can't get them down. Maybe you should just order me bacon and cottage cheese for every meal." I chuckled.

Francesca, didn't look amused. "Those are way too high in sodium."

"They'd be better than nothing, wouldn't they? Anyway, let's not talk about food any more. Let's talk about you for a change."

"Okay, I'll talk about myself, if you'll promise to drink your shakes. Is it a deal?"

"I'll try harder."

"I'm thinking of going back to school to study law," she said.

"Really? That's quite a change." Francesca never ceased to surprise me. As the days turned into weeks, I'd come to see her as more than just my dietician. We'd even talked about the crush she had on Dr. Brown, one of my medical doctors.

"I met him a few weeks ago when we both ended up sitting at the same lunch table in the cafeteria." She blushed.

"Have you talked to him since?"

"No, I haven't run into him."

Without saying a word, I began to formulate a plan. Each day when Dr. Brown came to check on me, I found a way to insert Francesca into the conversation.

"Dr. Brown, I know how concerned you are about my weight loss so you might want to talk to Francesca, the dietitian. She has some ideas on how to help me build muscle."

Dr. Brown's head jerked up when I mentioned her name. I made sure to put on my best poker face.

Meanwhile Francesca coaxed me to eat. She was my friend, so I wanted badly to reward her efforts. To please her, I attempted to force down the serving of lime-flavored protein powder Dave mixed in a glass of ice water every evening. The trouble was the kitchen workers brought two packets with every meal. Since I could only drink the one, Dave and Pierce tossed the leftovers in the corner.

"We'll take them when you go home," Dave said.

One afternoon as Francesca checked on me, she glanced across my room and spotted the growing avalanche of protein packets. Her brow furrowed. I cringed.

Caught

"I promise I've been drinking one every night, but they send too many," I stammered, knowing I'd let her down.

Without looking up, she dashed a note on her pad. "I'm ordering another serum albumen level on you. That test will tell us...."

"The status of the protein and muscle stores in my body," I interrupted, feeling chastised.

The results came back the next day and revealed, in scientific terms, what Dave and Pierce already knew. I'd lost an alarming amount of muscle in only three and a half weeks. The consequences could be dire if that trend continued.

A few days later, when I refused dinner again, Dave jumped on me with a line from Men in Black, one of his favorite comedy movies. "Edgar, you look like your skin's hanging off your bones," he said. His eyes glared with pent up frustration. I considered for a second he might be joking. He wasn't. "Lara, you're going to waste away if you don't eat."

"Mom, Dad's right. You're pissing us off. You're starting to look scary," Pierce added, giving me a defiant look.

Per my request, Dave began slipping me baggies full of vitamins, minerals, and protein rich herbal supplements from the local health food store to compensate for my starvation diet. I'd often volunteered there as a consultant on Fridays before the accident and knew the owner well.

"She gave me sacks of stuff when I stopped by," Dave said. "And she wouldn't take anything for them. She just wants you back soon."

"That was really nice of her." Then noticing the dark shadows under Dave's eyes, "but you look tired, sweetie. You should take some vitamins, yourself. Are you okay to drive?"

"Don't worry, Mom," Pierce chimed in. "I've been doing the driving for both of us. I'm not as tired as Dad."

"I'm okay," Dave said, looking much older than before.

Ann moved around Pierce, a carton in her hand. "I brought you some chicken and dumplings," she announced. "I hope you like them."

I opened the lid and peered at the pile of dumplings, floating in gravy. I took a small bite, but the gravy almost gagged me. Feeling embarrassed, I passed it to Dave, noticing a sad look on my mother-in-law's face.

"I'm so sorry, Ann. You went to so much trouble and I want to eat it, but I can't. I'm sure it's delicious though."

Another person who seemed concerned about my weight was Dr. Short, the resident who handled most of my medical issues. Dr. Short was young, handsome, and always took the time to answer my questions. He stopped by every day before lunch as he made rounds with an entourage of medical students in tow. They joined him at the foot of my bed with their backs to me and leaned in to hear what he had to say. None of them looked at me.

They're acting like I'm not even here. I fumed.

When they began asking Dr. Short yet another question about my nutritional status that I could have easily answered myself, I interrupted angrily. "I *don't* have an appetite and I *can't* eat, so I'm losing muscle mass and my albumen's low." The group jumped and stared at me.

I watched Dr. Short rifle through my chart till he spotted the latest lab results. His face registered alarm.

"You certainly aren't eating enough. Are you drinking the protein shakes?" Worry lines wrinkled his brow.

"I'm trying, but I can only gag one down a day."

"That's not enough. Why aren't you eating?"

"I'm not hungry and absolutely nothing tastes good, especially things that are sweet. I don't know why, but I can't force myself to swallow anything. I really don't understand it any more than you do. Maybe it's because I haven't been to the bathroom or maybe it's all the IV medications." Constipation had continued to plague me from my first week at County Hospital.

Dr. Short's face registered surprise. He quickly scribbled an order for an enema.

But the next day after the enema had done its work, I still couldn't eat. Dr. Short's eyes narrowed.

The nurse in me kicked in. "What about inserting a gastric feeding tube? Or how about hyperalimentation?" I suggested hopefully. Hyperalimentation was nutrition delivered through an IV.

"They don't recommend *hyperal* much anymore, and gastric tubes have other problems. We just want you to start eating."

Crestfallen, I stopped talking. *What the heck?* Didn't he care that I was starving? I couldn't fathom his resistance. Back in the 1980's when I'd nursed trauma patients, I hung bags of nutrients that infused through IV lines on nearly all of them. Apparently a lot had changed in trauma nursing since. I marveled at the new technologies that were saving my legs, among them the wound vacuum, hyperbaric oxygen, vena cava filter, and bone beads.

But even with all those and Dr. Norton, how can they expect me to heal if I can't eat?

A few days after the surgery to graft a big piece of my thigh muscle to fill the crater in my left ankle, the transplanted tissue looked like a piece of beef jerky. Most of the nurses and doctors wrinkled their noses as they peered at the graft.

"It looks bad, doesn't it?" Dave asked my nurse at the beginning of her shift.

"I agree with you. I'll get the surgeon to look at it right away."

The surgery had been a painstaking one. Dr. Wexler, the plastic surgeon who bore a striking resemblance to a favorite movie character of mine, inspected his work. He glowered and shook his head, without meeting my eyes.

The next day a transporter wheeled me back into surgery where the doctor excised most of dead tissue from the wound bed. The graft had died.

Weeks later, when Dave talked with me about the dead graft, there was little doubt in my mind what had caused it. I knew from my training to become a certified "wound nurse" that nothing could heal without the benefit of the right nutrients. Foods rich in protein, vitamin C, and calories were at the top of the list. Despite recently starting on the vitamins and herbs Dave brought me, weeks of eating a pitiful diet had taken its toll.

Dave wrote again to my good friend Barbara who lived in Wisconsin:

Once in a while, when Lara has a respite from surgery, she gets quite lucid and the old Lara comes through. I was hoping that today would be her last surgery for a while, but she will have to have another next week. Pierce and I have been running ragged trying to be with her whenever they will allow it. I'm trying to keep my job going and Pierce is working on finishing the police academy and then applying for a job in local law enforcement.

> As I said, Lara has mentioned several times that she wants to talk to you, but has been too weak or unconscious. She says to tell you that she loves you, and that she hopes to be able to talk to you soon.

Barbara wrote back:

> Dave, I have read your letters over and over, in shock and disbelief at first, and then, as the truth settled in,

feeling so concerned and upset for Lara, and for you and Pierce as well. I am so sorry to hear this news!

Is there anything that you need or that Lara needs, that I can do? Thank you so much for sitting down to write again. Of course, I would love to hear how she is doing, whenever there's an opportunity. And I will 'hold you all in the Light,' as Quakers say.

THE STRANGE LIFE ON FIVE EAST

On October 16th, after about sixteen days in the County Hospital Trauma Unit and three weeks after the accident, Dr. Norton deemed me medically stable enough to move to a room out on the Trauma Floor. They called that area Five East and transferring me there represented physical proof that I was improving. My new room looked more like a pie-shaped walk-in closet than a patient room, but that mattered little to me at the time.

Dr. Norton had cut my Hyperbaric visits to one each day. I felt elated until he promptly wrote an order for a new therapy to fill the gap. The physical therapist called the new one CPM, short for continuous passive motion, but I called it the *knee stretcher*. Not unlike a medieval rack, its sole purpose was to restore flexibility to my right knee. After the right leg reconstruction, Dr. Norton allowed my leg in its thigh-length cast to remain in a straight-legged position for a few days. In just that short time it stiffened. The first day on the new machine, Billy, my physical therapist, plopped the heavy piece of equipment on top of the bed and lifted my right leg into its cradle. He strapped my thigh down and set the motorized contraption on forty five degrees. He pressed Start.

I screamed as the CPM endeavored to force my stiff leg into a flexed position.

Billy hit the off switch.

"Don't even *think* about starting that thing again until I've had something for pain," I ranted. And while you're at it, next time *I* want to hold the controller."

Fifteen minutes later, after my dose of hydromorphone kicked in, I felt ready for another go. Billy handed me the remote and gave me a quick rundown on how to operate it. With a backwards glance, he walked out the door.

Two hours later he came back. He looked shocked to see I'd completed the full two hour session and even managed to bend my knee a little farther. With Billy's hands-off attitude and Dr. Norton's daily encouragement, I continued to make progress.

On Five East, my days started early with a trip to Hyperbaric. I was always happy to get it over with and happier still when the transporter wheeled me back to the safe haven of my little room. My nursing assistant had always changed the linens in my absence. I settled onto the clean, smooth sheets that covered my cloud-like mattress. After the long session, my legs throbbed. I punched the button on the call box.

"Will you ask my nurse to bring me some hydromorphone, please?"

I heard the nurse coming long before she entered the room. I saw her only twice during the twelve hour shift, so it felt like Christmas when she showed up. She wasn't alone. She pushed her constant companion, the COW, ahead of her as she walked. It was no secret that most of the nurses didn't care much for the awkward creatures. Personally, I liked them all.

COW, an acronym for "computers on wheels," was a metal drug cart that looked as if it had been designed by committee. Five feet tall and topped with a computer screen, the COW appeared tall and clumsy. Bins and drawers festooned the metal structure below the computer. The drawers brimmed with supplies and medications, and the COW clanked and banged her way along the uneven floor near my room.

Once she'd arrived, the nurse consulted the screen and typed something on the keyboard. The narcotic drawer sprung open and she grabbed a vial of hydromorphone. After drawing the liquid up in a syringe, she injected it directly into my central line on the right side of my chest.

The familiar rush of warmth spread through my torso, then into my arms and legs. With it came blessed relief. As I floated on my bed, it dawned on me how easily I could develop a taste for hydromorphone. I made a mental note to be cautious and tucked it away to consider later.

By my third week in the hospital, I felt the urge to write a note or two about the surreal world around me. I wanted to record what happened, in case I forgot.

"Dave, could you bring me some paper and a pen when you come tomorrow?"

"Sure, I've got a pad in the car you can have."

I started to jot down names and words on my pad. Most of them looked like scribbles, but those scrawls represented my first attempts to record my experience and feel more conscious in the world again. They gave me some sense of purpose.

More and more I interacted with my nurses and assistants. Most, I discovered, had honed their skills caring for patients with difficult and complex injuries like mine. Sadly, many looked stretched thin. Their brows knitted with worry as they came through my door. They squinted hard at the computer screen on top of their COWs, scanning the list of meds, current orders, and other details on my treatment plan. I liked most all of them, but a few stood out from the rest. When the charge nurse assigned me a really good one, I had high hopes I'd have them again. Sometimes that happened.

After a week on Five East, they rewarded me with an exceptionally industrious nursing assistant for three days in a row. She was a whirlwind as she tidied my room and changed my bed. No room at a five star hotel ever looked neater. Better still, every day she gave me a thorough bed bath. She didn't just hand me a wet wash cloth and go on her way, but scrubbed, rinsed, and dried my back and the other parts I couldn't easily reach. Then she applied lotion to my skin and combed my hair.

I considered a bed bath something special. Other than the one the nursing assistants had given me my first night on the Trauma Unit, I couldn't remember getting any others. That night they'd scrubbed my head and legs so forcefully, I'd cried. I guess they had to rub hard to get the dried blood off my skin.

Before they'd assigned me the industrious nursing assistant, it had already dawned on me that I hadn't had a bed bath in quite some time. Every night Ann brought me a warm washcloth for my face and a toothbrush and cup to brush my teeth. *What did other patients do in the absence of a family member like Ann?* I didn't judge the staff at all. I just figured they were way too busy. As a nurse, I knew what it was like to work without enough help. Consequently, I tried not to complain.

One morning, the charge nurse came by my room to do an informal survey. "I'm trying to assess how well the assistants are doing their jobs." She gave me a look that let me know she suspected more than she said. "Are you getting fresh water in your pitcher each day?

"Yes," I said.

"Are they changing your sheets each day?"

"Definitely"

"What about bed baths?"

"My assistant's been doing a great job these past several days." I smiled happily at her.

"What about the days before that?" She looked suspicious.

"I don't remember having any bed baths. Well, except for the one I had on admission."

"Hold on a minute. You've been here for a while. How long have you been at County Hospital?" Her eyes narrowed.

"I'm not sure. A little over three weeks, I think."

"That's unbelievable." She looked outraged. Then she let it slip. "I've suspected some of the assistants were charting baths without actually giving them."

Mystery solved. Now I understood.

Lunch arrived shortly after my bath and survey. I lifted the lid and gave it a cursory peek. I ate some cottage cheese and drank the carton of milk, before replacing the lid. Then I turned my attention to things that interested me. Eating wasn't one of them.

My mind drifted. Love and hope continued to infuse me, and as they did, I wanted to share those gifts with others. I'd spent years in nursing and mental health encouraging my patients. Now, as I lay immobile in my hospital bed, giving encouragement to others might help me feel useful again. I needed a sense of purpose almost as much as I yearned to walk.

As a nurse, I recognized the signs of burn out. At County Hospital, I saw those signs daily in some of my nurses and doctors as they made their rounds. They greeted me with vacant stares and rarely spoke when they inspected my wounds, changed an IV bag, or checked a piece of equipment. I wanted to help, but what could I do? I typically had less than a minute to interact with them before they left to see the next patient.

A nurse I'd never seen walked in. Without greeting me, she leaned over the foot of my bed to inspect the vacuum pump attached to my ankle.

"Is it doing okay?" I asked.

She jumped and looked up as if wondering from which direction the voice had come. When she saw me, she looked taken aback.

"I couldn't imagine who was talking," she said as if seeing a ghost.

I must look awful. She doesn't think I can talk.

Later a man in scrubs ambled in.

"Hi there," I said. With no expression, he grunted in my direction, leaning over my foot and peering at the muscle graft Dr. Wexler had embedded in my ankle wound. I recognized him. He'd visited my room before. His badge read "Dr. Smith." Since he'd never spoken, had he come out of something like morbid curiosity to gawk at my wound? His blank stare let me know he had no interest in talking.

"Are you doing okay today?" I asked undeterred. He glanced up again.

"Okay," he muttered, shrugging. He managed a grimace that might have been a smile. Then he turned and bolted out the door.

Though a few nurses and doctors, like Dr. Smith, responded with little more than a grunt, others smiled when I spoke to them. It gratified me to see the more disgruntled ones when they sometimes showed up hours later to talk.

One night about nine thirty, a particularly miserable-looking nurse shuffled into my room. The look on her face suggested she didn't have the smallest desire to be at work.

This one's going to be a challenge.

"Are you okay?

"Not really."

"You look tired? I bet you didn't get enough sleep?"

"No, I sure didn't." She sounded mad.

"I'm so sorry. I know how hard it is to start a nursing shift when you're already tired. I'm going to pray both of us get through the night okay." She gave no visible sign she'd heard me.

Around three in the morning I woke up and saw her dark form silhouetted against the light from the hall. I was well accustomed to my nurses coming in to hang IV bags. She surprised me when she sat down in the recliner next to my bed and broke the silence.

"I've got stage four breast cancer. I've just finished weeks of chemo and radiation.

"That must have been hard."

"It was. I'm also a single parent. When my sick leave ran out a week ago, I had no choice but to come back to work early. I had to have the money. I'm so tired I don't know if I can make it." She sighed loudly.

My heart ached for her.

"I'm so sorry you're having such a hard time. But I'm glad you stopped by. Do you have fifteen minutes to take a break and rest in my chair? It's very peaceful in here. You're more than welcome to stay as long as you'd like." In the dim light, I saw her joyless face soften.

We sat without saying anything for quite a while. Maybe she slept. When she got up and moved toward the door, I called after her. "Jesus brought me hope. I'll ask Him to look after you, too."

"Thank you," she said.

I wasn't always happy with what I had to endure in the hospital, but once I began to connect with the people around me again, I felt much better. Sometimes I even made a new friend. Andrew, the young male assistant who'd taken care of me in the ICU, often worked with me on Five East.

"This one size fits all gown doesn't flatter you much." He said, helping me into a fresh hospital gown one morning.

"What? You mean you don't like these tents they give me to wear?"

"It's so big, it's ridiculous," he laughed. "You might come out the arm hole."

I laughed as I pictured myself in the massive garment with the gaping openings for my thin arms.

"You remind me of my son," I said smiling.

"Well, you're like a whole different person from when I took care of you in the Trauma ICU. We thought you were bossy and acted a little strange."

"And I thought you and the nurse were trying to kidnap me," I said, half smiling, wanting him to understand how scared I'd been.

"No kidding? Well, no wonder you acted that way."

From my first days on Five East, I enjoyed a more mindless pastime. Each time someone ventured into my room I offered the same request as they turned to go.

"Just leave my door open."

"Are you sure?"

"Yes, please. Wide open."

My bed faced the door. When the door stood open, it afforded me a great view of the hallway beyond, like a wide-screen TV. What did I care about privacy, when all traces of modesty had left me weeks before? As I looked out my portal I felt reassured to know that I still felt connected with the larger, more vital world beyond. The idea of just lying in my hospital bed with only the four walls and my mind for company felt awful. Some of my thoughts scared me. Those that focused on the future frightened me most. It was best to avoid them.

The hydromorphone that coursed through my veins still impacted me. It made it easy to envision what I saw outside my door as a circus. The television couldn't compare with the drama that unfolded out there. Most afternoons, I witnessed a magician walking down my hall. He trailed a few feet behind the tall man in my circus who sported a large metal halo, encircling his head. The magician held onto the tall man's belt and guided him down the hall. I knew that the illusionist was really one of my physical therapists, and the tall man, a fellow trauma patient. It would be several days before I understood that his halo was actually a metal fixator like the ones on my legs. *A fixator attached to my skull would be a lot worse!* Meanwhile I let my imagination run with the stories I made up.

I watched the tall patient and realized that despite his fixator, I envied him. I felt the same way toward the sea of workers, visitors, and patients who ambulated down my hall.

They could walk. What could possibly be more magical than that? I sighed.

Sometimes I saw Billy, my wiry physical therapist, hurry toward another patient's room. Two enormous and well-muscled companions with buzz-cuts flanked him. They were the *strong men* in my circus, ready to demonstrate feats of strength to a waiting audience, just out of sight. Several days later, as I stared dreamily out my door, I witnessed two other massive *strong men* passing in tandem.

"Who were those big guys?" I asked my nurse, when she checked on me at the end of the shift.

"They were probably members of the County Hospital Patient Hoist Team. They help move patients."

I was also curious about the patients who sped by on stretchers. Were they new? Or, like me, had they called County Hospital home for a while? How had all of them come to be patients on Five East?

I bet they have some stories of their own to tell.

One evening they wheeled a young girl into the room next door. For the first twenty four hours, she screamed. I heard the nurses talk to her in loud voices. It sounded like they might be trying to make her more comfortable. In response, she screamed even louder. My heart wrenched as I lay in the dark and listened. After a while, she quieted down.

"She's a teenager who was in a car accident. She's in pretty rough shape," Andrew said as he rolled me onto my side to change the sheets.

"Do you think she'll be okay?"

"Not sure yet, but she's doing better today."

Evenings were my favorite part of the day on Five East. That was when Dave, Pierce, and Ann came to visit. They ambled in around seven, after dinner in the County Hospital Cafeteria. I looked forward to their coming and clung to them once they arrived. I felt safe having them there.

I'd been at County Hospital over three weeks and almost four weeks total in the hospitals when one evening Ann strolled in by herself. She handed me a warm washcloth and my toothbrush and gave me the latest news.

"I sent Dave and Pierce back home tonight. They both looked awfully tired. Would you like me to read your get well cards to you?"

"Yes, that would be great."

Ann read a card from her niece. I listened and felt touched by the kind words she'd written.

"That was so nice of your niece to write such a long note. I barely know her, but she sounds like she understands what I'm going through."

"You know she had cancer a few years ago."

"That's right. I'd forgotten you told me."

"She's okay now."

With all the cards read, Ann, a former stage actress and artist, penciled in an eyebrow on my face where she'd told me one was missing.

"You look so pretty," she said, after she'd finished.

I didn't exactly believe her, but it felt great to feel the love behind her words.

"Do you have a mirror?" I asked.

"Sure, here it is."

I let her place it in my hands and held my breath as I raised it in front of my face.

Not pretty at all, but not bad. I'd imagined worse. I scrutinized my face for a few minutes more. There were quite a few scabs and red scars around my eyes. The person who looked back appeared pale and thin.

"I look like the 'before' picture of someone in dire need of a makeover," I laughed.

"You're funny." She chuckled.

We enjoyed the light feeling for a few minutes more. Then I remembered that *night* was coming. It was almost time for her to leave.

"Ann, would you pray with me?"

"Sure, I will," she said.

"Lord, thank you for bringing Lara love and comfort as she heals." She went on, "Bring someone kind to take care of her tonight."

I began to feel fortified for the long night ahead. At nine o'clock a voice interrupted her prayer as it boomed over the loud-speaker in the hall. It announced in a sweet, but urgent tone, "Visiting hours are now over. Please exit through the hospital lobby." I'd learned to dread the sound of that voice.

Most nights, Dave and Pierce visited too. They brought a sense of normalcy to the strangeness of my hospital world. Sometimes they alternated nights with each other. That was particularly true once Dave returned to work.

"You're coming along, Mom. You just need to eat," Pierce said.

"You're healing. Just way too thin," Dave added.

To their credit, neither mentioned the extent of my injuries. It was around that time that I began to understand, in the lines between their comments and in the looks on their faces, how serious the damage to my body had been. How close I'd come to dying. What I saw in their eyes was not just affection, but relief.

One evening I looked up and realized something was wrong with Dave. He wore a shell shocked expression.

He's probably just tired.

I scrutinized his face more closely. *It's something else.*

"What's going on, Dave?"

"I can't stop thinking about how you looked on the ground that day. When I close my eyes, it's all I ever see.

"That's terrible. Now that I think about it, I only remember Pierce standing in front of me in the woods. I don't remember seeing you at all."

"I was behind you on the ground, holding you still. I thought your eye was gone and you'd bleed to death. I didn't know how to stop it." He looked as if he might cry.

As he spoke, the truth dawned on me. Pierce had heralded ambulances, hauled a jack to the woods, and hoisted the tree off Frances, while Dave had been on the ground right behind me, supporting my head and back, and taking it all in. The images from that terrible night had emblazoned themselves in his mind so forcefully that whenever he tried to sleep, they tormented him.

Dave had been my rock. Now he needed my help.

He needs to tell his story too.

"Sweetie, I think it would be good if you tell me some more about what you remember," I said, encouraging him.

"I really don't want to think about it."

"Please, Dave, I'm sure it will help."

Haltingly at first, tears in his eyes and a quaver in his voice, he began.

"You kept trying to get up," he whispered. "Something told me not to let you move, so I held you as still as I could. I knew I needed to stop the bleeding, but there were just too many gashes and I couldn't find them in the tangles of matted hair. I felt sick when I looked down and saw your twisted leg and mangled foot. Bones stuck out in every direction. I didn't know what to do except hold you. It didn't feel like enough."

He paused. Then he went on. "We waited in that awful waiting room all night as Dr. Bolling tried to save your life." He trembled and his eyes filled with tears.

I lay without saying a word until he paused.

"It sounds like you did an amazing job. What would I have done without you? I think you should tell that story to anyone who will listen. I promise it'll help." Tears rolled down my cheeks.

"I love you," I said.

"I love you, too."

I reached out and took his hand. In the soft light, I noticed his face relax. Dave had taken the first step to heal.

RIVER OF DOCTORS

It had been a week and a half since the kind woman had parked my stretcher in the corridor outside the Hyperbaric Unit and spoken to me. In the days that followed, I felt an overwhelming sense of joy when I recalled her simple but loving gesture. Unconditional love filled my heart for the many hospital workers who filed into my room day after day. Without knowing why, I knew those powerful emotions had come from God.

Would I have been able to cope this well before the accident?

I didn't think so.

Why had God chosen to lift my spirit in such an unexpected and powerful way?

What came to me was this. He wanted to bring me *hope*.

It was clear as a lake on a still day. Without hope, I would despair. A body filled with despair couldn't heal. Without hope, I would never mend. Jesus had brought me hope to save my life. Apparently, He thought I had more work to do. I vowed right then and there to do whatever it took to hold on to hope.

Increasingly, I realized how blessed I was to have been given some extraordinary doctors. Before the accident, with exception to our family physician, I had little use for many of the ones I met. They seemed far too focused on treating only my symptoms. While I preferred to try exercise and change my diet as a first line of defense, they handed me a prescription.

"You're wasting your money," they said when I brought up nutritional supplements.

After the tree fell, my body was in such a mess I had no choice but to entrust it to a group of physicians and surgeons I'd never met. To say my life was wholly in their hands was completely true. I'd made very few visits to the doctor before the accident, but now I had a physician for nearly every part of my body. Fortunately for me, my County Hospital doctors, like the Regional Medical surgeons before them, were amazingly skilled and caring.

With the help of hydromorphone, I stayed focused in the present most of the time, but sometimes I let myself fantasize about walking. Pangs of longing passed over me as I pictured myself on my feet and striding down the hall outside my room.

"I need to check your legs," Dr. Norton said, interrupting my daydream. He'd come in when I wasn't looking. As he gently palpated and studied my leg and ankle wounds, I noted a look of concern. I didn't ask any questions. Guess I was too afraid at what he'd say.

Dr. Brown also continued to look in on me.

"Let Francesca, the dietician, know about my albumen levels," I told him. After that, I waited to hear if he'd talked to her. Sure enough, a few days later Francesca mentioned it.

"Dr. Brown asked me if I had any more ideas on how to maintain your muscle mass. I wonder why?" She looked puzzled and happy.

"He must think you're pretty smart. Did he have anything else to say?"

"Not really, but he was friendly. Hold on a minute. Are you plotting to get us together?"

"Well, *plotting* might be too strong a word. I only told him you were trying to help me boost my protein stores and might have some ideas."

"Oh, I see." Her pale cheeks flushed red as she laughed.

Another of my primary medical doctors, Dr. Short, monitored everything from my blood pressure and blood sugar to signs of infection. He always took a minute to talk to me when he made his rounds. That told me I could count on him to be there.

One night around three or four in the morning, I awoke strangely disoriented and knew something was wrong with my bladder. I felt an uncomfortable and powerful urge to urinate for the first time since coming to the hospital. I struggled to orient myself. *I need to call for a bed pan.*

Then, I remembered I had a urinary catheter. Something was definitely wrong. I put my hand on my abdomen. It felt uncharacteristically round. I grappled for the call box and pushed the button.

My nurse that night, a particularly conscientious woman, hurried into the room. She rolled me onto a bed pan and pressed gently on my abdomen. Flushing my catheter with a large syringe full of sterile water several times, she tried to dislodge whatever might be blocking the flow of urine. That didn't help. She grabbed a smaller syringe and deflated the balloon that held the catheter in place. Finally, she eased the catheter out. Over a thousand *cc's*, more than a quart of urine poured into the pan. I sighed with relief.

"Call Dr. Short and tell him Ms. Easting's having a urinary crisis in room five eleven.

Minutes later, Dr. Short hastened into my room. "What happened?" he shouted at the nurse. That was the only time I'd heard Dr. Short yell.

"She's retaining urine. I just got eleven hundred cc's out.

"Get a urine culture and sensitivity, *stat.*"

He's worried I have an infection.

The nurse went over to the COW and keyed in the order on the computer screen.

After Dr. Short left and my nurse inserted a new catheter, I felt better. *Thank goodness that's over.*

Two nights later, when I awoke with the same symptoms, I began to worry.

"What's wrong with my bladder?" I demanded of Dr. Short when he appeared in the door.

He shrugged. "I'm hoping it's just tired of having a catheter. After all, you've had one for over a month. We'll see what your labs show."

The next day, two of my favorite doctors strolled in. 'I've looked at your labs and there's no evidence of bacteria in either specimen," the older one explained. "That's good news. No infection." His eyes twinkled.

"How could anything possibly grow in my urinary tract with all the antibiotics you've got me on?" I rolled my eyes and nodded at the rack of medication bags over my head. "If it's not an infection, what's causing it to block up. Whatever it is, I sure hope that's the end of it."

The two men were part of my team. They were specifically entrusted with keeping infections from growing in my body. The older doctor's hair was silver, while Dr. Lassiter's, a resident who hailed from Colorado, was brown. He couldn't have been more than a few years older than Pierce.

"What are you doing?" he asked when he noticed me trying hard to form letters on a small pad of paper with a dull pencil.

"I'm making notes. I'm thinking of writing about this strange experience when I go home, and I don't want to forget anything."

He hesitated for a moment. "You definitely should write a book. I've never known another patient who lived after injuries like yours. You need to tell all of us in the medical field what it's like to be a critically injured patient in the Trauma Unit, especially since you're one of us. We really don't know."

"I've learned a lot about being a patient, more than I ever wanted to know. I can tell you one thing. Knowing that someone cares makes all the difference. I'm talking about you, Dr. Lassiter."

"Hey, I want a copy of your book when you finish it. Don't forget, okay?" He looked thoughtful for a minute. "You know you're my favorite patient, right?"

"How come?" I asked, playing along.

He reflected for a minute and then looked more serious.

"Because you have a positive attitude and know who you are."

I was perplexed about the knowing who I was part and it must have shown, so he elaborated.

"The first time I met you, you were a new patient in the Trauma Unit. You could barely speak, and yet you described yourself as a *wellness nurse* and a *health nut* and informed me you were into herbal medicine and nutrition. I was surprised that anyone in such terrible shape could be so clear about themselves." He smiled.

I didn't have the heart to tell him that at least some part of my positive attitude likely came from the hydromorphone. His compliments bolstered me and made me feel he respected me, but I didn't feel one bit worthy of such high praise. I had only done what I believed I had to do to survive. Even in my most confused state, something deep inside had convinced me I needed to stay calm and hopeful if I wanted to live. That wasn't always easy.

By the fifth week at County Hospital, they'd taken me off enough medication that at least hallucinations and nightmares were not much of a problem. I'd had some great nurses the week before and began to think my trepidations about the night shift were well behind me when something shifted.

I'd been on Five East long enough to have had quite a few nurses assigned to me more than once. Most let me know that they knew I was an RN too. One night as I waited for my nurse to begin her rounds, she bustled in out of breath, looking stressed.

"We're really short tonight. In fact, I'm the only nurse on this end of the floor, and I have two brand new trauma patients. That's eight patients in all. I have no idea how I'm going to get through it." Her eyes looked wild.

For a moment I felt grateful that she'd entrusted me with her feelings, until I felt the old tightness return to my chest. I stepped back into my nursing role to try to calm her.

"You're a good nurse, but that sounds like way too many patients for *anyone* to handle. Have you thought about what you're going to do?" I tried to sound encouraging.

"No, not yet." She stopped in her tracks to look at me.

"Have you asked the Nursing Supervisor to send you some help?"

"I called her, but she has to see if someone can come in."

"If it were me I'd probably check the new patients first. Then I'd pass out bedtime meds to the rest of us. They might be a little late, but that's okay. You might not get a break tonight, but you'll get it done. I'll pray for everything to go well."

"Thanks, I might as well give you your meds while I'm here." She injected some hydromorphone into my central line and pushed the COW out the door, looking a little less frazzled.

"Lord, please give my nurse the help she needs tonight."

The next two nights when two other nurses said the same thing, I felt a lot less flattered. A tall nurse with a tough demeanor had a different attitude.

"Don't expect me to come in to see you every four hours tonight like I did a few weeks ago when I had you in the Intermediate Care Unit. I just won't have time." Her voice sounded gruff.

How dare she take this out on me? It's not my fault. The last time she had me, I was barely conscious and terrified. My blood boiled. I ranted at the four walls. "If I were in charge I'd tell everyone, 'Remember your patients are vulnerable no matter how strong they appear. Don't tell them you're not comfortable to handle their care, especially if they're a nurse or doctor.'"

My tirade over, I felt calmer and a little more compassionate. I began to pray. "Lord, please help my nurse and her patients get through this night. Oh and while you're at it, please watch over *all* the nurses and patients at County Hospital."

In the middle of the night when I called for something for pain, I waited over an hour for my nurse to show up. I trembled as I waited. *Am I safe here?*

She finally hurried in. "I'm sorry it took so long, it's just a madhouse tonight. I'm three months pregnant and I don't seem to have as much energy as usual."

"That's okay. I know you must be tired," I said, my fear and anger gone.

When she left, I felt stunned by the change I'd seen in her. *God had worked his magic again.*

THE OUTSIDE WORLD

Pierce and Dave stood by my bed.

"Dad, I wonder if Mom might be able to manage her cell phone now. Some of her friends are eager to talk to her. Gerry Ford calls two or three times a week. So do others. What do you think?" He cast a dubious look my way.

"I suppose so," he said, then to me, "Lara, do you think you can keep up with your phone now?"

"Yes," I said, not feeling at all certain. I did my best to remember what managing a cell phone entailed.

Pierce handed me the phone and plugged in the charger on the shelf next to my bed.

"How will I charge it," I said looking at the unit just out of my reach.

"Just keep the phone in bed with you, and we'll put it back on the charger when we come to visit," Pierce replied.

The hospital had become my whole world. I reflected little about life outside its walls. The phone that came with my room rarely rang, and when it did, I ignored it. It sat on the floor somewhere out of my sight, too far away for me to reach. Now with my cell phone, I began to think more about the people I loved. I also thought about my dog, Bob Marley, and realized I really missed his smiling face.

Having my cell opened up a whole new world of communication. By the end of October, once it occurred to anyone to check our minutes, the phone bill was well over a thousand dollars.

"That's terrible. How did that happen?" I whined.

"Well you know," Dave replied. "I have to call your mom every day. She's worried sick and wants to come down. I call her so she doesn't jump on the next plane. I love her, but it would be hard for me to have anyone else to take care of right now. Lots of your friends are calling too, now that they know they can reach you."

"But we just can't afford phone bills like that."

"Well, I think right now it's important for you and everyone to be in touch. So let's not worry about the bills. Okay?"

"Okay." I liked the sound of that.

Dave was right. Blessings arrived with each new call. As I related my progress over the five weeks and realized I'd gone from near death to mostly oriented and engaged, it amazed me.

"Hey Big Sis." My brother, Josh, rang from Washington DC. "I'm ready to come take care of you as soon as you go home."

"You would really come?"

"Try to stop me. I need a break from work, and I'd love to see Pierce and Dave and help you all out a bit. Do you know when you're going home?"

"I really don't know. No one's said anything about it."

Going home? No one had mentioned the prospect, let alone given me a date. As I looked at my legs, something told me it wouldn't be anytime soon.

"Well, just call me when you know."

Janelle, a longtime friend, called from her home on the coast.

"John wants to come help you for a week when you go home. Then, I'll take a turn after him." John was a retired nurse anesthetist and Janelle, a retired nurse and John's wife.

"Are you really sure he wants to do that?"

"He means every word."

"He knows I'm bedridden, right?

"That doesn't matter to him."

"Won't you and John want to come together?"

"No. If we come separately, you'll get a lot more mileage out of our visits."

I couldn't believe what she said. I hadn't seen John and Janelle in several years and now they were volunteering to drive ten hours and take care of me in the worst shape of my life. I could hardly take in their kind offer.

My boss called too. "Don't worry about your job. It's secure. We're prepared to wait."

When I hung up, I felt elated. I was "the nurse the tree fell on." I'd survived, but beyond that, no one could say what would be possible. Dr. Norton still hadn't told me if I would walk. I'd already surpassed my doctors' and family's expectations just by living. Now there was not only a glimmer of hope for my future, but for one that might have meaning, as well.

I began to envision myself, not just strolling in the halls, but walking into the factories and greeting the workers. I pictured myself performing hearing tests, teaching CPR, counseling workers, and bandaging work related injuries. Those images had such a powerful healing effect on my psyche, that I played them like a movie when I needed to brighten my mood.

Jenny, my closest friend from the plant, who'd encouraged me to trust in Jesus, drove over a hundred miles to visit me on a Saturday. She was just over five feet tall, but the power of her presence as she stood in that dark, cramped space at the foot of my bed overwhelmed me.

"You look beautiful," she said, tears filling her eyes. "Can I say a prayer for you?"

"Please," I said.

"Thank you, Lord, for protecting Lara and for saving her life. Continue to watch over and heal her. And thank you for our friendship. It means the world to me." After she left, her words hung in the air. I looked down in my hand to see the gift she'd handed me. I unwrapped it. It was a cross, perfect for holding in my hand while I prayed. A "clinging cross," Jenny had called it. I grasped it tightly in my hand and thought of her visit. What a lucky woman I was to have a friend like Jenny.

The next day Gerry Ford called. "You're life's going to have more meaning now than ever before. God has something very special in mind for you. I'm sure of it."

"You think so?"

"I know so. God has a plan for you."

How can that be true? How can God have a plan for me, when I can barely move?

Though I didn't really buy it, everything Gerry said as well as the promises that I could return to work, fortified me. I clung to them like a drowning woman to a raft.

Other friends called too. Barbara, my close friend and a practicing Quaker, rang late one afternoon from her home in Wisconsin. "I've been holding you steadily in the light," she said firmly. I felt the glow of that light warm me as she spoke. I had a good idea what she meant, but wanted to know more.

"Tell me more about holding someone in the light?"

"Well, when I hold someone in the light, I do a combination of old-fashioned prayer and a sort of visualization. I begin by sitting with my gratitude for the person and all that they mean to me and the world. I move to my hopes for them. I talk to God as I move from gratitude to hope. And I picture the person held up and surrounded by and inundated with God's light, which is radiant, the perfect temperature, healing, reassuring, and beautiful. I often hold my hands out, cupping the light and the person. It may sound a little theatric, but it feels exactly right."

"No, it sounds a lot like what I've been experiencing," I said.

We hung up, and I lay in the quiet room, smiling to myself.

Friends and family gave me support, and yet I often felt reluctant to talk much about what had happened with Jesus. For one thing, it was nearly impossible to put into words. The idea of a godly presence communicating with me was completely new and foreign to my experience. For another, some people, my husband included, fell silent when I told them about it. I'm sure they thought I'd gone a little crazy. After that, I was more selective with whom I shared that part of my story. I noticed that the ones who'd experienced God's Spirit for themselves didn't seem a bit surprised by what I said.

Ann brought me cards from her relatives who'd written me. "You're a miracle," many wrote. Others sounded even more optimistic. "God didn't bring you this far, not to bring you all the way."

One night during visiting hours, Ann quoted her favorite verse from the Old Testament. "I will never leave you, nor forsake you," she said. (Hebrews 13:5 KJV) Her words struck a chord. For years the fear of being completely on my own in the world had plagued me. In the first weeks after the accident, my most paranoid thoughts focused on being abducted and left to suffer alone. But now that I sensed God's presence alive and vibrant within me, I felt more secure.

Of all the many lovely and heartfelt notes I received, the letters that I got from Maggie, my sister-in-law, probably comforted me the most. In one she wrote:

> One night, the first week that you were at the hospital at Regional Medical, I awoke at four in the morning with a very distinct sentence-one sentence, spoken to my heart. I got up to write it down. Here it is, 'I am going to put this body back together.' I trust that was God's message to me for you. As the days have passed, I've gone back to where I wrote that down and I continue to thank Him for the team of healers that He has appointed to your care. One of the wonderful things about God is that no man can limit Him. He doesn't abide by the ICU visiting hours☺. He can come and stay for the duration. He is omnipresent. I have asked Him to show Himself to you as you come in and out of surgeries and consciousness, that you would sense his nearness.

Maggie wrote that letter my second week at County Hospital, just a few days before the angelic transporter had come to pick me up from Hyperbaric and given me hope. Since my sister-in-law had no idea what kind of relationship I had with God, she tried to fill me in:

> He cares about our brokenness and He's mighty enough to do something about it.

Then she spoke of a difficult time she'd experienced herself.

> He would inspire people to call or write at just the
> right time. The Bible says that God is near to the weak
> and broken hearted. I felt his nearness.

Just as for Maggie, I found that Jesus had done a lot of inspiring on my behalf. The amount of love that poured in even from people I hardly knew blew my mind.

But why was He giving me so much?

Maybe Jesus knew He had to overwhelm me with goodwill to convince me He was real.

And why was He answering *my* prayers and not the prayers of someone far more deserving?

Maybe Gerry was right. God really did have something special in mind for me.

Looking back, it was a good thing I felt confident in God's love as I started my last week at County Hospital. I was going to need it.

QUITTING HYDROMORPHONE

In my fifth and last week at County Hospital, they assigned me to a highly experienced float pool nurse named Cat.

"She tells it like it is," I told Dave when he visited me that night.

Cat had imparted what ended up being a valuable piece of advice. "Word to the wise, I don't know exactly when they'll discharge you from County Hospital, but I don't think it'll be long. Once they do, you won't be leaving here with your central line."

"What are you saying?" I asked, wrinkling my brow.

"I'm saying you won't have an IV anymore, and whatever facility you go to next won't give you hydromorphone." She raised her eyebrows and nodded at me to make her point.

I'd worked with the mentally ill and substance abuse patients in the past. It took me only a second to grasp her meaning. Hydromorphone was a powerful narcotic and highly addictive. *Would they take it away from me in my condition?*

It followed that any pain medication the doctors gave me when I left County Hospital would be given in pill form and in orders of magnitude less potent.

"Are you sure?"

"You bet," she said with a look that suggested she knew.

Her words jolted me. Having witnessed firsthand unpleasant drug withdrawals in quite a few hospital patients, I decided I'd better heed her warning. That night as my nurse injected my dose of hydromorphone, I silently vowed it would be my last till the next evening.

The next afternoon as I began to eat my dinner, a sudden wave of nausea gripped me and I retched so abruptly I didn't have time to move my plate. Then I felt fine.

What was that? I'm not sick, so what's wrong?

An hour later, when Dave ambled in, my legs were jumping and twitching on the bed. "There's something going on with my legs, Dave. I can't stop moving them."

"Oh I can see that, Lara. And that's not the only thing. You're talking a blue streak and acting a little crazy. How are you feeling?" He looked alarmed.

"I can't lie still. I feel like I'm coming out of my skin."

"When did you have your last dose of hydromorphone?"

"Last night," I said. "That's what it is. I haven't had hydromorphone for twenty-four hours. I decided to take myself off it and switch to oxycodone for pain."

"What? You didn't? Call the nurse."

The nurse came in pushing the COW. "What's going on?"

"My wife's neglected to tell anyone she's detoxing herself off hydromorphone. I'm pretty sure she's going into withdrawal."

"Why didn't you tell us?" She looked worried. "You've been on a lot of hydromorphone. You know coming off narcotics too fast can make you really sick?"

"I just figured I could do it on my own. Can I get hydromorphone in a half dose?"

"Sure, I can give you half. There's some flexibility in the order." She unlocked a drawer on the COW and retrieved the vial. I saw a look of admiration in her eyes as she injected the narcotic. In seconds, my legs stopped moving.

"Whew. That's better," I said, relieved.

Twenty four hours later when Dave came to visit again, my legs were back to doing a jig on the mattress. I chattered as if I'd guzzled three cups of espresso. Dave buzzed the nurse's station.

To my surprise, Cat showed up. "What's going on with you tonight?" she asked, looking curious.

"Oh, Cat, I'm so glad to see you. Since I saw you two days ago,

I'm almost off the hydromorphone. But can I have a quarter dose, please?"

"Coming right up." Cat looked pleased as she injected the reduced dose into my central line. That was the last one I needed.

I'd counseled countless patients who hadn't been quite so lucky. They hadn't been able to escape the hydromorphone, while others ended up hooked on other narcotics or massive dosages of opiates in pill form. I refused to let that happen.

Two days later, just out of surgery, I awoke in the Recovery Room and realized to my surprise I'd been dreaming about food. It was a BLT piled high with crispy strips of bacon and slices of garden tomato, slathered in mayonnaise. After five weeks in the hospital, it was the first hint of an appetite.

Where could I get a BLT? I had to have one. Then it dawned on me. Ann, my mother-in-law, often kept the fixings for treats like that. As soon as they wheeled me back to Five East, I called her.

"Hey, Ann. Are you coming tonight?"

"Sure am, darling."

"Well, believe or not, I'm hungry. Do you happen to have a tomato and some bacon to make a BLT?"

"I sure do. I'll bring you one."

That afternoon, I thought of little else. When she arrived with my sandwich, I opened the bag. Inside, I saw the sandwich of my dreams. I took a bite and swallowed it, barely bothering to chew. I'm sure I looked like a sight as I wolfed it down, but when I finished, Ann beamed.

"That was wonderful," I said smacking my lips. I didn't tell her I could have eaten a second or even a third. "I hate to ask you, but I will anyway." I laughed. "Could you possibly bring another one tomorrow?"

"I'd bring you a hundred if you'd eat them," she said, laughing with me.

Detoxing from hydromorphone marked the beginning of a shift in my appetite. It would be weeks before it fully returned.

NO PLACE TO GO

When Cat informed me about the hydromorphone and my central line, she'd also mentioned discharge. But discharge to where? How could I possibly go home this helpless and weak?

I never imagined they would take away my hydromorphone, let alone discharge me. It wasn't that I loved being in the hospital, but rather that I couldn't imagine how I'd make it anywhere else. Twenty-four seven, I lay on my back with the head of my bed raised halfway up and my legs weighted down with fixators. From that position I could eat, sleep, brush my teeth, and look out the doorway to the hall. That was it. Cat was the first to mention discharge, but soon others would follow.

Randi, a nice discharge planner at County Hospital, strolled in to see me first. "In a week, you will no longer qualify for care in this hospital. I'm meeting with Dr. Norton early next week to discuss plans for you." I stared at her like a deer in the headlights.

What does that mean? Still confused and agitated from coming off the hydromorphone, I had no idea, so I chose to ignore it.

The next day a stocky brunette from Regional Medical strolled in. "I thought you might need to see a friendly face," she said, shuffling over to my bed and wearing a flat expression. "I assess prospective patients for one of the units at the hospital."

I asked about the one thing I knew I desperately needed. "Will they give me physical therapy there?"

"That shouldn't be much of a problem."

So far, so good. I began to feel a little better about her visit.

"What treatments are you currently receiving?" she asked in an ominous tone.

"Treatments? You mean like IVs and surgeries?" *Why is she asking me? Is it a test to see what I know? Shouldn't she be talking to my nurse?*

"That's right." She nodded.

Confused, I looked down at my body and at the equipment attached to my legs and chest and tried to formulate an answer. "Well, I get hyperbaric oxygen treatments and IV antibiotics. I have a urinary catheter, an external fixator, a wound vacuum, and get wound care on both legs. I think that's it. Why?" *What's she driving at?*

As a nurse I should have known.

"Those won't be enough. You're too low-level medically speaking to qualify for my unit." Her voice was devoid of feeling.

"You mean they won't take me?"

"That's right, you don't qualify."

"What about the Rehab Unit? That's where I'd really like to go." Many years earlier I'd called on countless patients in that area to teach them how to manage their diabetes and colostomies. Their nurses had struck me as exceptionally caring and competent.

She hesitated. "You're not qualified for that place either."

"Why not?"

"Because you can't stand on at least one leg. That's their requirement"

I was starting to get the picture. "So, I don't qualify for your unit because I'm not sick enough. And the Rehab Unit won't take me because I'm too badly injured. Are there any other options? I can't stay here, and I'm certainly not strong or mobile enough to go home." My mouth felt dry.

"You might be eligible for a nursing home. I really don't know. I'd have to check with our social worker."

"And if I'm not?" I couldn't breathe.

"If not, you'll have to get someone from your church or your husband to take care of you at home."

"I don't belong to a church, and my husband has to work. He's trying to support us right now."

"I really don't know then," she said gathering her brochures into her satchel. She looked tired and depressed. *Another burned out hospital employee.* She shuffled out the door.

What the heck was that about? Where does that leave me? My heart raced as my thoughts spun out of control. If Dave stayed home he'd have to quit his job. I recalled a young male patient I'd called on at home years before. He'd been hit by a car, paralyzed, and had pressure sores from lying in bed. I'd gone to care for his wounds. His mother had been forced to quit her job, their only source of income, to take care of him. They lived in a one room apartment, filthy because she seemed too depressed to clean it. I could picture that happening to Dave and me.

Fear seized me. I saw myself lying in that bed with the stained sheets, in the windowless room. I pictured an even more worn version of Dave looking on. At five o'clock when my tray arrived, I pushed myself to eat. I retched again, this time out of fear.

How will we survive?"

Panic encircled my chest like the vice in Dave's workshop. I wanted to pray, but couldn't. When Cat came back, she found me sitting up in bed, chin resting on my chest, barely able to raise my head.

"What's happened to you? You look like someone died. When I saw you two hours ago, you were happy."

"I, uh, she uh," I struggled to form the words. "A representative from Regional Medical came today. She says I'm not qualified to be admitted there. She's not even sure I can get into a nursing home. She said my husband might have to quit his job and stay home with me. But what would we do then?"

"Stop." She put her hand up. "You can't go there. That woman gave you way too much information. She should never have said that to you. What the heck was she thinking? What was her name? I have half a mind to report her." Her face flushed with anger. "Hold on a minute. I'll be back." She bustled out of my room.

She returned five minutes later, holding a steaming cup of hot tea in a mug. "Here. My mother always said a cup of tea makes everything look brighter." She sat in the chair next to my bed and continued to talk in a soothing voice. "You've come a really long way. Don't let that negative woman knock you back down and don't think about what she said. You don't have all the facts yet. Do you want me to ask Dr. Norton for something to lift your mood?"

"Thank you, but please, no more drugs. I'm still struggling to detox from the last one."

"You're right," she said. "I forgot you just got off the hydromorphone. No wonder you're in such an emotional state."

I forced myself to focus on the warm cup I held in my hands. I let the steam and Cat's voice block out all thought. Slowly I began to feel centered again. When Cat left, I felt calm enough to pray.

"Jesus, I feel so weak. Please send me somewhere that will help me get stronger. You more than anyone else know what I need."

That night Dave wandered in alone. "What's the matter, Lara? You look depressed." I told him about the visit with the representative from Regional Medical. "Damn it. I hate that she upset you like that. You've been so happy. She could have called your nurse to get that information. Anyway, try not to worry about it. It'll be okay. Dr. Norton and Dr. Bolling won't let them throw you to the wolves." He reached out and gently squeezed my hand.

The following Monday, a representative from the Regional Medical Rehab Unit walked in. "Hi I'm Gigi." Unlike the representative from the other unit, Gigi flashed a broad smile and looked pleased to see me.

"All our patients participate in a full day of physical and occupational therapy every day except on Sundays. Typically they stay with us about two weeks, before going home. The family is also required to attend educational classes at the end of the program. Can you think of any questions?"

I took a deep breath. "Another woman told me I didn't qualify for the Rehab Unit. She said I had to be able to stand on at least one leg." I took another breath. "I know I can't stand, but my arms are strong. More than anything I want to go through your program. I know in my heart that's exactly what I need to get stronger. If you take me, I promise I'll work hard."

"It's true you're not technically qualified." She seemed to mull something over. "Every now and then they'll make an exception. That's why I thought it was important to meet with you face to face. I can see you're motivated, and you'd be a great candidate for our program. I'm going to present your case to our Medical Director and talk to the hospital's insurance carrier. Both would have to approve your admission." She headed toward the door. "I'll get back with you in a couple of days."

Gigi left me feeling more hopeful. I could tell she cared.

Toward the end of my last week at County Hospital, Dr. Wexler, the plastic surgeon, walked in and announced his plan. "I've decided to repair your ankle wound with something different. As you know the muscle graft didn't take. I'm going to try a synthetic product called Integra. It's a high-tech tissue scaffolding system that can help fill in deep, challenging wounds like the one in your ankle. I've scheduled your surgery for the morning."

The surgery on my ankle went well. Wednesday, the day after, Randi and Gigi continued to work on what to do with me. Randi scheduled a meeting with Dr. Norton and Dr. Short for later that morning, and Gigi met with the Medical Director on the Rehab Unit. The Integra surgery had been the last thing keeping me qualified to be a patient at County Hospital. Between the two planners, my life hung in the balance.

I awakened, obsessing over what would happen next. I started to pray but felt too distracted. I buzzed the nurse. *Maybe she's heard something.*

It was almost an hour and a half later when she walked in. By that time I felt exhausted from worry.

"I haven't heard anything," she said distractedly, looking harassed.

"Can I just have some lorazepam then?"

I felt defeated. I'd chosen a tranquilizer over trusting in God to help me.

Dr. Lassiter, the young resident from Colorado, strolled in for a visit. "Hey, are you okay?" He looked shocked to see me so glum.

"Honestly, I've been better."

"This isn't like you? What on earth's the matter?"

I told him.

"I'm sure it's all going to come out okay. You're such a positive person. They'd be foolish not to accept you on their Rehab Unit."

"Did you say *positive*?"

"Yes, and I meant it. Don't forget, I want a copy of your book. Promise me you'll bring me one." He flashed me a smile as he turned to leave. His kindness and encouragement meant the world to me. I didn't know it then, but it would be the last time I saw him.

My eyes followed Dr. Lassiter out the door and caught those of someone in the hall. A distinguished looking man about fifty made a sudden detour into the room.

"Hi, I'm a chaplain here at County Hospital. Did you want me to come in?"

"Yes," I said. "But you looked like you were headed somewhere else. Do you have time?"

"I certainly do. I normally cover a different floor, but I'd love to spend some time with you. It's funny. I rarely ever come this way. So tell me a little about what's going on?"

I felt an instant connection with the chaplain. I told him about the angels and how Jesus had brought me hope to help me heal. Then my fears came spilling out. As the chaplain listened, nothing I said seemed to surprise him. His eyes sparkled with love and understanding.

"Thank you for sharing your story. You've been through a lot, good and bad. I'd like to say a prayer for you. Would that be okay?"

"Yes, please. I haven't been able to pray for myself these past few days."

"Please God, bring hope to Lara again. Your hope and your love have fortified her and kept her from despair. Now she faces new challenges and she's afraid. More than ever she needs to know that you are still with her, empowering her as she goes through this new phase of her recovery."

His prayer felt just right. "Thank you so much. That was just what I needed to hear."

"Here's my number. You can call me any time." He took my hand and gave it a gentle squeeze, smiling, before he turned and walked slowly out the door.

Later that same day when Bailey, my friend from Surgery, dropped by to visit, I still felt calm. "I'm so glad you came," I said. "I'll be leaving County Hospital soon, and I wanted to tell you how much your friendship has meant. I know you're going to make a wonderful nurse anesthetist, but I'm going to really miss you."

"What? Where are you going?"

"Don't know yet." I shrugged.

"Call me when you get settled." She handed me her cell number on a piece of paper.

"Thanks," I said as she leaned over to give me a hug.

The following morning Gigi called from Regional Medical. "The Medical Director approved your admission to Rehab. Now I need to get the okay from the insurance company. They'll make their decision soon." She sounded hopeful.

I took a breath, trying to focus on God's Spirit within me. "Please Jesus, let the insurance company approve my admission to the Rehab Unit."

My words sounded hollow. They lacked power. Something on the TV caught my attention. The only show I'd ever watched at County Hospital was *Little House on the Prairie*. It was the only one that comforted me. Now a pastor strode back and forth across the screen preaching. I turned up the volume.

"If you're not positive something can materialize, it will not become a reality. Pray with confidence," he boomed.

"Okay, let's try this again," I whispered. I turned the volume down. "God, I know you are more powerful than the insurance company that seems to hold my life in its hands. I know you want me to heal. Please open the way for me to go to the Rehab Unit. You've done everything possible for my good so far. You've brought me wonderful surgeons and people who have loved and supported me when I needed them most. I know I can count on you to help me now."

That's more like it. Moments later the phone rang. Gigi. "The insurance company approved your admission. You'll be in room 306 on the Rehab Unit."

"I can't believe it. I was just praying when you called. Now you and God have answered my prayer. Thank you for everything."

I called Dave at work. "Hi Sweetie. Guess what? I'm going to Regional Med Rehab Unit. Can you believe it? They're taking me today."

"Really? That's great. Wish I could talk right now, but I can't. I'm covered up. Pierce and I will see you there tonight. Take care, honey. I love you. Bye."

No sooner had I hung up when Randi the discharge planner hurried in. 'The ambulance is going to pick you up in thirty minutes. I'll tell the nurse to get you ready." She started to leave.

"Do you have a second?" I asked.

"Sure," she said, coming over.

"You know, Randi, I've been scared to death these past few days. The worse thing was, after days of feeling so connected with God, I felt detached and alone. Then, a few minutes ago, I prayed for His help again. I thanked Jesus for all the people like you who've worked so hard to help me. And I asked Him to send me to Regional Med Rehab Unit. Now, thanks to all of you, I'm going."

Randi took a swipe at a tear that started down her cheek. "Thank you, I really needed to hear that what I'm doing makes a difference. I've been kind of discouraged lately, thinking nothing I did mattered. Sometimes I feel I'm no match for the insurance companies or hospital policies." Her face glistened as she smiled through her tears. I reached out to hug her, before she turned to leave.

A few minutes later, someone else knocked on my door. It was the night nurse who'd struggled with cancer. Her cheeks now glowed with a rosy color and the corners of her mouth turned up slightly when she saw me. "I just wanted to say goodbye and tell you I'm doing a little better." She came over and handed me a card with a picture of a cherub on the front. "Thank you for giving me hope," it said. "I've been carrying it around for days."

"We're on some strange journey here, aren't we?"

She nodded.

"Lately I've come to believe that we're not in this alone. God is with us. Take good care of yourself, my friend." I squeezed her hand tightly and looked into her sad eyes.

Then, just as Cat had predicted, two nurses descended on me and carefully pulled out my urinary catheter and the central line. One placed a pressure dressing over the small holes left in my chest and applied pressure. The other disconnected the wound vacuum from my left ankle. "It belongs to the hospital," she told the other nurse. Finally they buzzed the nurse's station to call Billy to pick up my ankle stretcher, the CPM.

They were about to take off my hospital gown when I protested. "I don't have anything else to put on."

"I guess it'll have to go with you then." One nurse slid a piece of paper in front of me to sign. I didn't bother to read it.

I glanced over at the shelf above my bed and noted my few possessions. "Could you hand me those things?" The nurse passed me my cell, the charger, my toothbrush, and my note pad and pen. That's all I had with me.

As suddenly as the tree had crashed to the ground, they discharged me. *So this is it?* Stripped of everything but the hospital gown, I was too happy to care.

God had proved once again that He called the shots. Now it was time for me to see what I could do to get stronger. I looked down at my body. I'd never been this weak or thin in my life. I would need a few more surgeries down the road to finish the job my trauma surgeons had started. Now it was up to me to heal.

ALMOST HEAVEN

The ride back to Regional Med felt magical. I gazed out the back of the ambulance, mesmerized by the flaming fall colors and rays of bright sunlight that flashed by. After five weeks without so much as a glimpse of the outside world, I couldn't tear my eyes away. The day looked glorious, and no one felt happier than I to see it.

A pretty young woman sat beside me in the back of the ambulance. "I'm Rosa. I'm in training to be a Paramedic. What happened to your legs?" she said looking over at my leg cast and fixator. I offered her the short version, preferring to concentrate on the view out the windows.

An hour later we pulled into the ER entrance of the hospital. The EMTs rolled my stretcher into the lobby, up an elevator to the third floor, and down a long hall, before stopping in front of room 306. When they opened the door and wheeled my gurney in, I gasped. "This is so beautiful."

My new room, unlike any of the previous ones, looked like a spacious bedroom in a nice hotel. A giant picture window at the far end treated me to a view of hills dotted with red, yellow, and orange trees. I was back where I belonged, almost home.

"Thank you, God, for bringing me here." My eyes welled with tears of joy.

A minute after I arrived, Janice, the nurse who admitted me, went to work. First, she checked every inch of my skin and found a tiny raw area near my tailbone. "That looks like a skin tear, probably from having been slid sideways in bed."

"Oh no." I sighed, concerned. I'd seen how quickly bed sores, even small ones, could grow. I'd once called on an elderly homebound patient with a hole in his hip the size of my fist. His wife told me it had grown from a blister in less than two months.

"I know you've been lying on your back," Janice said, "but I probably don't have to tell you better stay off it."

I looked at my external fixator with the awkward metal spikes jutting out from the bones on my left leg and the massive full leg cast on the right leg. How would I ever get comfortable on my side?

Janice weighed me on a bed scale and subtracted what she estimated to be the combined weights of my vacuum pump, external fixator, and right leg cast. "You can't weigh any more than ninety or ninety-five pounds. How much did you weigh before the accident?"

"A hundred twenty-five." I quickly did the math. "Oh my God. That's thirty pounds. I've lost a quarter of my body weight." I felt stunned, but not nearly as shocked as when I caught sight of myself in the full-length mirror across from my bed. The reflection of a much older, skeletally-thin woman stared back. *Is that really me?* I'd always had an athletic build. Now, I saw someone I didn't recognize.

My appetite came and went. It had improved when I first detoxed off the hydromorphone, but it still wasn't good. I told myself whether I felt hungry or not, I had to eat.

"God, please give me back my appetite so I can heal and get stronger," I prayed, believing He would help.

Janice, a thirty year veteran on the Rehab Unit, was on top of the situation. "I got you an order for Megase," she said.

"Isn't that the medication they give cancer patients to stimulate their appetites?"

"Yes, I gave it to my husband when he had cancer several years back. I'm pretty sure it'll help you too." Janice handed me my first dose. Then she turned to other matters. "They just took out your urinary catheter this morning, right? Have you gone yet?"

"No, I tried, but couldn't. I had some problems going a few nights ago. Do you think something could be wrong with my bladder?"

"I'm not sure." Janice hurried out the door. Minutes later she returned with a straight cath, a small catheter to relieve my bladder.

A tall, lanky urologist sauntered in as soon as she'd finished. "Janice tells me you've had some problems."

I nodded. "I retained a quart of urine a few nights ago when I still had my catheter. They told me it wasn't an infection." He raised his eyebrows.

"We need to do an ultrasound to make sure you don't have a *fungal ball*."

I didn't ask what that was. I could guess. Yeast and funguses proliferated in the body when a patient took antibiotics. A fungal ball sounded ominous.

"Not another bladder problem," I grumbled.

He hesitated for a moment. "I hope not either, but I'm far more concerned that retaining that much urine might have damaged your bladder."

"What would mean?"

"In the worst case scenario, you'd have to catheterize yourself every six hours when you go home," he said, looking grim.

"You mean like patients who've been paralyzed?"

"Uh huh."

Catheterizing myself wasn't an option. Not only did I feel too weak, I lacked coordination.

In the Ultrasound Department, a radiologist read the film and told me what he saw. "I don't see any evidence of a fungal ball." He smiled. I felt relieved until I recalled the urologist's warning. *That much urine might have damaged your bladder.*

Back in my room, I buzzed Maureen, my nursing assistant, determined to prove the urologist wrong.

"I have an idea," I said when she walked in. "Would you bring me a pan of warm water and a bed pan?"

"Sure, coming right up." She nodded as if she understood.

I rolled onto the bed pan and forced my mind to concentrate. Then I slipped my hand into the warm liquid. The old remedy worked like a charm. I beamed at Maureen. "God is definitely good."

That evening, I had a visitor. A good looking man with wavy brown curls and sparkling blue eyes bounded into my room and towered over my bed. He appeared to be in his early thirties and looked excited to see me. "I've been following your progress through Dr. Norton and waiting for you to come back. Do you know who I am?"

I studied his face. "Well, you must be either Dr. Court or Dr. Bolling." I remembered Dave's glowing remarks on the surgeons at Regional Medical.

"I'm Dr. Bolling. Dr. Court and I actually do look a lot alike, but I'm the more handsome one." He grinned in a way that suggested he didn't take himself all that seriously. Then he surprised me. "Did they tell you at County Hospital, I came to see you?"

"No. When?"

"You'd only been there a week when I was driving back from a family reunion. I stopped by the Trauma Unit to check on you. They told me you were having a treatment in the hyperbaric area, so I marched down there, but the staff in the Hyperbaric Unit wouldn't let me in."

"No one ever mentioned it." I frowned, the heat in my face rising. "I wish they had. I could really have used another friend in that place."

"Well, they probably didn't believe I was a surgeon. I came straight from a picnic and was wearing shorts and a t-shirt." He laughed.

We talked for a few more minutes before he looked at his watch. "By the way, I need to let you know I won't be back for a few days. My wife is scheduled to have a baby in the morning."

"That's wonderful. Congratulations to you both. Is this your first?"

"No, our second. We have a son." He wore a big grin.

"I can't believe you came by this late with all that going on. And thanks for checking on me at County Hospital. I only wish I could have seen you."

He took my hand, and then turned to leave. I lay quietly in the fading light and contemplated how lucky I'd been to have someone as kind and diligent as Dr. Bolling that terrible night in September. Or had it been something other than luck?

"You know Dr. Bolling was a theology major before going to medical school," Pierce had informed me one night at County Hospital. I now reflected on that and a smile spread across my face.

Maybe there are no accidents.

As night approached on the Rehab Unit, I began to feel uneasy. Not long after eight, I looked up to see an attractive woman in scrubs towering over me. I must have looked apprehensive because she hurried to reassure me. "Don't worry, honey, we're gonna take real good care of you. My name's Nora and I'll be your nurse tonight.

Nora brought over my personal care supplies and helped me get ready for bed. After I turned on my side, she placed two pillows between my legs to keep the fixator spikes from gouging me.

"Just call me if you need anything." she said and turned toward the door.

True to her word, in the middle of the night, when I buzzed for something for pain, Nora appeared in minutes.

"I'm impressed. You're fast," I said, relieved.

She handed me a pain pill. Then I turned on my side and Nora tucked a few pillows behind my back for support.

"I can see I'm in good hands. There were so many times at County Hospital when I felt scared on the night shift."

"Well, you're safe with me. Anyway, I'll let you know if I'm tied up. If that happens, I'll find someone else to help you."

"Thank you."

The first day on Rehab had been an emotional one. Now I could relax.

I awoke the next morning feeling happy. The door opened. "Hi, I'm your nursing assistant. It's time to wake up. Did you sleep okay?" She hit a lever on the side of my bed, raising my head.

Still mostly asleep, I blinked at her. "I slept pretty well. It's a little tough getting comfortable on my side though."

As the room came into focus, I could see my nursing assistant better. She was a willowy blonde who looked about Pierce's age. She carried over supplies for a bed bath and placed them on my over-bed table.

"We want you to do as much as you can yourself. That's the philosophy on Rehab. Then I'll help with the rest."

I washed with a wash cloth and dried myself. The nursing assistant and I did our best to wrestle on a pair of men's pajama bottoms. They didn't want to go over the sharp fixator spikes. My transfer had happened so fast, Dave hadn't known what to bring me to wear. The assistant and I struggled to get the pants on for a good fifteen minutes, before I lost patience. "How will I ever do this myself?"

"There's got to be a better option than those pants," she said. "I'm new at this, but your external fixator would make it hard for anyone."

"I'll call my son and ask him to bring a pair of his stretchy athletic shorts tonight," I said. "Those should be easier."

The assistant placed my breakfast tray on the over-bed table. My stomach growled. By eight- thirty, I'd eaten half of the small box of cereal and a banana. Maybe the Megase was working. I hoped the kitchen would send up macaroni and cheese for lunch. The thought of it made my mouth water. Hospital food was starting to sound good.

"Now it's time for you to learn how to transfer from the bed to the wheelchair." The nursing assistant produced a wooden board.

I'd transferred many wheelchair bound patients using a sliding board. But now that I *was* the patient, I realized moving myself from one seat to another using only my arms and a board involved a certain level of trust. The sliding board was about three feet long and spanned an open gulf between the bed and the chair. One end of it went under my bottom while the other rested on the wheelchair seat. It looked a long way down.

I began to inch my way across, in jerky motions, my arms held straight at my sides. I felt dizzy and off balance. What if I hit the floor?

"I'm right here," the assistant said, apparently sensing my fear.

With my first transfer under my belt, I found myself sitting so bolt upright, the room lurched sideways. I slumped back into the wheelchair to avoid falling forward.

"You okay?" she asked.

"Dizzy," I said.

"That's to be expected. You've been in bed for weeks."

She pushed me down the hall and into the therapy room. Light flooded the beautiful space, but nausea distracted me. The assistant handed me a ginger ale.

"Thank you." I said, grateful. "You must be psychic." A few sips later my stomach settled.

A young woman with a calm demeanor approached me. "Hi. I'm Hanna, your occupational therapist. I want you to start with exercises that'll strengthen your arms. You'll be relying on them completely to get around for quite a while."

Per Hanna's instructions, I raised and lowered my arms, holding two pound weights. For the first thirty minutes they felt strong. I was glad I'd entertained myself at County Hospital, pulling on the stretchy bands Billy had tied to my bed rails.

The strong feeling didn't last. My arms began to tremble when I lifted them. Soon I could barely control them.

"That's enough of those," Hanna said gently. "Rest a few minutes. Then I want you to try some pushups on your wheelchair arms."

I rested. Then I pushed up eight or ten times, before I had to stop. 'I don't feel very well," I said. My whole body started to shake.

A therapy assistant wheeled me back to my room. I felt so weak and defeated I broke into tears as she rolled me through the doorway. The kind woman put her arm around my shoulder.

"I'm too weak to exercise," I sobbed. A deep sadness washed over me and my heart felt heavy with grief. I'd prayed for the chance to come to Rehab, but now, I didn't think I could do it.

"You'll be okay. You're going to get stronger every day. I promise. That's what happens to everyone who comes here."

I don't know how many minutes I sat there with the assistant's arm around me while I cried. Eventually I took a deep breath and dried my eyes.

I took advantage of the time in my room to rest and regroup emotionally. In an hour when the assistant reappeared at my door, I felt stronger, more determined.

Back in the therapy room, I met my physical therapist, Karen. She had her hands on her hips and wore a serious expression. It was obvious she meant business.

"Now, you're going to work on your legs. I can see you've lost a lot of muscle mass in your thighs and butt. Those muscles, as well as your abs, will be vital once you start walking. It won't be easy today, but I know you can do it." She gave me an encouraging look.

I raised and lowered my legs in three directions. I felt surprised to find I could lift the leg with the fixator so well. Then I worked on my abs. Maybe I still had some strength left after all.

After two hours, Karen put up her hand for me to stop. "That's enough. You did well for your first day. I'm not surprised you're tired." She gave me a look that let me know she admired the effort I'd made.

Karen wheeled me back to my room. From the wheelchair, I struggled to transfer into bed. "Don't forget to stay off your back," she said in a no nonsense voice that reminded me of Cat, my nurse at County Hospital.

"I really haven't figured out how to get comfortable on my side yet."

"I can imagine." She wrinkled her brow as she glanced down at the spikey fixator. In the muted light it looked like metal scaffolding.

Despite the late hour Karen stayed to help. Before I could say another word she'd stuffed six pillows between my legs, behind my back, and under my head in various trial arrangements. To make sure the night staff knew the plan, she took pictures and posted them on my wall. Not only was Karen thorough, it was plain she cared. My heart swelled with gratitude.

Two days later when Saturday arrived, I felt spent but satisfied. I'd made it through my first two days in therapy. What I managed to accomplish in that short time filled me again with hope. The therapy assistant had said I'd get stronger if I worked at it each day. I believed her. It was a truth that would guide me in the months to come.

A feeling of peace fell over the unit. While Rehab had operated like a boot camp for the injured during the work week, the schedule relaxed on Saturday and Sunday. Dave and Pierce wouldn't visit until evening. They were working at our house with Dave's brother, trying to figure out what changes to make to our family room. They had to make it ready for when I would come home in two weeks.

I don't want you lying around all weekend, Karen's voice echoed in my head. I could tell from her tone she meant it. After lunch I took advantage of the free time to wheel myself around the unit. I soon found to my delight I could propel my chair without difficulty using my arms. For someone who'd been stuck in bed for six weeks, it felt thrilling beyond measure to be mobile again. What may have seemed a small thing to others, felt like nothing short of a miracle to me.

I ended my journey just inside a tiny glass chapel that jutted from the side of the hospital building. I gazed down at the park below. Rays of sunlight poured through the windows, warming my face and legs. I completed a few sets of arm exercises for good measure and began to pray. As I did, tears of joy and relief streamed down my face. I'd survived the accident and the ICUs. Now I would get stronger.

"Thank you, Jesus, from the bottom of my heart for my life and for Pierce and Dave. Thank you for bringing me to this wonderful place and for giving me the strength and the appetite I need to get stronger. Thank you especially for Dr. Bolling, for Karen, Janice, and Maureen and for all the rest of my doctors, nurses, and aides. For letting me feel your love and comfort. I love you. Amen." As I prayed, warmth filled my chest and spread throughout my body. Then came an incredible peace. Knowing I could return to that place of peace again made me feel safe, content.

Back in my room, I phoned my mom at her home in upstate New York. From the time the tree had hit, Dave called her daily, but up until now I hadn't felt strong enough to have a lengthy conversation with her. We'd always been close, maybe too close. Her worries had often fueled my own. For that reason, I sometimes needed to keep a healthy distance. Now, I looked forward to talking with her.

"Oh, Lara. It's so good to hear your voice. How're you feeling?" She sounded relieved.

"I'm doing great, Mom. I'm so glad to be here. I wish you could see this place."

"Dave said you had a hard time at the other hospital."

I considered what to say and decided to tell her about the angels. No telling what she'd think. I inhaled deeply before I began.

"Mom, some of what happened at County Hospital might sound a little strange. But it felt as real as anything I've ever experienced. I was at my lowest point when a tired-looking woman showed up to push me from the hyperbaric center back to my room. The pain was almost unbearable and I really didn't think I could keep going. Out of desperation, I called out to God and asked Him to help me. Then the tired-looking woman spoke to me in a powerful voice. 'You're going to be okay, God's going to heal you. You don't need to be afraid.' Just those simple words completely calmed me and filled me with joy. As crazy as it might sound, I knew it was Jesus' Spirit who spoke through her. I think He did so to give me hope."

"That's wonderful. I'm glad you got so much support from the people there," she said, missing my point.

I chuckled at her reaction. It was obvious she thought it was more about the kindness of strangers, than God.

I'd shared my story with a few others who responded the same way.

"Were they giving you lots of drugs at the time?" one asked.

"Maybe you felt so desperate you wanted to believe God spoke to you?" another said.

Then, there was my favorite. "When the tree fell on you, did you have a concussion?"

I laughed when I played those back.

Their reactions really didn't matter. What I'd said didn't sound rational, but what I'd experienced had been real. I hadn't lost my mind.

GAINING STRENGTH

Time was going fast. It would only be a week and a half before they sent me home. There was so much left to do. I worked hard in Rehab, while Dave and Pierce labored to overhaul our family room. It was the only part of our log home located on the ground floor that could be converted to a space for someone in a wheelchair. No one knew if or when I might walk or climb the stairs to the main part of our house again.

Greg, Dave's brother, and Maggie, his wife, drove in from a neighboring state to help with the project. As a contractor, Greg was well suited for the job, but Dave expressed concern when he called.

"Neither Greg nor I really know what you'll need. I guess I should talk to your physical therapist. My brother's talking about doing things like putting in a handicapped toilet and a shower and widening the bathroom door down there." He sounded weary. "I don't know if I have the energy for all that."

"Just tell him," I suggested. Dave's plate was already full. "Why not stick with the original plan of rearranging rather than remodeling the family room. That sounds like plenty to tackle until we know more. Anyway, I'm not planning to stay down there for long." The family room was a neglected space, primarily used when we had an overflow of company.

"Do you think you'll need a hospital bed?" he asked, looking more hopeful.

"No, I'll be fine with a regular one." I pictured myself sleeping downstairs alone. The image of lying in the dark, cut off from Dave and Pierce, conjured fearful thoughts. It was shades of the night shift at County Hospital all over again.

The next morning in therapy I talked to Hanna.

"Why not get your family to move your king-sized bed downstairs. That can be your new master bedroom. Then you and Dave can sleep together."

"That's it. Why didn't we think of that?" I couldn't wait to tell Dave.

I called him after therapy. "I like it," he said and sounded brighter.

Saturday evening, after working at our house all day, Maggie, Greg, Dave, and Pierce burst into my room on Rehab for a visit. By the smiles on their faces they'd been having fun together.

"What have you four been up to?" I asked, their energy contagious.

"Mom, we moved your king-sized bed downstairs. Unfortunately, we had a little problem." Pierce gave me a half smile.

"What happened?"

"We got the bed stuck in the stairwell for a good half hour." He laughed.

"I hope you didn't leave it there," I giggled.

"Lara, you'll be glad to know we moved your desk and computer down too," Dave added, looking pleased.

"That's great." I considered the joy of emailing friends and smiled.

"That's not all. Maggie relocated your favorite paintings and pottery from the living room to brighten your space."

"Oh, thank you, Maggie. That was so thoughtful. You know how much I love bright colors."

Maggie walked over to the bed. I'd looked forward to telling her about the amazing gifts God had given me at County Hospital. I felt sure she would understand.

"When I prayed, Jesus answered. He sent people from all over to give me hope." I could hardly contain my enthusiasm.

"It's obvious that you've been filled with the Holy Spirit." Maggie's eyes widened.

"Is that what you call it? The name certainly fits. It brought me so much joy I still feel happy whenever I think of it. I think the Holy Spirit might be why I survived."

Once again it dawned on me how fortunate I'd been. I'd met others in physical therapy who hadn't been so lucky. One depressed looking woman, who might have been in her forties, suffered fractures to her legs and arms in an auto accident. Her arms, in braces, rested uselessly in her lap, making it impossible for her to transfer, wheel, wash, or feed herself. My heart ached for her.

Another young man with metal external fixators on his arms and a brace on his back shared his story. "The ambulance that picked me up asked me where I wanted to go. They said it should be County Hospital or the trauma center in the big city. I'd never heard of County Hospital, so I chose the other. What a big mistake! No one answered my call button or came to help me. I developed bed sores and a staph infection. After two months, I begged them to send me here." His face was contorted with pain and anger.

Seeing others in worse situations made me reflect on just how far I'd come. I'd been incredibly fortunate. I reflected on the hundreds of prayers that friends and total strangers had offered on my behalf. Had their prayers brought me a miracle? I felt positive they had.

By the time I'd arrived in Rehab, I couldn't remember anyone shampooing my hair in over a month. Granted, they'd probably worried about disrupting the many sutures, cuts, and scabs I could feel through my curls. Looking in the mirror, my ringlets appeared to lay matted with blood and were sticking out in every direction. It didn't take long for me to notice the sign that read "Beauty Parlor" a few doors down from my room.

"Is that really what it says it is? I asked the therapy assistant.

"Sure is."

"Can I do it with my injuries?"

"Shouldn't be any problem."

"Well, sign me up." The assistant made me an appointment for the following Tuesday.

I was like a child waiting for their birthday to arrive. On the appointed day, she wheeled me into the tiny room. The hairdresser, a cheerful woman, smiled and greeted me. "Hi, a wash and trim for you today?"

"Yes, please." I felt elated.

"Do you want conditioner?"

"Definitely. Give me the works."

"Do you have any neck problems I should know about?"

"No, just a back that was broken and a foot long laceration on my head that is still tender," I said.

"I can work with those. Don't worry, I'll be gentle."

The hairdresser leaned me back over the sink and lightly scrubbed and massaged my scalp. If I'd been a cat I would have purred.

"Are you sure that doesn't hurt the cuts on your scalp?"

"No, it feels wonderful." I wanted to sign up with the hairdresser every day of the week.

When she finished, I cast a cautious glance in the mirror. My curls framed my face in a short bob. "I think I'm starting to look more like my old self. Thank you. How much do I owe you?"

"Twenty dollars."

"Wow, what a deal." Only twenty dollars to feel like a new woman.

While having my hair washed felt heavenly, getting the stitches in my right leg taken out was anything but. Miranda was one of my favorite nurses on the night shift. She bustled in at around eight. "I need to look at your stitches." As she peered down at them, I looked too. They covered an area about ten inches long down the side of my shin and were crusted over in scabs.

"Just as I suspected, they need to come out. Quite a few of them look like they're imbedded." I knew that meant the skin had grown over them.

With complete focus and calm Miranda began to work. I could see she was having a hard time grasping the stitches with her tweezers.

"Ow," I cried. She pressed on. It hurt. I yelled again loudly enough to be heard down the hall. Then I started to cry. I'd had my share of pain, but this felt awful. Miranda paused.

"I'm sorry. I know it hurts. I have to dig them out. Do you want me to stop?"

"No, I'm sorry. Let's just get it over with."

"Not a problem." Miranda pressed on for another ten minutes, while I did my best to take some deep breaths. Finally she was done.

"Thank you," I said, relieved.

"You did well. I could see it wasn't going to be easy. They'd been in there way too long."

Miranda was both compassionate and a true professional.

After six weeks in the hospital and a week on Rehab, I continued to gain strength as I slowly regained my appetite. I suspected it had something to do with the Megase Janice brought me every morning. Or maybe it was because everyone who visited tried hard to fatten me up. Coworkers lavished me with lunches from my favorite restaurants when they visited. A friend who ran a Mexican restaurant in town even brought me a platter of chicken enchiladas, beans, rice, chips, and salsa one night in the middle of a downpour. I'd only previously managed to eat a few bites at each meal, but when my friend handed me my dinner, I ate everything on the plate. My appetite had returned with a vengeance.

"What do you want me to bring for lunch?" Jenny asked when she called.

"Visiting me at County Hospital was more than enough, but a chicken salad sandwich on wheat from The Lunch Place would be wonderful if it's not too much trouble," I answered, laughing. I had my order down.

I knew I shouldn't encourage the people who loved me to buy meals for me, but I couldn't help myself. Those chicken salad sandwiches fueled my fantasies. No doubt, it was my body's cries for protein.

Sunny, my current dietician and former colleague sent up extra thick sandwiches and chocolate shakes from the hospital kitchen and treated me to a veggie plate from a restaurant I liked on Main St. I loved their collard greens and jalapeno corn bread.

Even Dave and Pierce were under strict orders to pick up macaroni and cheese from the hospital cafeteria when they stopped there every night for supper. I was shameless.

Anyone could see after a week on the Rehab Unit I'd gotten used to being pampered. I had so many people indulging me that Janice, my nurse, came in at lunch just to see what I was eating.

"I have to admit I'm a little envious," she said one afternoon as she looked longingly at the Reuben sandwich, piled high with corned beef and sauerkraut, sitting on my table.

"Would you like some?" I mumbled, wolfing it down. She took a bite. I'm ashamed to say I didn't offer her a second one.

It struck me again how much everyone was doing for me. Friends told me they wanted to help, so I let them.

One evening, Pierce had had enough. "Mom, you're getting spoiled. Don't get the idea that you can expect such preferential treatment when you come home. Dad and I are both completely worn out. We're not gonna be able to drive back to The Lunch Place every day to bring you a chicken salad sandwich." Pierce's aggravated expression suggested that Dave wasn't the only one who felt stressed.

His words stung, but I understood. Dave and he had grown weary after weeks at County Hospital trying to coerce me to eat. They'd felt sick at the sight of my frail body wasting away as I sent plates loaded with food back to the kitchen. But it wasn't my fault. I'd never been a picky eater, but to Pierce I'd been a bit obstinate in my refusal to eat. My body, in starvation mode, had rapidly broken down muscle, while I could do nothing to stop it. Later they both realized it had been the hydromorphone.

At Regional Medical and eating with gusto, I felt sorry for other patients who, owing to medication, stress, or illness, couldn't force themselves to eat.

In Room 306, visitors flooded in to see me. Doris, the person I reported to at Great Foods Manufacturing, trudged in and grimaced at the sight of the metal external fixator sticking out of my left leg and foot.

"Oh, God, that's awful." She cringed and looked like she'd be sick.

"Does it really bother you that much? I've grown so used to looking at it."

Doris's adverse reaction was the first of many I would encounter in the weeks to come.

Most days I pushed my body so hard in physical therapy that by three o'clock it took great effort to inch my way across the sliding board back into bed. I even had to ask Doris to tell my friends at the plants not to visit for a while. I didn't want to offend anyone, but I just wasn't up to having company. I began to realize I was not just physically weak, but emotionally drained. I felt exhausted, yet wound up tight like a spring. Even chatting with my closest friends sometimes wore me out. At my job I'd counseled workers on how to improve their health. Now when they visited, I still made an effort to hold up my end of the conversation, to be "on," like the hostess at a party. It never occurred to me to let them know how I felt. I guess I worried they'd think I didn't care.

Despite warnings from Doris to the workers at GFM, my friends outside of work still showed up. Their visits persuaded me I still had a life. Liz, a wonderful nurse I'd worked with many years earlier in the hospital, also walked in one afternoon as I was working out in physical therapy.

"I know you don't remember when I visited you in the ICU, but I wanted to tell you how impressed I was with Pierce. He was so good with you, always patting your arm and telling you you'd be okay. You would have been proud."

"I am proud. I remember him saying just what I needed to hear under the tree and later at County Hospital. He kept me from panicking."

"I could also see how worried Dave was. It was obvious how much he loved you."

"I think you're right. He was terrified I wouldn't be the same person if I lived at all. I'm so blessed to have him. You know what they say, Liz. Opposites attract. Dave goes with the flow while I push the river. He sees the glass half empty, while I think it's half full. He researches everything while I fly by my feelings. We're different, but it works."

I felt touched to hear what Liz said. Since she'd retired from nursing she'd taken to writing. Her award winning short stories inspired others. I showed her the pile of notes I'd scribbled at County Hospital. Liz had a strong faith in God, so I decided to tell her about the dark days at County Hospital and how Jesus had brought me out of the fog and into the light.

After I'd told her, she beamed. "I hope you'll write about everything that happened after you get home. Your story will encourage others."

"You think so?"

"I know so."

The next Saturday when Dave and Pierce were visiting, Perry bounded in. Frances limped behind him, sporting a walking cast. It was the first time I'd seen them since the night of the accident, seven weeks before. They took turns hugging Dave, Pierce, and me. Their love energized us. Even Dave perked up and smiled.

"We're like comrades who survived a battle," I said, aware that a special bond now existed between us. I turned to Frances. "I'm tired of talking about myself. I want to hear how you're doing."

"I'm much better, just a little sore. The cast comes off in a week." Frances always looked on the bright side.

"I'm just so sorry you got hurt, too. Bet you'll think twice the next time we invite you over to dinner." We both laughed.

"Well, you sure look a lot better than I expected," Perry exclaimed, scrutinizing me. "I was definitely prepared for the worst."

"I must have looked pretty bad then, the last time you saw me." I chuckled.

"Well, yes, you did." Perry raised his eyebrows.

"We've got some news to share," Frances said. "Anthony got the job on the night shift at Colson Police Department."

"Lucky guy," Pierce said with a half-smile. Anthony was Pierce's best friend from the police academy. Interrupted by the accident, Pierce had yet to finish the program. To be honest I wasn't all that eager for him to complete it.

Conversation grew animated as Perry regaled us with a few larger-than-life tales from his thirty years in law enforcement. Pierce, who'd long since grown weary of my questioning his desire to work in that field, avoided looking at me. But as Perry's stories focused on the anger, frustration, and pain he'd witnessed in the inmates, they reminded me of my own earlier work counseling the mentally ill. For some reason the parallels between the two professions had escaped me. Now, I began to relax into the conversation. As I listened to Perry's yarns, I got it. Law enforcement was a lot like counseling the mentally ill with the added protection a gun provided.

The guys continued to talk together and Frances moved in closer to me. "Do you remember much from that day?" she asked in a quiet voice.

"Well, I remember lingering in the kitchen after the four of you went outside to shoot. You know I've never been wild about guns."

"I know," she whispered. "And if we hadn't brought the twenty-two over, you wouldn't have gone outside and gotten hurt." Her eyes gave me a sad puppy look.

"I went outside because I wanted to spend time with you, not because you brought the gun."

"Mom went outside because I told her she needed practice," Pierce chimed in. "If it was anyone's fault, it was mine."

"It's no one's fault," I said in a loud voice that made everyone jump. "It just happened."

After that, the conversation flowed more easily. The afternoon passed too quickly, and soon everyone left and I lay alone. It was getting dark outside the window.

"I'll bet you didn't think I'd come," Gerry teased when he walked in around nine and handed me an envelope. I opened it and found four hundred dollars from the employees at GFM.

"Good heavens, Gerry. Pierce told me you already gave him some money from everyone at work."

"You're just getting back the love you've given. Don't forget what

I told you. God has something really special in mind for you." His blue eyes flashed with his grin.

I smiled back at him, but felt confused. It was one thing to believe Jesus had fortified me with his loving Spirit, and another to think He had a blueprint for my life. Hadn't I already been doing important work, motivating workers to lead healthier lives before my accident? How could Jesus have something better in mind for me now that my body was broken? After Gerry left, I settled back in bed and contemplated what he'd said.

I was still thinking about it the next afternoon when the chaplain at the hospital strolled in and informed me, "There's an inspirational channel on TV you might enjoy." That night I found the remote and selected the channel. I settled back onto my pillows to wind down. Lush scenes of grassy mountain meadows, brooks and trees, filled the screen. Flocks of wooly sheep meandered into view, as *Ave Maria* filled the air. I let my body relax more deeply into the bed. A man's voice boomed in resonant tones.

"Yea, though I walk through the valley of the shadow of death, I will fear no evil: for thou art with me; thy rod and thy staff they comfort me...." (Psalm 23:4 KJV)

For the first time in days, I felt completely calm.

"Thank you," I said when the chaplain wandered back in a few days later. He sat in the stuffed arm chair in front of the picture window.

"I'm glad it helped. Do you feel like talking?"

I nodded.

"I want to know how the accident has affected you. How're you doing emotionally?" He gave me a penetrating look.

"I'm not sure I know yet. I'm over my dread of the night shift, but lately it's been hard for me to relax. Sometimes I cry in response to the smallest things. Then I feel euphoric when I sense God's presence and am struck by the fact that I'm still here, that I survived. All in all, I think I'm doing okay."

He gave me a look that seemed to question how *okay* I really was.

"I've had my own journey with health problems," he said

unexpectedly, as a sober look replaced his smile. "It's not been easy." For the first time I saw pain in his eyes. Then more gently, "I'll be interested to touch base with you after you've been out of the hospital for a while. I'll want to hear how you feel about life and God then."

His last remark startled me. It hinted at bigger challenges to come. A chill in the air made me shiver. I felt his note of warning and sensed he was right.

My body and spirit grew stronger. Just as at County Hospital, I enjoyed an unusual bond with a few of my caregivers. I felt closest to Maureen. She was a jovial mother of three, and there was something comforting about her. Thanks to Maureen, I looked forward to nights on Rehab. We laughed and joked as she gathered the things I needed to help me get ready for bed.

"Two years back, I started college, but had to put it on hold. My youngest son was having some problems then. He's doing better now with my help." She looked a little sad as she spoke. "I also really need to lose some weight. It's driving up my blood pressure."

"You know, Maureen, that's one of the main things I do at work. I teach workers how to lose weight."

"Would you be willing to help me?" She said, looking hopeful.

"Well, let me consult my schedule." I paused in mock deliberation. "Guess what? I just happen to have an opening." I laughed. "No really, just say the word. I'm available any time you want to talk. I'll give you my number so you can call me." I scribbled my name and number on a scrap of paper and handed it to her.

"Thanks," she said, looking pleased.

One night, during my second week on Rehab, I lay in bed for two hours without going to sleep. My nurse handed me two lorazepam to remedy the situation. I had taken that medication at County Hospital but at half the dose.

On Rehab that night, the lorazepam, in combination with my oxycodone, made me want to chat. I remembered with delight that Pierce, being the most reliable night owl in the family, would be awake. Sure enough when I dialed his number, he answered.

"Hey, Pierce. Just felt like talking. What are you doing?"

"Mom? Why are you up so late? You all right?" He sounded concerned.

"Couldn't be better. How about you?"

"I'm finishing up some loose ends for the police academy. I should graduate in another week."

"Oh, that's right. You have to pass their driving test. I've been so wrapped up in Rehab, I'm afraid I forgot."

I prattled on, slurring my words and regaling him with one story after another. No one had ever had so much fun in the hospital.

The next evening when Dave and Pierce strolled in, my son looked sideways at me.

"Mom has been drunk-dialing me," he told Dave. His comment didn't sound complimentary. Apparently I'd not only been slurring my words, but talking for well over an hour. "You were ready to party." He sounded like my father.

I felt embarrassed. I'd never been really drunk in my life. My extreme sensitivity to the medications had gotten me in trouble again.

After a week and a half on Rehab in Occupational Therapy, Hanna gave me an assignment. "Today, I want you to wheel around the hospital. I'll go with you in case you get tired."

I'd been wheeling myself for ten minutes when I got an idea. "Could we go to the ICU so I can visit Larry? I want to thank him."

Hanna looked at me and raised her eyebrow. "Sure, let's do it."

It had been two months since I'd been a patient in the Regional Medical ICU. As I rolled through the double doors into the unit, I saw the big nurse across the room with his back to me. Sensing my eyes on him, he turned and glanced briefly in my direction, then looked away.

"You don't recognize me, do you?" I asked.

He turned and looked back at me. The lines in his face softened in recognition.

"The tree lady?"

He ambled over, gathering me into a bear hug.

"Thank you for taking such good care of me. I'm sorry I gave you a hard time about eating. I know you were only trying to help," I said, my face still buried in his side.

Larry was quiet for a minute. Then he looked me in the eye. "You were the worst trauma case I'd seen in my fourteen years in the ICU." He wore a grim look. That was saying something coming from a seasoned nurse like Larry.

The momentous day before I was to be discharged, the unit manager, a stylishly dressed woman, bustled into my room. "I have a surprise for you. Tomorrow morning, the police academy wants to hold a special graduation ceremony just for your son right here. That way you and your husband will be able to see him graduate."

"One just for us?" I said. *Oh my goodness. Tomorrow morning is going to be busy!*

At seven the next morning in the conference room on the Rehab floor, Pierce raised his right hand and swore the *Oath of Honor.*

"I will never betray my badge, my integrity, my character, or the public trust. I will always have the courage to hold myself and others accountable for our actions. I will always uphold the constitution, my community and the agency I serve."

With those few words he graduated. Perry and Frances, minus her cast, were with us to cheer him on. So were several others including a reporter, a few nurses from Rehab, and Dave and I.

The reporter took pictures. "Can you say a few words on how you feel?" she asked, directing her gaze at me.

"Me?" Wasn't Pierce the one graduating? Put on the spot. I struggled to organize my thoughts. "I'm happy to see my son complete one of his long held goals. I know he wants to be of service to people in our community. I'm very proud of him."

The reporter smiled and scribbled something on her pad. Then she turned to talk with the college president.

Pierce walked over and leaned in to whisper. "You know I held my breath when you started to answer. I was afraid you might say something that would embarrass or incriminate me."

"Would I do that?" I said, taken aback.

"Well, yes, lately."

Apparently, he still had my many drug-induced conversations on his mind. He obviously didn't trust me to say the right thing. That made me sad. At work, I'd excelled in the art of diplomatic communication. Now my son considered me a loose cannon. I loved Pierce. The last thing I wanted to do was embarrass him.

"I'm so sorry I worried you."

"That's okay, Mom. It's not your fault. Anyway, you're much better now that you're off the meds." He squeezed my shoulder and gave me a smile.

It was time for breakfast. I wheeled over to a table full of donuts and chuckled as I thought of the lame old police joke. Pierce had counseled me never to tease anyone in law enforcement with that unflattering stereotype. I bit my tongue. Maybe my judgment and sense of restraint were improving.

I had just turned to Frances when Hanna rushed in. "I've got to do some last minute training with you and Dave before you go home today."

"I'm sorry, Frances. I hoped we could talk," I said. "I'll call you in a few days when I get settled."

Hanna directed us to a handicapped bathroom down the hall. "I want you to practice transferring to a real toilet." Up to then, all my experience had been with a bedside commode. "Back your chair in next to it," she instructed.

I backed it in and positioned the sliding board. Then I worked my way gingerly across with my arms rigid at my sides until I reached out and planted one hand on the opposite side of the toilet seat. There was nothing Dave could do. He fidgeted, watching me struggle until I finally swung my body over and landed with a thud on top of the commode.

"Ugh. That was tough." I grimaced. "I hope the ones at Dr. Norton's office are easier." I began to worry about what lay ahead. Dave and I had an appointment to see the good doctor later that morning.

"You can do it," Hanna said and hugged me.

"Thank you, for everything." I said, watching as she hurried down the hall toward the therapy room.

It was barely nine-thirty, when they rushed me back into my room. My nursing assistant and Dave were already packing my things onto a cart, while one of the hospital wound nurses began changing the dressing on my ankle one last time. She took the long piece of tubing that attached on one end to the ankle dressing and inserted the other end into a portable wound vacuum that would be going home with me.

"Whew!" I said, looking at my husband. "This morning is insane. There's so much left to do before they discharge me."

By ten, Dave pushed me in my wheelchair to the front entrance of the hospital, where Karen instructed me on how to transfer into the passenger seat of my compact car. After transferring onto the toilet, sliding into it was easy. I took Karen's hand. "Thank you. You've gone above and beyond. I won't forget all you've done." Tears welled in my eyes.

"I'll miss you, too. You've done a good job. Maybe we can go to lunch, when you get back to work," she said, smiling.

"I'd like that."

After pulling out of the parking lot, Dave pointed our car north toward County Hospital Physician's Center for a checkup with Dr. Norton. Then, we would be heading home. My insides did a flip. Dave and I were on our own.

PART TWO

THERE'S NO PLACE LIKE HOME

Dave and Pierce had worked themselves to a state of near exhaustion converting our downstairs family room into a suitable space for me while I was confined to the wheelchair. They'd visited me daily and waited through thirteen surgeries, talking to scores of doctors and social workers to help coordinate my care. My husband's face sagged from not eating and stress, while Pierce's showed tiny worry lines where none had been visible before. My son was only twenty-one at the time. The accident had launched him overnight into an adult role. He'd reassured me with his calm presence, while chauffeuring Dave to the hospitals and back, when his father was too tired to drive. It would be weeks before I fully understood how hard things had been for them.

After leaving the hospital at eleven on discharge day, Dave drove me a hundred miles up the highway to see Dr. Norton. The good doctor pronounced my legs "healing well" and informed me it would be time to remove the big metal fixator from my leg when I came back for my next visit.

"In your office?" I asked. "That sounds painful. Isn't it screwed into my bones?"

"Well yes, but it won't take long to take it off."

His words didn't reassure me much. The picture of his unscrewing it made me cringe.

"Do you think you could remove it when Dr. Wexler does my skin graft? I'd be asleep then."

"Sure. Just have him call me when he's ready to do the surgery."

I made a mental note to talk to Dr. Wexler as Dave and I got back in the car, this time heading south. An hour later, we veered off the

Interstate and continued out into the country. It was dark by the time we turned into the long winding drive and drove up the hill through the trees to our house.

Dave stood by my car door as I slid into the wheelchair. He rolled me through our entrance, struggling to get me over the threshold and into the family room.

I looked around. It had been two months since I'd been home.

"It looks beautiful, sweetie," I said, trying to take in the big room in the dim light.

Marley, my dog, backed off from the wheelchair and kept a safe distance. Did he remember me? I'd probably picked up some hospital scents along the way.

"Marley, come here baby. It's okay." I tried to coax him with some baby talk, but he was having none of it and settled down around the other side of the bed.

More troubling than my dog's indifference was the nagging realization that at home Dave and Pierce would have to take over my care. Dave especially looked beyond tired and depressed. I worried about him. How would we manage without the help of my nurses' aides?

That evening we both moved in slow motion, trying to finish our unfamiliar chores. From the wheelchair I unpacked the medications and wound care supplies from the big plastic sack and arranged them on my dresser. Dave mixed hydrogen peroxide and sterile water in a glass jar to make the solution needed for doing my pin care. That night and those that followed, using a Q-tip soaked in the solution, Dave cleaned the deep holes in my skin where the metal rods screwed into my bones. The sensation of the cotton tips swishing in those tender holes made me cringe. Dave forged ahead. When he was done, he assembled the bedside commode and positioned it next to my side of the bed.

On Rehab, Maureen and Nora and the rest of my industrious nurses and assistants, had answered my pages. Now I hated having to ask Pierce and Dave for help. Both had that haunted look that spoke of trauma and too many sleepless nights. Dave had just completed his final chore of the evening and sat down when I remembered something else.

"I hate to bother you, but I need a glass of water to take my pain pill."

Dave exhaled loudly, then snapped. "You just enjoy having someone wait on you, don't you?"

His remark stung and ignited a spark.

"How can you say that? I hate asking for help."

"Is that right?" He didn't look convinced.

"Yes, that's right. I'd much rather be doing things for myself. In fact, I'd much rather be taking care of you. Maybe we could change places. That would be just fine with me," I said, raving.

Dave got up slowly and trudged into the bathroom. We both needed a lot of rest.

I turned onto my right side, still wearing the full length leg cast. It was almost December and chilly in our downstairs room, but I only needed a sheet to stay warm. I wasn't sick. My body must have been generating extra heat to heal my legs. From that position, I struggled to organize my six pillows as my assistants in Rehab had done. As I moved my left leg into position, the spikes sticking out from the external fixator ripped a long gash in the new sheets.

"Darn that thing," I fumed, focusing what remained of my anger on the metal monstrosity. Dave wearily got up one last time to fetch the duct tape from the workshop next door. I patched the rip, while he padded the prongs. That was as much as we could do. Then we slept.

The sun had been up for hours when I heard the familiar sound of Marley snorting. He was exploring me from a safe distance. I held out my hand, but he didn't come.

"That's okay, boy. I'll wait till you're ready.'

I savored a sense of triumph, knowing Dave and I had made it through our first night at home. Rays poured through the window illuminating our big bed and highlighting the beauty of my new space. It was only then that I fully appreciated how much work Dave, Pierce, Greg, and Maggie had put into making it feel like a place I'd enjoy. Every surface sparkled from their cleaning. Many of my favorite paintings, photographs, and brightly colored pieces of pottery graced the walls and shelves. I realized those were Maggie's thoughtful touches. At the far end of the room, Dave had set up a tiny refrigerator next to a new bookcase. He'd stacked the top shelves with dishes, silverware, a can opener, and napkins. Below, there were boxes of cereal, crackers, tea, and nuts. A new microwave, a gift from Frances, perched on top of the refrigerator. I had a kitchenette. I lay back for a minute and marveled.

Dave reached over to caress my arm. His touch aroused feelings buried deep inside. I rolled onto my left side as he turned to face me. The warmth of his body on mine and the familiar scent of his skin sent passion surging through me. He kissed me. For the moment my fixator was forgotten.

Afterward, we lay just holding each other for a long time. I melted into the safety and comfort of his arms. Some things were still the same.

Dave got up, stretched, and stood by me as I transferred into the wheelchair. He hung the wound vacuum onto the back of my chair. Then he draped the six foot length of tubing that connected the vacuum to the deep wound on my left ankle, over my shoulder and across my chest.

"You gonna be okay?"

"Fine." I gave him a smile that I hoped conveyed confidence. He tramped upstairs to get dressed.

Eager to find ways to be more independent, I wheeled around my spacious room. I was happy to find I could easily make a modest breakfast right from my chair. Leaning over, I lifted the carton of milk out of my tiny refrigerator and poured it on top of the cereal in my bowl. I was thankful Dave had thought to place so many things within reach. With a banana and some walnuts on top, it was a breakfast fit for a queen. I savored each bite. So far, everything was going well.

I wheeled through the bathroom door just far inside enough to reach the sink. Filling it with warm water, I soaped the parts of my body I could reach with a wash cloth. After rinsing and drying, I rifled through my dresser, locating a stretchy black skirt with an elastic waist. I pulled it over my head, delighted to find I could still dress myself so long as I didn't bother with pants or underwear. A turtle neck minus a bra completed the outfit. It didn't look like much, but I felt comfortable.

Heartened, I reached down to wheel myself over to the desk where emails, letters, and bills vied for my attention. A sharp twinge jabbed my ankle wound.

"Ouch," I yelled, grimacing. Looking down, I saw the long hose that attached to the vacuum pump had gotten hopelessly tangled in my wheels. If I continued, I'd yank the dressing right off my ankle. It was a complicated dressing and not one Dave or I could easily replicate without help from the home health nurse. Stuck, I pulled out my cell.

"Dave, could you come downstairs? I got the vacuum hose caught."

A few minutes later Dave appeared, looking amused. "Well, Lara, you really got yourself in a mess this time." He unwrapped the tubing. "Next time, be careful to move it out of the way before you take off."

"I will, thanks," I said, embarrassed.

Next, I dashed off some notes to friends and as I did felt more connected to the outside world than before. Bills and the checkbook came next. I'd managed our finances before the accident. Now, I was on a roll. Each new success empowered me to try something else. Being confined for so long, it didn't take much for me to feel good about what I accomplished. I could manage fairly well with just a little imagination.

I thought of Karen, my physical therapist, and started exercising. Her voice reverberated in my head. "Right leg up and down. Not too fast. Don't forget to breathe. And repeat."

"Not bad for my first day at home," I said when Dave appeared twenty minutes later. Under his watchful eye, I inched across the sliding board and back into bed. I still didn't feel safe transferring alone. I was more off-balance and dizzy than I wanted to admit, and the linoleum floor below looked a long way down and unyielding. What if I fell? The image of splintered bones flashed unsolicited across my mind, making me shudder.

"Stop!" I said out loud. Dave jumped. In my imagination, I held up a stop sign in my mind to block the fearful thought. It was a relaxation technique I'd learned years before.

Dave called his boss and arranged to take two more days off. After those, he could take no more. Meanwhile, Pierce filled out applications for law enforcement jobs. Very soon it would be hard to count on either of them for help.

How would I manage alone?

HELP ARRIVES

Oh the sisters of mercy, they are not departed or gone.

They were waiting for me when I thought that I just can't go on.

And they brought me their comfort and later they brought me this song.

Oh I hope you run into them, you who've been traveling so long.

Leonard Cohen from The Sisters of Mercy

Before the tree fell, I couldn't have named a single person, other than Dave, who would have been ready, willing, and able to care for me once I came home. In the summer of 2009, a few months before the accident, my one close local friend, a woman I'd met weekly for breakfast for almost seven years, decided to take a break from our friendship. She didn't reject me with a diatribe, listing reasons she no longer wanted to hang out; she simply stopped showing up. As bad as that felt, I'd had no choice but to accept her wishes.

I turned the matter over to God. That was the first time I trusted Him to handle a personal problem. Allowing the situation to play out, I let Jesus do the rest. That approach turned out to be best. Her actions had hurt and stunned me, but after a short while, I had to admit that at least for the present, the friendship had run its course.

With that friend out of the picture and other friends and coworkers at least forty minutes away, I couldn't imagine how I would ever make it to doctors' appointments and physical therapy sessions when the time came for me to walk. It would be weeks before Dr. Norton would let me drive.

After our first night at home, and Dave and I settled into a new routine, I remembered the offers to help I'd received at County Hospital. Would those people still want to come, or had they thought better of their proposals? I hesitated, my cell phone in hand. Then I dialed Janelle and John who lived near the coast.

"Janelle, in the hospital you mentioned something about coming to help….."

"I was just thinking about you," she said. "We still want to help. John can come first. Then I'll be there after Christmas. When do you want him?"

"Would the end of November be too soon?"

"No. I'll let him know."

When I hung up, I felt astonished by their willingness to drop everything to help. I quickly dialed my brother, Josh, in Washington, DC.

"I can't wait to see you," he said.

By that weekend, my first helper arrived. My brother was a stocky man with dark curly hair. He worked as an electrical engineer, designing and installing underwater turbines, powered by river currents, to generate energy. He was so eager to help I was a little concerned he might feel let down once he discovered the reality of caring for someone in a wheelchair. But like Greg, Josh came bursting with lavish plans and endless enthusiasm.

"I think we better keep it simple." Dave advised after hearing his ideas.

Josh looked crestfallen. "Aw, come on Dave. You mean I can't remodel your whole house while I'm here?" He laughed.

"Thanks, maybe next visit," Dave chuckled.

Josh moved on to his next idea. "Hey Sis, do you think you could play keyboard and sing if I accompanied you on your electric guitar."

"I'll try," I said, not really sure I could sit that long at the piano. My back muscles still ached, where they'd cut through them to insert the stabilizing rods.

Josh hauled amplifiers and instruments downstairs. I wheeled in front of the keyboard. We played a few Neal Young tunes with fair success, before my back gave out.

"Let's do it again tomorrow," he exclaimed, looking pleased.

Josh entertained us with his good humor, and before long, we all felt truly cheered. Dave and Pierce had looked depressed before his arrival, but after a week with my brother, they were back to laughing and joking and telling stories. Pierce, especially, enjoyed teasing his uncle, in honor of their long tradition of hurling insults at one another.

"You need to work out more," Josh joked, squeezing Pierce's bicep.

"Well, you need to get a haircut," Pierce retorted and lunged at his uncle in a mock wrestling move. They tussled for a minute. Then Josh turned to me.

"Hey Sis, I'd really like to take a look at the infamous tree. Don't you want me to wheel you down there so you can see it, too? Who knows, it might give you some closure."

"You can't push the wheelchair through the woods, but maybe Pierce could take some pictures for me."

"I haven't even been back to look at it since it fell. That was two months ago. I wouldn't mind going with you," Pierce said.

When they returned, my brother looked impressed.

"Whoa, that was some big tree," he exclaimed.

"Mom, it looks like a battlefield down there with the left over medical trash and scraps of clothing everywhere," Pierce added. He held up a scrap of blue fabric from the jacket I'd worn and one of my brown suede shoes, both covered in blood.

He turned on the camera screen to show me the pictures he'd taken. I stared in awe at the huge pine lying on the ground, denuded of bark. Four-foot spikes jutted out from its formidable trunk. Looking at his photos, I shivered and thanked God again for sparing my life.

A home health nurse came three times a week to change the

complex dressing on my ankle. Her visits broke the monotony of my days. Despite her obvious skill, it took well over half an hour for her to fit the new dressing to the wound.

"I'm sure glad we have you. I don't think Dave could manage it right now," I said as she cut out the first layer. The dressing material was permeated with a silver solution to discourage bacterial growth in the wound.

"No problem. I did lots of these when I worked in Trauma."

I stared down at the vacuum hose and the ankle dressing and realized how much I longed for the day I wouldn't need them.

With Josh visiting, Dave and Pierce looked happy again and my own spirit grew lighter. Then when he'd been with us a week and a half, he flew home. I hated to see him go. What would we do without his sunny disposition to cheer us?

That same afternoon John drove in from the coast. As close as I could remember it had been fifteen years since I'd seen him. I felt a little nervous about his coming. Would it feel awkward asking a man who wasn't my husband for help? I'd felt relaxed with Josh, but Josh was my brother.

Though John was seventy years old and sported a shaved head, he looked like a much younger man. His love for motorcycles and travel was surpassed only by his enjoyment of the two together. Dinners with John were lively events. Dave had set up a long card table at the bottom of the stairs so we could all eat together. Our guest enthralled us with stories from his adventurous treks across the country and up into Alaska. I watched my husband's face as he listened and could see how much he yearned for a motorcycle of his own. Long before Pierce was born, he'd ridden a BMW, but had been forced to sell it to buy a Travel-All to haul his tools for a job. I wished I could buy him another.

Something else stayed with me from John's visit. He'd spent years working as a nurse anesthetist putting surgical patients to sleep, and only recently retired. He captivated us with anecdotes from his work with patients. One evening, after talking for a while, he paused and shook his head. "I saw a lot of patients with injuries like yours. I just can't believe you made it out of those hospitals without an infection or a blood clot. Do you know how unusual that is? In fact I'm amazed you kept your legs at all."

Dave looked alarmed. John's comments grabbed my attention, too. I was fresh out of the hospital, but still not out of the woods. Dr. Bolling had made it abundantly clear I could still develop an infection or throw a clot. Every morning, I gave myself a shot in the abdomen to keep my blood thin and swallowed handfuls of vitamins and herbs to prevent infections and promote healing. I also prayed.

John continued. "Some of my patients wasted away in long term care institutions for years, battling one infection after another. Their wounds didn't heal. A few never made it out at all. You were incredibly lucky." He nodded in my direction.

I didn't think luck had had much to do with it.

"Sorry, I didn't mean to worry you," he apologized, noticing Dave's frown.

That evening I noticed something else. As John spoke, I could barely make out what he said. *Why is he talking so quietly?* I looked over at Dave and Pierce, but they appeared to hear him just fine.

"John, could you speak up? It sounds like you're whispering." I said from across the narrow table. Dave and Pierce turned to look at me.

"Sure," he said. "People tell me I speak in a quiet voice."

"Lara, I think you've lost some hearing," Dave interjected. "Half the time you don't answer me. In the hospital I thought you were just out of it from the drugs, but now I'm thinking it was also because you couldn't hear."

"Hmm, I'll bet it's the holes they made in my ear drums," I said. "Come to think of it, they never took the ear tubes out, did they?"

A surgeon at County Hospital had implanted them my first week in the hospital to equalize pressure in my ears during hyperbaric treatments, and no one had mentioned them since.

"I'll bet you're right," Dave said. "You should ask Dr. Baker if she can take them out when you see her next week. Maybe then the holes in your ear drums can heal."

"I will." Dr. Baker was the young female surgeon who'd performed amazing repairs on my face, scalp, nose, eyelid, and outer ear the night of the accident. She'd know what to do.

I enjoyed watching Pierce and John as they chatted. They obviously liked hanging out together. "Pierce, you've got the right personality to be a good nurse anesthetist, yourself. It takes someone who can get along well with difficult people. I'm talking about the surgeons." He laughed.

I needn't have worried about feeling awkward with John. He accompanied Pierce and me to my doctor's appointments and made a great stir fry at home.

John's visit reminded all of us that new possibilities awaited just outside our door. We were happy to hear life would eventually be about something other than my broken bones.

As we moved into December, people all over and at a few dozen churches continued to pray for me. They were often folks I didn't know. Maggie wrote that every Monday night someone in her Bible study also prayed aloud for me.

> Be assured that people haven't forgotten you here.
> They may not know you, but they still care.

Had it been all those prayers that prompted God to lift up my spirit and fill me with so much hope at County Hospital?

CHEATING DEATH

I'd seldom gone to the doctor before my accident, but now the number of visits I logged astonished me. I'd been a little critical of people who constantly ran to their physicians, but by early December I began to feel like one of them.

Going for a checkup involved the long trek to the County Hospital Physician's Center, attached to the hospital. It also involved the challenge of negotiating their handicapped restrooms. Prior to my injury I'd given little consideration to the difficulties faced by those who couldn't walk. I assumed handicapped bathrooms were designed in some special way to make them easier to use. That was not always true.

On my second trip to the Physician's Center, I made a pit stop in one handicapped restroom where I found the sink stationed so close to the toilet, I had to climb on from the front.

"What were they thinking?" I grumbled as I reached across to place my hands on the toilet seat. Pushing up with my arms straight, my body, now airborne, rotated in midair. When it landed hard on the seat, my external fixator smacked the tile floor, sending shock waves through my fractures. I yelped in pain.

Later that day in another bathroom, I found the individual stalls so small I couldn't squeeze the wheelchair through their doors. After that, I dreaded travel to new places where the poor designs of the restrooms would cause me difficulty.

By my third trip to the Physicians Building I had scoped out the most user-friendly facilities and grown more adept at negotiating them. I also remembered to bring along neoprene gloves for a less germy transfer. The difficulties I faced in the County Hospital

Physician Center's lavatories were no different than the challenges faced every day by thousands of others with injuries and disabilities. If those restrooms were indicative, what would handicapped facilities be like in restaurants and stores?

My friend John was still with us when Pierce drove me up to see Dr. Wexler, my plastic surgeon. That day I was feeling more apprehensive than usual. The muscle and skin graft in my ankle wound had long since failed. Dr. Wexler had implanted something called Integra my last week at County Hospital. It was a synthetic material designed to fill in deep wounds. In the three weeks since coming home, I'd visited him twice to see how well it was doing.

"I hope he says it's ready," I said to Pierce as he pulled the Scion into a handicapped space in County Hospital's enormous parking garage.

I'd grown weary of the large open cavity in my ankle, of tangling the long vacuum hose in the wheels of my chair, and of the tedious dressing changes the home health nurse had to do three times a week. If the Integra had filled the wound cavity, Dr. Wexler would be able to close it with a skin graft. I wouldn't have to fret over those things again.

"Don't worry, Mom. When your home-health nurse came on Monday she said it looked good," Pierce said as he hoisted my chair out of the car, rolled me through the lobby and into the surgeon's office.

The aroma of fresh-brewed espresso wafted through the building. On a different day I would have asked for a cup. Today I thought only about what Dr. Wexler would say.

Several people in the waiting room stared in horror at my external fixator, but I didn't care. I was used to their stares by now.

"Lara Easting," a nurse beckoned from the door. I wheeled over and followed her into a treatment room. She peeled off the layers of my ankle dressing and gave the wound a satisfied look. "I think the Integra has worked its magic."

"I agree," Dr. Wexler said as he peered over her shoulder, smiling. "Schedule her for surgery next Monday."

"Could you see if that day works for Dr. Norton, too? He told me he could take the fixator off at the same time." I kept my fingers crossed.

"No problem. I'll call him and set it up."

I let out a whoop. I suddenly understood what that surgery meant. No more gaping holes in my ankle and no more wound vacuums or large metal fixators. No more ripped sheets or tangling hoses. The long wait was over.

A week later, after John drove back home, Mom flew in. She was eighty-three, worked out with weights, walked two miles most days, and was eager to help. She was also a world-class worrier.

"I'm glad to take you to your surgery tomorrow, but I don't think I can manage anyone else," Pierce announced.

When she arrived I tried to think of what to say. I didn't want to hurt my mother's feelings.

"Mom, tomorrow I have some minor surgery at County Hospital. Pierce's taking me, since Dave has to work. It would be wonderful if you could stay here and make us some stuffed cabbages. That way Dave won't have to cook when he comes home. Next week you'll be able to come with us when we go back to see Dr. Norton."

"Are you sure? I'd be glad to go with you tomorrow?"

"Yes, I'm sure. Dave bought everything for the stuffed cabbages."

"Okay. I'm here to help any way you want." She smiled broadly.

"Thanks for understanding, Mom." I sighed in relief, touched by her generous spirit.

That night before bed I prayed. "Jesus, you've seen me through thirteen surgeries and blessed me with the most incredible surgeons. Today I'm asking you again to guide their hands. I'm turning all my fears over to you and asking you to fill me with your peace. Amen." Warmth spread throughout my solar plexus whenever I prayed. Peace followed. That let me know God was with me. Prayer was like hydromorphone for the soul.

On December seventh, Pierce and I checked in with the receptionist in the Out-Patient Surgery Department at County Hospital. Ann joined us. I changed into a gown and the nurse inserted an IV in my hand.

"You can go ahead and move onto the stretcher," she said. I worked my way over and she covered me with a sheet and wheeled me into the surgical staging area. It was a place I'd seen many times before. She parked me in the first stall at the end of the long row of cubicles. Familiar faces smiled down at me. The nurse anesthetists were the first to stop by. My friend Bailey, the student, was with them.

"Wow, you look a lot better than the last time I saw you," she said, smiling.

"Thanks, I'm doing really well. How about you?" I beamed back at her.

"I finally graduated." Her face lit up.

"I wanted to thank you for taking the time to visit me and making me feel like I still mattered. It felt good to know I had a friend like you at County Hospital."

Drs. Wexler and Norton strode over. "How are you feeling?" Dr. Norton asked.

"Good. I appreciate your taking the fixator off while I'm asleep."

"You bet." He nodded and patted my arm. His kind manner always made me feel he cared.

When the anesthesiologist injected some Versed into my IV, I knew I'd be out soon.

"Lord, keep me safe," I whispered.

I awoke in what seemed a matter of minutes and squinted down at my left leg. I yanked the sheet off to get a better look. The vacuum hose and metal fixator had vanished and in their place was a boot. I sighed with relief.

The post-op nurse saw me stir and rushed over to raise the head of my stretcher. I struggled to rouse myself. "Time to wake up so you can go home," she said. Her voice had a melodic quality to it.

Dr. Norton strode in and smiled. "As you've probably noticed, after I took off your fixator, I put on a walking-boot. That will serve as a cast now that you don't have a fixator anymore. But just because it's called a walking boot doesn't mean you can walk in it. Remember, your fractures are still healing. Are you with me?"

"Got it," I replied, feeling drowsy.

Dr. Norton left and Pierce and Ann appeared at the door. A transporter soon arrived with a wheelchair, and my mother-in-law leaned over to hug me goodbye.

Nothing could dampen my spirits as Pierce drove me back down the highway. No doubt the narcotics in my system played a role in my joyous state, but more than the effect of any drug, the removal of the fixator and closing my ankle wound marked a milestone in my recovery.

"I'm so happy," I shouted, taking in the colorful lights that hung on the trees down our road. In two weeks it would be Christmas.

At home, Dave and Mom greeted us as Pierce pushed me over the threshold and into my bedroom. "How'd it go?" they asked together. Our smiles answered for us.

"Why don't you sit down and I'll dish up," Mom said. "The stuffed cabbages are ready. I'm afraid they aren't quite as good as usual. I'm a little out of practice." She came over to hug me.

"They look wonderful," Dave assured her, looking relieved and diving into his plate. Pierce joined him.

"They do, but I better not eat any." I said, wheeling into my place at the table. Just out of surgery and back on oxycodone, I didn't have much of an appetite.

"Aren't you hungry?" Mom asked, looking concerned.

"Just a little queasy from the pain meds and anesthesia." I smiled to reassure her.

When they finished eating, I wheeled over and climbed into bed. It felt good to lie on the crisp, clean sheets without the external fixator. I could finally move my legs without ripping them.

"Thank you, Jesus, for bringing me through the surgery and for carrying us safely home," I whispered before falling asleep.

The next morning, Mom came down to check on me. "Are you feeling better today? Can I fix you some breakfast?"

"Yes, much better. If it's not too much trouble, eggs sound great.

I'm going to try not to take any oxycodone today. That should help my appetite even more."

Mom bustled back up to the kitchen. Thirty minutes later she came down with a plate of scrambled eggs and toast. When she'd set me up at the table and I wheeled over to eat, she joined me sipping some tea.

We made small talk about Pierce and Dave. Then she asked gently, "Do you ever think how different things might have been if you hadn't gone into the woods that day?"

I paused only a moment before answering. "I try not to. Thinking about that might drive me crazy. What I do think about is why on earth I'm still here. Ever since that day in County Hospital when Jesus' spirit visited me, I've believed He brought me back for some purpose."

A strange expression crossed my mother's face.

"What is it, Mom?"

"You know, that wasn't the first time."

"What do you mean?"

"It wasn't the first time you cheated death. Do you remember the other?"

I let my mind search back, way back to remember what she was talking about. Then, it came to me, the whole episode vivid in my mind.

I was twenty-four when it happened. I'd just rented an old house in a quiet neighborhood and finished my first week on the job counselling hospital psychiatric patients.

Friday night after my shift I pulled up in front of the house after midnight. Exhausted, I opened the car door and sat staring out the front window before gathering my things. That's when I saw him. His dark form shuffled slowly up the road in the oncoming lane. *Just some old guy out for a walk.*

I watched him lumber along until he came up even with my car.

Then, without warning, he turned and with the speed of a jackal hunting prey, crossed the road, stopping just inside my open door.

"Get out of the car," he whispered.

"What?" My chest tightened.

"Get out of the car." It was more of a growl, ominous.

My throat went dry.

Kick him in the groin. My father's voice prodded me into action.

I pivoted in my seat, leaned back, and flexed my knee. I kicked out at my assailant with all the force I could muster in that awkward position.

The man grunted and recoiled backward.

I was grappling wildly in the dark to close the door when a hand like a vice-grip shot out and grabbed my arm. With one swift yank, it jerked me out of the car and onto my feet. The force of that motion told me all I needed to know. Clutching me tightly against his side, he pushed the cold barrel of a gun hard against my temple and walked me up the road. Though it was a chilly night, I broke out into a sweat.

"I'm sorry I shoved you, but I thought you were going to take my car." I said, trying hard to appease him.

"Shut up," he hissed through tightly clenched teeth. "Shut up or I'll blow your head off."

My legs went weak. His grip tightened.

Then I remembered something. My purse was still in the car. He didn't want my money. Terror clutched my chest.

With my right hand, I pushed the gun away from my head and turned to face him. "You don't want to hurt me. I've never done anything to you."

"I told you to shut the hell up." His cold eyes glinted with hate.

My stomach turned inside out.

We'd walked a half a block and rounded the corner. I was about to lose sight of my house. That's when I made up my mind. I would fight to get away or die trying.

"Lara?" In the distance, my roommate's voice rang out.

The man lurched to a stop.

I slapped the gun away from my temple, screaming like a woman possessed.

"Lara!" My friend's cry pierced the darkness again.

I twisted around to see her striding across the lawn.

For a split second, my assailant loosened his grip.

This is it. I jerked away and rolled on the ground. Would he shoot me?

Jumping to my feet, I sprinted in a zigzag, moving target fashion, speeding through the blackness toward the beacon of light and my friend.

Together, we sprang up the steps onto the porch and into the house. Then, I fell into her arms sobbing.

"It's okay. He's gone," she said, holding me.

For weeks after the attack, whenever I'd thought of my escape, I felt euphoric. The trees, shrubs, and clouds had taken on an otherworldly glow. Their colors pulsed, electric and vibrant. Even the buildings and cars looked surreal. The world had never appeared so beautiful or so full of promise. It was great to be alive.

Despite all my failures, God had reached down a hand to save me. But why?

Not knowing the answer, I'd thrown myself into working even harder with my mental health patients. Spurred on by the conviction that God wanted me here, I'd poured every ounce of energy into loving them.

Gradually, the weeks had turned into months. The late work hours and drama of my twenties had taken their toll, and the memories of that night and God's gift faded.

Until now.

I came back to the present and my bedroom where my mother sat staring at me.

"Apparently," I said slowly, "God's been working for a long time to keep me here. Now, I just have to figure out why."

DELAYED HEALING

A week later, Pierce, Mom, and I drove back up to the County Hospital Physician's Building, to see Dr. Norton. As Pierce wheeled me in, I felt my spirit soar. They'd decorated the atrium from floor to ceiling for Christmas. Crafts and goodies were on display. The smell of coffee and baked goods wafted in the air. This time my son pushed me into the coffee shop to let Mom and me indulge in a cup of the steaming brew and a cheese Danish. Pierce ordered pound cake and hot chocolate. I handed the money to the clerk who'd come around the counter to serve me and passed my coffee to Pierce before wheeling myself back into the atrium and the direction of Dr. Norton's office. Without the fixator, no one stared down at my legs as they passed by. Instead, they smiled at me as I propelled my way deftly through the crowds of patients and workers in scrubs who'd gathered to shop.

In the middle of the atrium, I spotted a counter with a sign that read "Transporters." I stopped short. A woman was talking on a two way radio. She looked up. "Can I help you?"

"I hope so," I asked, leaning toward her, my heart beating faster. "I was a patient in this hospital just a few weeks ago. I had some wonderful transporters, but I still remember one in particular. I'd really like to thank her, but I never got her name."

"Oh my goodness! We have dozens of transporters, so I'd have no way of knowing which one she was." She turned away, dismissing me, to take another call.

"Thank you," I said, slumping back into my seat, disappointed.

Dr. Norton's office was packed when Pierce pushed me through the door.

"Mom, it looks like a wheelchair convention," Pierce warned me.

Half the people in the tiny waiting room sat in wheelchairs, while it was standing room only for those who accompanied them. Most of the patients wore long hinged casts like the one on my right leg. Others had walking-boots like the one on my left. The walking-boot stopped just below my knee and with its massive sole looked like something Frankenstein might have worn. How would I ever walk in it? "I know it's called a walking-boot, but don't put any weight on your feet yet," Dr. Norton had cautioned me.

Only one man had a metal fixator. In fact he had two. One attached to his lower leg and another to his arm. He made an effort to shift his massive weight in the chair without success. The corners of his mouth drooped as his wife strained to help him get comfortable. *Poor man.* Few of the other patients smiled as I scanned their faces. I felt sorry for the ones who winced in pain. It didn't seem quite fair that I felt so good.

The door to the exam rooms opened, and a friendly face burst through it. He rushed through the maze of wheelchairs and leaned in from the side of my chair to embrace me. It was Kenneth, my guardian angel from Hyperbaric. Back then he'd mentioned he worked part-time with Dr. Norton, but it hadn't registered.

"You've got a really sweet mother," he said to Pierce, nodding at me.

I flashed him a smile. That meant a lot coming from the man who'd seen me at my worst.

"The ladies in Hyperbaric asked about you. I told them you were coming today."

"Tell them I said hello. They all seemed nice, but you were definitely my favorite."

My visit with Dr. Norton began with x-rays. Kenneth wheeled me through the door to the treatment rooms. He spoke to someone just out of view.

"Hey Hercules, this is Lara Easting. She's ready when you are. She's my friend so try not to drop her, okay?" He winked at me.

The person to whom he spoke lumbered around the corner.

Hercules was an enormous man with massive arms and black curly hair. He had an equally broad smile and was built like the young men I'd met on the Patient Hoist Team.

"I would never do that, Ms. Lara." He gave a gentle punch to Kenneth and reached out to shake my hand.

"Glad to meet you. Is it Hercules?"

"Naw, he's just playing with you. My real name's Eddie. You can call me whatever you like." He leaned over my chair and scooped me up into his big arms as if I were weightless. Gently, he placed me on the x-ray table. When the technician finished, he settled me on a treatment table in a small room across the hall.

After a few minutes Dr. Norton strode in and shook hands with Pierce and my mom.

"And how're you feeling?" he said, looking intently at me.

"You know I'm always good." I gave him a smile.

He took a few minutes to admire Dr. Wexler's skin graft before seeing how well my right knee could bend. "Looks good," he said. "How far have you gotten with the CPM?"

He was talking about the motorized knee-flexing machine I used at home.

"I maxed out the machine at one-hundred and ten degrees of flexion." I beamed.

I'd come a long way since the County Hospital Trauma Floor, when I could only manage forty-five. Though my right knee would never bend like the left, I could flex it enough to eventually be able to walk.

"You've done a great job." He looked impressed as he took a seat at the computer to look at my x-rays.

I waited for him to speak.

"Well, it looks like you can definitely put a little weight for a second or two on your left foot when you transfer into the wheelchair. Just be sure to wear the walking boot."

He turned to study the films of my right leg and stared at them for what seemed an eternity without speaking. I looked at the side of his face trying hard to read his thoughts.

"And the right one?" I asked, growing uneasy.

Dr. Norton raised his eyebrows and gave me a sheepish look that suggested bearing weight on that leg was a different matter. He pointed to a light area on the x-ray that apparently illustrated a problem. I felt my stomach do a flip.

"There's delayed healing in your tibia, the shin bone, probably because of significant *debridement* in that area. I'm sure right after the tree fell on you they had to remove bone fragments to prevent infection. I want you to start using a stationary bike every day to increase circulation in your lower legs. I'm also going to send you home with an ultrasonic device called a bone stimulator. That should help the tibia heal faster."

He handed me a small cylindrical device roughly the size of a remote controller. "You need to use it every day."

I wasn't really listening to his instructions. I was busy stewing over the problem with my tibia. It was the primary weight-bearing bone in my lower leg. Without it I wouldn't be able to walk.

On the ride home, Pierce tried to reassure me. "Mom, with all the nutritional supplements you take and your healthy diet, your shin bone should be doing fine by your next visit. Don't forget how happy Dr. Norton said he was with your skin graft and left ankle. He thinks the stimulator and cycling will help, too."

By the way Pierce spoke, I should be better in a week.

CHRISTMAS FROM A WHEELCHAIR

I took the bone stimulator from its case and presented it to Dave.

"Merry Christmas," he laughed, taking it from me and inspecting it to see how it worked.

"Very funny," I said. "Oh, by the way, Dr. Norton wants me to get a stationary bike to improve circulation in my legs. Only one problem. How will I get on it?"

"I'll see what I can find on the internet." Dave was great at researching things.

Sure enough, Dave found a pedaling unit I could use while sitting in my wheelchair. He ordered it the next day.

"Merry Christmas again," he said, showing me the picture on our computer.

"That's a lot of money." I said. Our funds were low.

"You need it. So there's nothing more to discuss."

I looked at him in wonder. You had to love a man like Dave.

As Christmas approached, I tried not to think about my leg. "Delayed healing" Dr. Norton had called it. What if my bone didn't heal? I asked that question once before putting it out of my mind completely. It did no good to worry.

Despite my positive mental outlook, an uncomfortable dizzy feeling often tormented me. The room tilted off kilter any time I shifted my position in the wheelchair, turned my head to the right, or looked down. At times, it took real effort to hold myself upright in the chair, and I just gave up sitting and climbed into bed. Lying still was the only way I got relief.

In the evenings when dinner was done, Pierce, Dave and I talked and watched movies together. Despite their thoughtfulness in other areas, more and more I noticed they chatted without bothering to include me in their conversations.

"I can't hear you. Can't you speak louder," I said, feeling frustrated.

"Sorry, I'm just too tired to repeat everything," Dave said.

"You know I'm just hard of hearing, not brain-damaged. I'm still interested in what you have to say." I felt the heat rising in my face as I suppressed a sob.

"Sorry," Dave offered.

I kept thinking of Jesus. There was no doubt in my mind it had been His love that had seen me through the hospitals and brought me safely home. Now, he would carry me through the vertigo, the deafness, and every other hurdle I encountered. I had to remember that.

One afternoon before Christmas, three women burst through our front door when Mom opened it. "Merry Christmas," they shouted together.

Doris, my supervisor at Great Foods Manufacturing, and Hope, a nurse I knew from Regional Med, walked over to where I sat at the card table. Hope handed my mother a large glass pan. "It's meatloaf, mashed potatoes, and vegetables."

"That's dandy," Mom said, taking it and carrying the heavy pan upstairs to the kitchen.

"Thank you," I said, surprised. "We all love meatloaf and mashed potatoes in this family."

But that wasn't Hope's only gift. She handed me a thick envelope. I opened it and discovered it full of bills from a fund raiser she'd helped organize.

"When did you ever find the time?" I asked, incredulous.

"I worked on it during lunch."

Then Doris slipped me a check. It read, "Merry Christmas from GFM." It was made out for five hundred dollars.

"It's your bonus for going above and beyond the call of duty as our wellness nurse," Doris boomed. Though Great Foods

Manufacturing was not technically my employer, they treated me like one of their own.

My eyes glistened with tears. "Wow. This is unbelievable. What can I say? Maybe I'll get that hot tub after all." I laughed through my tears and wheeled around the table to pull all three into a hug.

"Merry Christmas," I shouted after them as they waved and headed out the door.

Now we would not struggle to pay our bills.

The next day, Pierce drove Mom to the motel where she would catch the shuttle to the airport. I rode along to see her off. When it was time to go, Mom rushed around to the passenger seat to hug me goodbye. I clung to her, like a homesick child heading to camp.

"Mom, thanks for coming and for all your help. I love you so much." I sniffed.

"I love you, too, dear. Just wish I could stay longer." Tears welled in her eyes as Dave took her elbow and helped her into the van.

Mom flew home, leaving an empty space at the table and a lonely place in my heart. For almost two weeks she'd catered to my every whim as only a mother could do. What would I do without her?

Back at the house, that afternoon, Pierce came in carrying a big box. "Merry Christmas, Mom. I found the perfect one for your room."

He hauled out a small Christmas tree decked in colored lights and set it on my dresser.

Dave disappeared into the workshop and brought out an old box of my favorite ornaments. "Where do you want this one?" he asked, holding up one of my favorites, a small pink wooden pig with wings.

"Oh, that's Pig Angel. I want him on this side of the tree so I can look at him.'

"Your wish is my command," Dave said, humming.

After hanging the ornaments, Dave plugged in the small village of ceramic houses that graced the shelf over my dresser. Lights shone from their little windows.

On Christmas Eve, I heard a big truck pull up in front of our house. Fed Ex.

"Oh man, look what Aunt Dorothy sent us," Pierce exclaimed as he bounded in the front door, holding up a big package, smoking with dry ice. "Fillet mignons!"

He disappeared up the stairs with the box. An hour later, he reappeared alongside his father, both carrying steaming platters. Medium rare steaks with stuffed potatoes, broccoli, salad and apple turnovers. I wheeled into my place at the card table, my mouth watering.

"Thank you, Lord for our wonderful dinner. And thank you for Aunt Dorothy," I said.

We ate in the glow of the colored lights, while Norah Jones played softly from the other end of the room.

Overflowing with Christmas spirit, Pierce had also bought a few presents, wrapped them, and arranged each under the little tree. On Christmas morning, Dave and I opened our gifts.

"The original <u>Moby Dick</u>?" Dave exclaimed, opening his package to find a DVD.

"I knew it was one of your favorites," Pierce said.

"You were right." Dave looked pleasantly surprised.

"Yum. Shortbread cookies." I said, after opening my package and popping one of the buttery cookies into my mouth. I glanced over at Dave and Pierce, feeling overwhelmed with love. The path before me was uncertain, but those who mattered most were still with me. I was truly blessed. It felt good to relax and feel happy, at least for the moment.

JUST WANTING TO FORGET

A few nights after Christmas, Dave and I lay in bed talking. It was the first time I'd spoken about the hospitals since coming home. As I rambled, I was back in the County Hospital Trauma Unit and feeling lost.

"I'm sorry it was so hard," Dave said gently. "If they'd just let us visit more often, maybe you wouldn't have been so scared."

"It's not your fault. I'm thankful you came as often as you did. Your visits kept me going."

I went on talking for quite a while and as I did, the trickle of words became a torrent of sorrow. Weary, I paused. Heavy breathing from the other side of the bed told me Dave, exhausted, had fallen asleep. I lay alone with my grief.

Turning on my side, I fell into an uneasy sleep. I dreamt I was back in the Trauma ICU. The nurses and aides were speaking to each other. They didn't seem to know I was there.

"Hey, I'm right here," I shouted.

They kept on talking, ignoring me.

My heart pounded in my chest as I awoke in a blind panic.

I'd escaped death in the hospitals and cried little in the weeks since coming home. It had made me feel good to think of how strong I'd become. But tonight, while Dave slept, I wept inconsolably in the dark. Apparently, some of what had happened still haunted me.

After a few minutes, the tears stopped and my mood shifted. Something else took hold of me. It was the impulse to write.

Write? Where was that coming from?

"You definitely should write a book," Dr. Lassiter had said at

County Hospital when he saw me scribbling illegible notes on a pad. Later, my friend Liz had agreed.

Despite their encouragement, in the weeks since coming home, I hadn't wanted to think about the hospitals, let alone document what happened there. I was still trying to recover from my many injuries. My hearing was so bad, I could barely make out what Dave and Pierce said when they spoke to me. I felt dizzy whenever I turned my head. I couldn't walk or stand and some part of me hurt whenever I sat in my wheelchair. I was completely wheelchair bound, and Dr. Norton still couldn't tell me if or when I might walk. Life had been good before the tree. Now it looked as if it was destined to be a lot harder and certainly more painful. How could I think of writing about my life when I could barely face it?

This is for life.

Was that what the chaplain at Regional Medical had warned me about? Had he known I'd eventually have to face it? A feeling of dread crept into my stomach.

"Stop thinking about the future," I shouted at the silent space around me and shook my head. I forced my attention back to my beautiful room, the soft bed, and the loving presence I felt within me. It was only with that presence that I felt safe.

For weeks in the hospital, I'd patiently answered the hourly question, "What happened to you?" I'd come to be known at County Hospital as "the nurse the tree fell on" and enjoyed what celebrity that title afforded me. Telling and retelling my story had presented a way for me to connect with people again. It gave me the sense of purpose I'd lacked as a hospital patient and helped sharpen my mind.

But writing about the Trauma Units or Hyperbaric might be different. Heat burned my cheeks when I reflected on how indifferently some of the staff in those places had treated me. Would going over it make me feel worse?

Safe in the confines of my downstairs room, I wanted to forget. I played back what Liz had told me. "Make sure you write your story."

I contemplated the inexplicable drive that pushed me to put my memories on paper. Even when I could barely hold a pencil, the motivation to record them had been strong. *Why, Jesus?*

Would writing be God's way of purging my demons? Would it help me make sense of all that had happened? Would it keep me sane? Would it give me and others hope? However difficult it might be to put the indescribable into words, I decided to honor my desire and formulate a plan to write. I would begin just as soon as the holidays were over and my helpers had gone. I'd commit an hour or two each morning to sitting at the computer. After that, I'd see what happened.

EMPATHIZING MORE, BLAMING LESS

Two days after Christmas, Janelle drove the ten-hour drive to our house. Janelle was John's wife, about five years my junior, and a wonderful friend. She'd managed more than one successful career, first as an ICU nurse and later as a realtor. More recently she'd completed another degree and started a job as a research librarian near the coast. It was there she and John lived in a house they'd built by the water.

The day she arrived I was feeling more physically off balance than usual, like a new sailor trying to adjust to life at sea. Was the vertigo getting worse? As if that weren't enough, my left ear felt full of water and a whooshing noise made it even harder to hear. I crawled into bed determined to get some relief, but it was Janelle's calm presence that soothed and distracted me.

While John had entertained us with stories, Janelle made it her primary mission to pamper me. On the first day, she did three loads of clothes, shampooed my hair in the bathroom sink, massaged my aching shoulders, and then cooked breakfast and lunch. She did it all before two o'clock. As icing on the cake, she presented me with a pound of gourmet coffee, brewed a pot, and brought a cup for me to enjoy. I had only recently learned how to make tea in my microwave downstairs, but it was coffee that I craved. I cradled the warm cup in both hands, savoring its rich aroma.

"I love coffee, Janelle, but Dave and Pierce don't drink it. They already do so much I don't want to ask them to make coffee too."

When my husband and son came home that afternoon I couldn't wait to tell them about everything Janelle had done.

"Hey, you won't have anything left to do tomorrow," Pierce said, laughing. "You'll be bored."

"You're hired," Dave added. "You're definitely one of those workers who requires little supervision. I'll bet your boss loves you."

Despite the jokes, I understood how much Pierce and Dave respected my friend.

In addition to her other talents, Janelle could make one heck of a salad. She searched our big pantry and refrigerator for ingredients. Then she chopped, diced, and tossed them into a huge bowl over a bed of lettuce. Each creation was unique and brimming with color, texture, and flavor. By the end of the week all of us agreed, if we gave an award for the "Most Industrious" volunteer, that honor would have to go to Janelle.

The next few days Janelle and I spent more time just hanging out. It was during those quiet moments when we talked.

"What was it like being a trauma patient in the units?" she asked and settled back with a cup of tea in her hand to listen.

"Well, most of what I remember from my first week in the ICU wasn't bad," I began. "But when they transported me to the Trauma Unit at County Hospital things were different. I felt lost and abandoned, like I'd been cast adrift." I took a deep breath and let it out. "You know, I've searched my memory, Janelle, but for the life of me, I can't remember the nurses or aides there ever saying anything to encourage me. It scared me to think I was completely at their mercy." My chest felt heavy.

Janelle paused a moment before she spoke. "By the sound of your voice, I can hear how hard it must have been. I'm sure it would have been a lot easier if they'd been able to talk to you a little more," she said gently.

Janelle spoke from experience. She'd done ICU nursing herself and dealt with many compromised and unconscious patients of her own. "I'll bet your nurses were very task oriented. They had to be. Their job required minute by minute monitoring of equipment as well as keeping up with the needs of their critically injured patients." She paused. "And I'll bet they assumed, however wrongly, that you were too out of it to benefit from conversation."

"Maybe so, Janelle, but I didn't want conversation. I would have been happy with just a pat on the arm or a kind word to let me know they had my back. I'm sure you reassured your patients." I was surprised at how angry my voice had become. Did Janelle think I was overreacting?

"Well, I did try to tell them what I was going to do before I did it. That's just good nursing."

"Exactly. And I know you well enough to believe you said it in a way that convinced them you cared. Sometimes it's not so much what someone says as how they say it. My nurses could probably have told me almost anything if they'd just said it in a soothing way. I guess I just didn't feel the love in there." I sighed again. "I see your point, though. The nurses had to stay focused. Just wish they'd reassured me a bit more in the process."

"Is it possible that the drugs in your system and the blow to your head influenced your perception?" Janelle had a look of pure love on her face.

I considered the devils and demons I remembered seeing in Hyperbaric and my fear that the nurses in the Trauma ICU were kidnapping me. Slowly, I began to see my caregivers in a more positive light, to empathize with them more and blame them less.

One morning in late December after staying a week, Janelle drove home. Pangs of sorrow gnawed at me. I loved Janelle and would miss her terribly. I was also keenly aware that she was the last of my helpers scheduled to come stay. Left alone, there would be little to distract me from my thoughts.

Things had been going well, maybe too well. At times, despite feeling optimistic, I found myself waiting for the other shoe to drop. It was strange how my thoughts were trying to undermine me. I would have to keep watch on them.

I prayed, feeling that now familiar sense of warmth in my heart. It came to me that having time alone might actually be a gift. It would give me a chance to write. It might even make me stronger.

Too often before the accident, I'd worried. Since my awakening at County Hospital, I felt stronger, more solid, knowing that Jesus' Spirit was with me, empowering and guiding me.

I thought about all the friends and family who'd sacrificed time to care for me. I reflected on my sister, Hillary, who'd come in the beginning to support Dave and Pierce, and Janelle, who'd just left. All of them occupied a special place in my heart. Now, for better or worse, I had to learn to be on my own.

DR. W. MARLIN BOLLING

In early January, true to my word, I spent my days writing for hours at the computer. More and more the process seemed to help me make better sense of all that had happened in the hospital. Maybe one day, I'd even understand why the tree had fallen on me.

Marley sat at my feet. He'd long since gotten over his fear of the wheelchair and the strange hospital smells. Delta and Daisy, his feline buddies, joined him on the floor, vying for my attention. Every now and then, Daisy, who was deaf, jumped on top of the keyboard, typing some strange words and distracting me in the process.

"Get down, Daisy," I nudged with my elbow. "It's hard enough to remember what happened without *you* helping me." Daisy just sat on the keyboard, refusing to move.

"You're being naughty. See how nicely Marley and Delta are sitting on the floor?" I gave her a shove. She landed next to her sister and began to wash.

Late in the afternoon, Dave trudged in the front door, carrying his briefcase.

"Here's something that might help you, Lara. I kept a journal of sorts during your early weeks in the hospital."

Dave handed me a large three ring binder.

"That's wonderful, Dave. I had no idea you'd written anything." I felt excited to take a look inside. Maybe I'd be able to go back and find out what really happened.

I held the notebook in my hands for a minute before opening the cover. Something made me hesitate. Did I really want to see what my husband had written? After all, it was during those early weeks in the hospital when I'd been out of my mind. What would it say?

I slowly opened the cover and read the first page. It was handwritten and a treasure trove of doctors' names, dates, treatments, and surgeries. There was also a list of some of the more bizarre remarks I'd made, the names of nurses I liked, those I argued with, my pain level each day, and other key pieces of information.

"Wow, this will definitely help me fill in the gaps," I exclaimed.

"Good, I was hoping it might be useful," Dave said. "I know you didn't have a clue what was going on back then."

As I looked through his journal, the phrases "brain damage" and "not making any sense" appeared on more than one page. It was obvious Dave, more than anything else, had been worried about the state of my mind. From his notes I could see he'd asked my County Hospital doctors to repeat the MRIs and other tests that had already been done at Regional Med to rule out brain trauma. Apparently, he wasn't convinced the earlier results were right. It began to dawn on me just how scared he'd been, wondering if I would be the same person he'd married. No wonder he'd looked shell shocked from worry when he visited.

I spent the next day reading his notes. The week after the accident, he and Pierce had been numb with exhaustion, traumatized, and too overwhelmed to eat, yet what Dave wrote was detailed and perfectly clear. How had he done it?

"Funny, you'd never kept a diary before. Why now?" I asked.

"I don't know, just knew I wouldn't remember anything if I didn't."

"Sweetie, you probably won't buy it, but I think God may have been guiding you."

"You think so?" He looked doubtful.

"I know it sounds strange, but I do."

Dave was quiet. "Well, I pray to God all the time, but never seem to get an answer." He frowned.

I should have known he felt that way. I'd been so excited at County Hospital when I'd felt Jesus' presence. In hindsight, I wasn't paying much attention to how uncomfortable Dave had been with all my comments about God. I was still pretty wrapped up in myself. Later I would have to face the truth.

Pierce was out more than usual after New Year's, seeing friends and going to job interviews. He was happily getting on with his life as a twenty-one year old that just happened to rent a room in his parents' house.

Some days, it felt a little strange being alone at home in my wheelchair. I was accustomed to being on the go. Not wanting to think about it, I pushed myself each morning to start my routine. First, I thanked God for all of my blessings. Then I worked my way across the sliding board into the wheelchair, rolling over to the sink to give myself a sponge bath. I ate a bowl of granola, exercised with ankle and hand weights, called insurance companies, answered emails to friends, and wrote. Whatever I needed to do, I did it. Staying with that structure gave me a small but vital sense of accomplishment. It also kept me calm.

By mid-January, all I could think about was regaining my ability to walk and going back to work. A single happy image hung at the forefront of my mind. I was standing in the entrance hall of the larger of the two factories as the workers greeted me with big smiles. I could feel their love. Now the only two things that stood in my way were my broken tibia and the vertigo.

Dr. Norton's reference to delayed healing still weighed heavily on my mind. It would be three more weeks until I saw him again. Despite my best efforts, I started to feel anxious, so I made an appointment with Dr. Bolling for a second opinion.

Pierce drove me the forty miles to see him. I hadn't seen Dr. Bolling since he'd visited me on Rehab. "I can't wait to see him. Dr. Bolling feels as much like family as he does my surgeon. I know you and your dad feel the same way. Without him, who knows what would have happened.

"I agree. Not taking away from the amazing reconstructions Dr. Norton did after that, but we were lucky Dr. Bolling was the doctor on call that first night." Pierce pulled into a handicapped space. "Not many surgeons would have stayed at the hospital for three straight nights to do surgeries and make sure you were okay."

Pierce wheeled me into the examining room. A few minutes later Dr. Bolling bustled in, stopping just inside the door to smile at me. He turned to shake Pierce's hand and then continued across the room to hug me.

"It's so good to see you. Please give my best to Dave," he said, releasing me.

"I will. He really wanted to come, but couldn't get off work."

I handed Dr. Bolling the x-rays from Dr. Norton. He studied them with interest. "Wow, this is some amazing work Dr. Norton did," he exclaimed, shaking his head in wonder. That's exactly why I sent you to The Wizard."

I laughed at his reference to Dr. Norton. As he spoke, I noticed that while Dr. Norton had often expressed his emotions through facial expressions, Dr. Bushy communicated his with words. That was a quality I really appreciated in a doctor.

"Dr. Norton wrote me about the problem with your tibia," he said, a more serious look crossing his face. "Sometimes with severe compound fractures like yours, the bones just don't knit together."

"So there *is* something wrong with my tibia?" The words caught in my throat.

Never one to mince words, Dr. Bolling came right to the point.

"You might need a bone graft."

"As in another surgery?" I blurted, alarmed.

No doubt sensing how his remark had struck me, he elaborated. "Just an outpatient surgery. With all you've been through, it shouldn't be that bad."

"Any surgery sounds awful right now." I frowned, "I've had fourteen already, and I need to get back to work. I told my boss I was shooting for the end of April. That's only three months away. Another orthopedic surgery would push my return date back even further. Bottom line is I don't know if she'd hold my job."

"You'll see Dr. Norton again at the end of the month. I'm sure he'll have a better idea how your leg is healing by then. Be sure and let me know what he says."

He walked over and gathered me into a hug. "No matter what happens, Dr. Norton and I will be with you every step of the way."

His words gave me hope. I collected myself. "Thank you. I'm not going to lie. You haven't told me what I wanted to hear. But I also came to see you because I needed the truth. We all love you and appreciate everything you've done." I managed a smile.

Pierce drove us home. My mind reeled. Not knowing was hell. I whipped out my note pad and updated my to- do list. Making a plan always helped me deal with worry.

1. Use the bone stimulator <u>twice</u> a day
2. Pedal twenty minutes, <u>varying pace</u>
3. <u>Increase</u> nutritional supplements to strengthen my bones
4. Pray for healing

With the new plan, my shin had to heal.

That night as we lay in bed, Dave tried hard to comfort me. "We still don't have any idea what's going to happen. Anyway, even if you do end up having to have another surgery, we'll get through it. I'll take care of you." He wrapped his long arms around me and pulled me close. For a time, I just lay enveloped in his warmth and listened to the slow, steady beat of his heart.

VERTIGO

The end of the holiday season had always left me feeling let down, knowing there would be no time off from work until May. Now, Dave was in the same boat. With our helpers gone, the cooking, cleaning, and all the rest of the chores fell squarely on him. That meant when he walked in the door from work, he headed straight up to the kitchen to start dinner and clean up. It was hard for me to watch, knowing there was nothing I could do.

It had been two months since coming home from the hospital and I was still stuck in the wheelchair. I couldn't get upstairs even to shower. On his days off Dave toted a big tub of warm water and placed it on the floor in front of my chair. He squatted, scrubbing my feet and legs.

"Thanks, Sweetie. My feet have never looked this bad."

As he scrubbed, layer upon layer of loose skin floated on the water. "It's just dead skin. How about some lotion?"

"Great"

Dave massaged my feet until I was in heaven. When he finished, they felt smooth as a baby's. It was another of my husband's many labors of love.

But by the middle of January, more than the impact of anything else, it was the vertigo that threatened to derail me. When had it started? I'd first noticed the spinning in the Trauma Unit when they'd rolled me onto my side to change the sheets. Back then, the funhouse effect amused me. I didn't give it another thought until it showed up again in Rehab.

"Your body's probably trying to adjust to sitting after lying for so long," the Medical Director had said when I asked her.

The vertigo that came when I rolled onto my side was soon joined by a more chronic state of feeling off-balance. It was with me whenever I sat up in the wheelchair or bed and didn't go away after they sent me home from the hospital. Would it make me fall off the sliding board? Vomit? An annoying ocean sound, like a giant seashell, whooshed through my ear and made me feel as if my ear had water trapped inside. Despite a round of antibiotic ear drops, the water in the ear feeling persisted. Now, two months later, neither the vertigo nor the rest of it was fun anymore.

Pierce drove me to Dr. Baker's office to see what she could do. With all the extraordinary repairs she'd done on my face, eyes, ears, and nose, I had high hopes.

"I can't stand this awful feeling. It's like being drunk without any of the fun. And I can't hear," I complained when she walked in.

"Before we go any further, I want to check your hearing," she said.

The test result soon revealed what Dave and Pierce already knew.

"You have moderate hearing loss," Dr. Baker said.

I'd tested the worker's hearing at GFM. Moderate loss was never good.

"Well, no wonder you can't hear, Mom," Pierce said. "I know you can't help it, but Dad and I are really tired of having to repeat everything."

"And I'm tired of feeling left out of the conversation," I said, hurt. I turned to Dr. Baker, "I think the problem has to be the ear tubes they left in my ears after hyperbaric treatments. Can you take them out? Maybe then the holes in my ear drums can heal and I'll be able to hear."

"Sure," she said without a hint of emotion. She looked to Pierce, "Hold her head and don't let her move." She meant business.

"You mean right now, without something for pain?" I started to panic.

Dr. Baker didn't act as if she heard me. She seemed intent on searching for something. From her tool cabinet she selected what looked like a pair of needle-nosed pliers. Pierce held my head firmly over to one side. I braced myself for what would come next.

"Don't move," she said. Poking the end of her pliers into my left ear, she grabbed the tube and yanked hard.

I yelled as I felt a sharp pain in my ear. Though it was winter, beads of sweat covered my forehead.

Dr. Baker dabbed at my bloody ear with a gauze pad and firmly pushed my head over to the other side. "Hold her head," she said again to Pierce. I could feel his hand on the side of my face, pushing down.

The pain was unbearable. I reached up to swat her arm away, but she was too quick for me.

"I've got it." She sounded triumphant.

A flood of emotions hit me. Relief, shame, anger. "Sorry I moved," I stammered. "But that hurt like crazy."

She dabbed at the blood trickling from my ear, apologizing. "So sorry if I hurt you. I'll see you in a few weeks to see if the holes have closed. Make sure you don't get water in your ears." She turned and left.

I stared after her, while Pierce gawked at the table where she'd dropped the ear tubes.

"Holy cow! Look at those things. They look like big rivets with jagged edges. Are you okay? You look like a sheet."

"Yeah, I'm okay. But no wonder that hurt."

"Yeah, no wonder." He raised his eyebrows, looking pale himself. "That was awful."

In the next few weeks, I hoped for the best, but by the end of January the dizzy feeling and the whooshing noises were worse than ever. I couldn't help but notice that feeling physically off-balance had a way of making my thoughts and emotions off kilter, too. I struggled to write and socialize with friends. How would I ever concentrate when I went back to work? How would I have enough balance to walk? Those thoughts sobered me.

I willed myself not to despair. Had God already handed me my quota of miracles? Had He grown weary of answering so many big requests from one small woman? I pictured Jesus as the giver of all blessings and the supreme Spirit of Love, and yet....

"Jesus, I know you haven't brought me so far to leave me like this," I cried.

Pierce took me back to Dr. Baker.

"The dizziness has gotten worse," I said when she walked in.

Dr. Baker picked up her otoscope and inspected my ears.

"Neither hole has healed. The one in your left ear drum is huge and jagged. I doubt it'll heal on its own."

I remembered the pain I'd felt. It was the same ear that always felt clogged and roared like a giant seashell.

"I've been doing an exercise my sister taught me that's supposed to correct vertigo," I said. "It seems to help a little, but the relief never lasts."

"I'm going to send you to a physical therapist to make sure you're doing it correctly. I'm no expert, myself."

Pierce drove me to Out Patient Rehab at Regional Medical. I recognized my physical therapist right away as one I'd had in the hospital Rehab Unit.

"Hi. Good to see you again. I'm Terri. Don't worry, I've used vestibular exercises with lots of folks with vertigo and they work." She was smiling.

"That's what I wanted to hear." For the first time in days, I relaxed and felt hopeful.

"Sometimes with a blow to the head, tiny crystals called otoliths are forced from their little pouches in the inner ear into one of the semicircular canals. That makes you feel dizzy when you move," Terri explained.

I transferred from my wheelchair to sit on the padded treatment table she indicated, stretching my legs out in front of me.

"First, I'm going to tilt you backwards," she continued. "It's a maneuver called the Dix Hall-Pike and will give me a better idea of what's going on."

She slid her arm behind me and quickly tipped me backward until I lay flat. As the room spun wildly, I grabbed the sides of the table to keep from falling on the floor.

"Did the spinning start immediately or was it delayed?" Terri asked.

"Immediately."

"I think the crystals might be stuck in the little hairs in your semicircular canals. I'm going to do another maneuver called the Semont, to loosen them."

Terri sat me up, this time with my feet hanging over the side. With my head turned to the left and a firm grip on my shoulders, she flipped me onto my right side. She counted to thirty. Grabbing my shoulders again, Terri flung me from my right side to my left until I stopped, my face resting on the soft table. When she finally sat me back up, the room rotated before it came to a stop. Apparently, Mr. Semont didn't mess around.

"You'll feel dizzy today, but I want to see you again at the end of the week."

I was still feeling woozy when Pierce and I reached the car.

"That Semont maneuver was a bit violent," he said, raising his right eyebrow and giving me an ironic look. That was saying a lot coming from a guy who'd just graduated from the policy academy.

Despite Terri's warning, for the next few days, I felt better. Then the dizziness returned. This time I experienced delayed spinning when I rolled onto my side.

"Delayed spinning should mean the little crystals are floating freely now," Pierce said, referring back to what Terri had told us.

On our second visit to physical therapy, Terri tried another exercise.

"The Epley maneuver will move the loose crystals back where they belong."

She tilted me backward, this time rolling me over to my left. After the Epley, though I felt a little better, I was still not right.

Will I ever be free of the vertigo? "Lord, I'll do whatever it takes."

"Drink plenty of water," Maggie advised me over the phone when I mentioned my problem. "That's the message I'm getting from Spirit."

"Hey, I'll try anything."

Every morning before I got out of bed I repeated the Epley Manuever, followed by two glasses of water. Little by little the strange off-kilter and spinning sensations seemed to diminish. I began to feel some sense of control over the vertigo.

One afternoon I got an unexpected call from my sister, Hillary.

"I need some advice," she said.

Hillary rarely asked for advice, so when she did, I felt honored.

"Lord, please guide my thoughts and words," I whispered under my breath.

As we talked, I concentrated on my sister's problem, and a strange thing happened. I felt my fears and much of what remained of the vertigo fade.

"How's the writing going?" Hillary asked.

"It brings me peace. Whenever I sit down at the computer and the memories come flooding back, even the painful ones, writing helps me remember how lucky I've been."

"You focus on your gifts."

"Exactly. In every chapter of my story, I've found at least one blessing in the midst of the pain. It's obvious, Jesus wants me to be here, so He's giving me hope."

I hung up and understood how focusing my heart and mind on someone else's needs and on my own gratitude calmed my worries and soothed the vertigo.

When I went back to Dr. Baker, she had another plan. "I know your vertigo is a little better, but the holes in your ear drums aren't. That's why you still can't hear. You're going to need an ear patch surgery, a tympanoplasty. I'll take muscle from your jaw to reconstruct your ear drum. The next opening I have isn't until late March, two months away. Do you want me to put you down?" She rapidly recited a long list of potential risks, including hemorrhage and deafness, in a monotone.

"How likely is it that the graft will take?" I asked.

"Good," she said, sounding confident.

I looked at Dave and a silent understanding passed between us.

"Let's do it," I said.

On the ride home, checking in with my feelings, I was glad I'd gone ahead and scheduled the tympanoplasty. I'd witnessed firsthand Dr. Baker's extraordinary skill as a surgeon the night she'd repaired my face and scalp and reattached the top of my ear and eyelid. I had tremendous faith in her. If anyone could restore my hearing, she could.

THE WIZARD

Later that same week Pierce and I headed up the highway to see Dr. Norton. It had been six weeks since I'd seen him. After the recent appointments with Dr. Baker and Dr. Bolling, I prepared myself for more bad news, this time on my legs. I fidgeted in the passenger seat and made an effort to calm myself.

"Jesus has his own time table for your healing," Maggie had said when I spoke with her on the phone. I decided to consider what she'd said the next time I prayed.

"Jesus, I don't know your specific plan for my healing. I just ask that you continue to bring me hope." Fortified with God's powerful spirit of hope, I would be fine.

By the time Pierce wheeled me into Dr. Norton's office, I felt at peace with whatever happened next. We waited only a moment before they called us back. Hercules carried me across the hall for another set of x-rays. He had just picked me up for the second time and gently deposited me on the treatment table, when Dr. Norton strode in.

"How're your legs feeling?"

"Good."

"Are you pedaling and using the bone stimulator?"

"Every day."

He studied the x-rays. First, he looked at the left ankle and, giving it the nod of approval, he moved on to the picture of my right leg. He enlarged the image on his screen to scrutinize the tibia.

"None of the hardware has moved. That's good. Let me run some numbers." He grabbed his calculator and did some figuring. "Thirteen weeks since the reconstruction. The left ankle and foot are as healed as we can probably expect."

I held my breath as he looked at the tibia again. He seemed to be weighing his options. Apparently the answer wasn't cut and dried.

He came over to where I sat on top of the treatment table. He squeezed and pushed on various parts of my shin bone.

"Does that hurt? Does this? How about that?" he asked as he pressed hard.

"No."

Then he asked me to bend my right knee and push with my foot as hard as I could against his hands.

"What about that?"

"No."

He walked back to the computer and said the words I will never forget. "I *think* I see some healing in the tibia."

"You do?"

"I do, and any way, I've got an awful lot of hardware supporting that leg, and weight bearing should make it stronger. I guess it's time to see what it can do."

"Really?"

He looked at me. "You're ready to start physical therapy for gait training with a walker, just make sure you back off on it if you have a lot of pain."

All I heard was *you're ready to start physical therapy for gait-training*.

"Are you sure?" I asked, excited.

"I think so. Let's see how it feels when you stand. Swing your legs over the side and rest your feet on the floor."

I maneuvered into position with my bare feet flat on the cold floor.

"Pierce, you get on that side of your mother and hold her under her arm, and I'll support her on this side." My pulse raced. Would it hurt?

"Go ahead," Dr. Norton said. "We've got you."

I was on my feet. No pain, no dizziness, just the sheer joy of standing.

"How does it feel?" he asked.

"Not bad." I held my breath waiting for something to happen. Nothing did.

"Okay, let's see if you can take a step. We'll hold you."

I stepped out a few inches with my right foot and grinned as tears streamed down my face. The long wait was over.

Later I wrote to friends and family:

> Good news! This week I was sanctioned for another round of physical therapy, this time for gait-training and stair climbing. Hey, it may not be pretty, but I am going to walk! It's hard to believe the time has finally come after four months in a wheelchair. Thank you for your love and prayers. You're always in my thoughts and heart.

Liz wrote back:

> Lara, what wonderful news! Your positive attitude is remarkable, and I'm sure it has been a big factor in your progress—that along with your loving family, prayers, and God's love and healing power. Your joy almost jumps out of the computer. Yes, I believe you will walk too, and it will be **BEAUTIFUL!**

Jenny wrote, too:

> Just keep on trusting in God and have faith. He will see you through this. Remember that He loves you even more than you love Pierce. Isn't that amazing?

FIRST STEPS

I was in high spirits by the time we reached the house and then Pierce's cell rang.

"This is Pierce ....Yes, Sir......Good.... I will....Okay.....I'll see you then."

Pierce parked in front of our log house, pumped his fist in the air, and let out a loud whoop.

"The police department offered me a job. I start next week." After months of putting his life on hold, Pierce could move forward.

"That's wonderful. Congratulations," I said, feeling proud and grateful.

Pierce's new job, though certainly welcome, resulted in a major loss of transportation for me. I'd been so concerned about my leg I'd almost forgotten my friend, Sandi, had called. Over the years, I'd lost touch with her, renewing our friendship only six months before the accident. The minute Dr. Norton sanctioned me to go to physical therapy for gait-training, I wasted no time in calling her.

"When do you need me to take you?" she asked.

"Is Monday too soon?

"No. I'll be there. Just email me the time."

On Monday morning, I got up early. It was the first day of physical therapy, and I couldn't sleep. Thoughts whirled through my mind. How would it go? Would it hurt? Would I really be able to walk on a leg that had been broken in fifty pieces, hardware or not?

I ate a bowl of cereal and cinched the Velcro™ stays tightly on the hinged cast that ran the length of my right leg. I buckled the new plastic "stabilizer" around my left ankle to make sure the ankle wouldn't turn over when I tried to stand and put on a pair of shoes. All this I did in preparation for walking.

Sandi pulled her little blue car up in front. A retired nurse anesthetist, she was adept at wheeling me over the threshold of our front door and out to her car. I transferred into the passenger seat, and Pierce loaded the wheelchair into the back. Sandi and I were off.

Her presence comforted me. She was one of those rare people who made me feel completely accepted, no matter what my state of mind. She was also one of the most accomplished women I knew.

"You're looking well, but are you ready for this?" she asked, scrutinizing me.

"Yes. I just can't believe I'm really going to walk." Butterflies fluttered in my stomach.

I talked to Sandi on the drive and told her about the angels in the hospital. "I know you didn't know it then, but you were one of the people who motivated me to seek a closer relationship with God this past year. You told me that knowing Jesus had forgiven you helped you feel much better about yourself, that He'd empowered and changed your life. I often thought about what you'd said."

"I had no idea." She smiled. "I guess we never really know how the seeds we plant and the kind words we say make all the difference?"

As we drove, I thought about how much Sandi was like Dave. When something interested him, he set about learning to do it well. He'd built beautiful and useful things out of wood for our home in his shop, taught himself to play drums and bass guitar, cultivated a beautiful garden, made a painstaking study of wildlife, maintained our computers, and fixed the cars and motorcycles. Most of those projects had gone by the wayside after the tree fell. Since that time he'd done his best to be a good caretaker, pampering and cooking for me. Now I was determined to give him his life back.

Like Dave, Sandi loved animals. She was a skilled equestrian, owning a small horse farm. She was also an accomplished oil painter. Many of her beautiful creations graced the walls of her living room. Among her many accomplishments, Sandi loved to cook, often treating friends to lavish meals. Dave and I counted ourselves lucky to be included.

Earlier in January, when I was still struggling with vertigo, Sandi walked in one morning bearing a basket. "I hope you haven't eaten."

She laid a table cloth on my card table and decorated it with a center piece and china plates. She pulled out a mixed green salad, along with homemade chicken salad, fruit, and bread. "Good heavens, Sandi. You'd put Martha Stewart to shame."

"Well, I could tell you needed a lift," she said, smiling. "Anyway, someone's got to fatten you up."

A lurch in the car yanked me out of my daydream. "We're here," she said, turning into a parking space. A sign over the door read Out-Patient Rehab. A soft-spoken physical therapist named Joe met us in the lobby. I wheeled after him into the big therapy room to begin my first session.

"It's time to see what you can do."

Was it me or did he look a little nervous too?

"Will it hurt?"

"I don't know, but be sure to tell me if it does."

He led the way to the parallel bars. "Every day, the first thing you'll need to do is stretch your calves and ankles." He demonstrated.

I stood and tried to stretch them by leaning against a pillar. My ankles and calves felt incredibly stiff, my feet, sore as if they had no padding.

"Now, stand between the rails, holding on, and try to walk to the other end."

I took small, careful steps, supporting most of my weight on my arms. I made it the ten feet to the other end, taking a moment to look out across the room. The view was beautiful. Strangers had stared down at me in my wheelchair, often talking to me as if I were a small child. Now, I felt elated, more in control.

I made five or six passes on the parallel bars leaning heavily on the rails. No pain in my legs. When I finished, I sat in the wheelchair.

"How did that feel?" Joe asked.

"Not bad, so long as I don't put much weight on my legs."

"That's enough walking for your first day. Wheel over to the padded table and let's work on exercising your ankles and knee some more. Then we'll ice you."

Tuesday I was back in therapy. Joe met me in the big room, carrying a walker. "I want you to ambulate from here over to that wall. That should be about thirty feet."

I stood and leaned forward, hunching over the walker, putting a lot of my weight on my hands. I stepped out with my right foot. Then I brought my left foot even with the right. Right forward, left together. Right forward, left together. My lower back as well as my legs hurt as I shuffled.

"I think my back hurts because I'm leaning over so far." I looked at Joe. He nodded. "Trouble is I can't help it. My legs hurt like crazy if I don't support most of my weight on my arms. Is that normal?"

"You've had some bad breaks. Hopefully the pain should get better." Despite the confident sound of his voice, he looked concerned.

"My doctor ordered me a back brace in the hospital. Do you think it would help?" I asked.

"It might help the pain, but if you wear a brace, your thoracic muscles won't get any stronger."

I was glad to hear him say that. I hated the uncomfortable metal contraption. From what he said, the pain in my back should get better the more I exercised it.

When Sandi drove me back to the house, everything hurt. I iced my right leg and left ankle as well as my back and sat on the love seat to look over the long list of therapy appointments. There were eighteen sessions on the schedule and all an hour's drive away. It was then I remembered another person who'd offered to help.

Hope was a retired cardiac nurse. "Don't forget to call when you're ready to start therapy," she'd said back in December. Though I'd barely known her then, I admired her. Hope was the kind of woman who was thoughtful, generous, and outspoken.

Now it was early February, and I called Hope back. "The doctor wants me to go to physical therapy two or three times a week. The number of appointments is overwhelming, and anything you can do will really help."

"I can take you whenever you like. Just give me the dates."

"Would once a week be too much?"

"No, but I can do more if you need me to."

"Hold on. You've been to my house when you brought us the meatloaf and the money from your fundraiser. You know how far it is. But in case you've forgotten, it's forty miles."

"I know, but it's something I want to do." Evidently she meant it.

"I don't know how to thank you," I said, humbled. "You don't even know me all that well, yet you're so willing to help."

"When I heard people talking about what happened to you, I could tell you were a good person at the end of her rope. I've been there myself. If it hadn't been for the people who offered to help, I don't know what might have happened to me or my kids. Like you, I live in a remote area, don't belong to a church, and have few local friends outside of work. I shudder to think what I'd do if something like this happened to me. At least, my husband is retired. So let me do this for you. Someday, you can do something to help someone else. Or you can do something for me. Hey, I figure you'll owe me." She laughed.

"God has sent some wonderful people my way, and you're right at the top of the list." I could hardly get the lump out of my throat.

"I'm not much of a believer, but I think sometimes God whispers in someone's ear to help. I guess this time he whispered in mine."

"Thank you," I said, my eyes brimming with tears.

Hope drove me to therapy on Wednesday. It was my third consecutive day, and I was already in pain. She sat and watched as I shuffled, hunched over the walker, around the perimeter of the large room. I'd made my way in a jerky sort of fashion twice around the room before my therapist stopped me.

"Try to stand up a little straighter," he said.

I moved again, struggling to stand taller.

Pain burned in my right shin, forcing me to put more weight on my arms. I kept going.

"Okay, why don't you take a rest, then we can work on your balance."

I relaxed before making my way to the parallel bars.

"This time I want you to try to take a few steps without holding on."

"Are you serious?" I couldn't believe what he was asking.

"Just see if you can."

I already knew what would happen. I steadied myself and lifted my hands from the bars. Shifting the weight to my left leg, I strained to step out with my right. Without help from my arms and with full weight on each leg in turn, I cried out in pain. I lost my balance and grasped the rails. The joy of my first steps evaporated. It would be a while before I walked without support.

Hope dropped me off at home. I wheeled over to the sofa and dropped heavily onto the cushion.

"God, thank you for helping me walk." Tears moistened my eyes. "I know with your support it'll get easier every day, but one question. Does it really have to hurt this much?"

That evening and the next day I practiced in my room. Even a few steps sent sharp pains through my feet, ankle and shin. Was something wrong?

"What do you think, Dave? Call Dr. Norton?"

"I think you're trying to do too much," he said.

"I guess I thought the harder I pushed, the sooner I'd get back to work. I should have known three days in a row was a bad idea. My legs need recovery time in between sessions, but it was all Out-Patient Rehab had to offer on short notice. I won't make that mistake again."

I didn't have to go back to therapy for four days. By then my legs would be better. I was counting on it.

"I've come up with a new strategy. I'm only going to practice a few steps at a time," I said to Dave when he came downstairs. "That should help with the pain."

It had to.

THE TORNADO

It had rained several inches by the time night fell. Water saturated the ground as high winds hit our neighborhood. We were watching TV downstairs, when the power went out. The temperature in our bedroom plummeted. Quickly, Dave piled more blankets on the bed and handed another to Pierce who stretched out on the couch. Through the night, the wind whistled and pounded us. Despite the raging storm, our log house was built into the side of a hill and felt secure.

The next morning the lights and heat were still off, and the wind was howling when Dave and Pierce drove down the driveway to go to work. Minutes later they burst through the front door again. I saw from their faces that something was wrong.

"There are at least ten trees piled across the driveway. We're blocked in," Dave exclaimed, panting from his walk up the hill. "We couldn't get our cars turned around, so we left them down there."

"That's not the worst of it, Mom," Pierce added. "There must be another hundred trees down on our property by the road. It's the biggest mess I've ever seen."

"Oh my God. Did a tornado hit?" I frowned, remembering the big one that had devastated our community in the early nineties. "I didn't hear anything last night, but you know I still can't hear that well. Do you think the neighbors are okay?"

"I don't know what the heck it was, but we're not the only ones with a problem," Dave said. He wore a grim expression. "We walked a little way down the street. It looked like the Apocalypse has hit. Trees were tied in knots across the road, and there was nothing left standing in the yards that we could see. Our friends next door have a huge pine leaning on their house."

"That's terrible. Are they okay?" It was worse than I imagined.

"Their house looks all right, but they're going to have to get a tree surgeon out here right away."

Our lovely wooded neighborhood was a wreck. I sat in dazed silence, trying to picture it. Dave and Pierce hurried to the workshop, returning moments later carrying their chainsaws. "We have to clear the trees on the drive," Dave said.

"What, right now? The gusts are whipping the tops of the trees around out there. It's dangerous. A limb could come down." What was he thinking?

"It's not a problem for me, but this is Pierce's first day working at the Police Department. It wouldn't look too good if he didn't show up," Dave said. "Anyway, we'll be careful."

Before I could argue, Dave rushed out the front door with Pierce in tow.

"What the heck? Are they mad?" I wheeled over to the bedside table and fumbled around for the matches in the dark. My hands shook as I lit the lantern by my bed and tucked a blanket around my legs and feet. Shivering, I sat bolt upright, stiff with fear and cold and tried to pray. When I couldn't, I started muttering at the walls.

"Here I am, sitting in the basement, stuck in this chair, barely able to hobble, and they go out there! How could they do that?" For a brief deranged moment I thought about trying to go after them with my walker.

The more the wind howled, the more I kept ranting. "Why didn't Dave listen? What if something happens? A tree falls? The chainsaw kicks back? They get hurt. My God. They could get killed. And I wouldn't even know?"

I'll call them.

I dialed their numbers. No answer. My heart raced. I tried hard to calm it.

All morning the storm raged, pelting my small window as Dave and Pierce worked outside. Now and then, the log house shuddered and groaned. I couldn't see them working, but I could see the tops of trees down the hill near the drive swirl violently in the wind. "Jesus, don't let anything happen to my husband and son," I pleaded.

By afternoon I was really going crazy. "Why does this keep happening? Why is it always trees? We're surrounded by them. Maybe we should move? That's it! We need to move somewhere with no trees. Anywhere! I've got to convince Dave. I'll make him understand. One of us crippled by a tree is enough."

What seemed like hours later, I still sat in the dim light, numb with cold and limp with fear. The door opened. Dave and Pierce trudged into the house, both of them talking and laughing.

I sank back into my chair, relieved.

"Well, we've cleared an opening big enough to get a car through, but the road is still blocked," Dave exclaimed.

"Dave! You both could have been killed. Why didn't you let me know you were okay? All day I've had to sit here and wonder, while you were out there having fun." Rage and relief played tug of war with my heart.

"I don't know about having fun. Aw, I'm sorry we worried you, but we're okay. We didn't want to stop until we got it done." He stroked my cheek.

That evening the lights came on. Power meant that the power company had cleared the road and repaired the downed wires. The three of us huddled around the electric heater, drinking soup and talking.

"The other news isn't good," Pierce said. "It looks like more than a hundred more trees are down at our entranceway. A tornado must have cut a two-hundred foot swath down the road."

"I can tell you this now that we're done, Lara. You were right to tell us not to go. Sawing into that twisted heap of pines was a bit terrifying."

"And dangerous," Pierce added.

"We never knew which way a tree would move when we sawed it. A few snapped back upright when I cut through them," Dave said, looking wide eyed.

"Twice Dad had to jump out of the way," Pierce added soberly.

A chill ran down my spine.

On Sunday, we slept in later than usual. Neither Dave nor I could muster the energy to get up. "I'm treating you to breakfast out," I said at ten, peering over the covers at Dave. "We both need something to cheer us up."

"You're right." he sighed. "Can you make it out to the car with the walker?"

"I'm pretty sure I can."

Dave inched the car slowly down the drive until we reached the opening he and Pierce had made through the massive pile of trees. I held my breath, not certain I wanted to see what lay ahead. Emerging into the light, I gasped. What they'd described earlier did nothing to prepare me for what I saw.

The aftermath of a hurricane could not have looked any worse. I stared in horror. The entranceway of our once beautiful wooded six-acre lot looked like a war zone. Dave pulled out onto the road. All down the country lane the story was the same. Mountains of trees littered the yards.

My eyes searched ahead to the first house. It stood in the midst of the rubble, apparently intact. So did the next.

"I can't believe it," I said, relieved. "Thank you, Jesus."

Monday we paid a tree surgeon five-thousand dollars to remove the trees that still hung precariously over our drive. Hundreds more lay in an ugly tangle at the front of our property. We pondered what we could afford to do. A neighbor suggested we talk to the loggers who worked on the cleanup a few doors down. I made a mental note to call them.

NO PAIN, NO GAIN

Thursday, Sandi picked me up. It had been a week since I'd gone to therapy.

"Good heavens. I almost missed your driveway," she said looking shocked. "I didn't recognize your place."

"I could cry just looking at this mess," I said as she turned from our drive back onto the road. "We've lost some precious friends in these trees. Dave says it will be generations before new ones take their places."

"I'm so sorry," she said, biting her lip.

It was then that I realized I'd been operating under a delusion. Without recognizing it, I'd been thinking Dave, Pierce and I had already paid our dues. God had handed us our trial by fire, and we'd proven ourselves to be up to the task. Life was supposed to be easier for a while. It wasn't. Apparently there was no cosmic tally of trials or good deeds, no blueprint that outlined a just plan for our lives. Life just went on, and bad things kept happening. My spirit sagged. I prayed for hope, but my usual sense of buoyant optimism was in short supply. God was there, but farther away than usual.

"Why, God?" I asked. "Is there a message?"

I didn't sense an answer.

My first day back in physical therapy, I had a particularly rough session. Sandi took me out to eat at the Italian Villa Restaurant afterward, to give me a lift. With some delicious soup and warm coffee in my stomach, the world looked brighter. I shared more about what had happened at County Hospital when I'd felt Jesus' Spirit fill me with His healing energy.

"This lunch out was just what I needed, though it was a lot to ask of you," I said, smiling at my friend. "I've been so down over the trees. Thank you."

"The day was yours, and I was honored to be able to do something for you. Anyway, I feel blessed to hear your testimony. You lifted my spirit."

Over the next few days, I continued to grieve. Loggers carted the hundreds of tree bodies away and smoothed out the field left in their wake. We handed them the rest of our savings. Most of our neighbors followed suit.

It began to look a little better at our end of the road. That weekend, Pierce walked down the drive to check it out. When he came back in, he stopped by my room.

"Mom, you'll never have to worry about that dead pine again. The other trees have taken their revenge and pounded it into the ground when they fell. It's gone." He smiled broadly. Obviously, the news made him happy.

"That's good to hear," I said, understanding his need for closure. I was still working on mine.

I contemplated what he'd said. Maybe, the dead tree was a metaphor. Perhaps it *had* died to make way for something new. I'd just have to see.

By the end of February, I'd been in physical therapy for three weeks. They transferred my therapist, Joe, to another center and assigned me a new one named Sasha. I soon found Sasha was a bit of a slave driver, prodding me to push harder through my pain.

"Plop," went the walker as I threw it out in front of my feet and swung my right foot forward. My rhythm was as jerky as before.

"Try to ambulate with a more normal gait," Sasha instructed.

I tried to picture the way I'd walked before the accident. I began again, and then stopped.

"It's the pain that's making me move this way. I haven't forgotten how to walk," I said trying to make her understand.

"Oh, I know," she said, not seeming to know at all.

Didn't anyone understand how much it hurt?

While Sasha pushed, Hope supported me from the sidelines. Like Sandi, Hope always managed to say exactly what I needed to hear. She continued to watch my efforts quietly as I took each hobbling step, wincing in pain, and made my way at a snail's pace around the big room. When I'd limped four or five times around, Sasha finally sat me down, and an assistant wrapped ice around my swollen legs and ankle, signaling the end of the session.

Hope wandered over to join me. "It was all I could do not to jump out of that chair and scream at that woman that you'd had enough for one day," she exclaimed, her face red. "Was she trying to kill you?"

Her indignation on my behalf cheered me.

"Okay, so where do you want to go today?" she asked, regaining her composure.

"Don't you need to get home?"

"No, I have all the time in the world."

Between Sandi and Hope, I felt like a princess. "Would you take me to the Pastry Supreme? They have the best rolls and coffee."

"Your wish is my command."

I'd been a regular at the Pastry Supreme before the accident. Once a week I'd gone there for coffee on my afternoon break. Now as I hobbled, leaning on my walker through the door, it felt good as smiling faces greeted me.

"What the heck happened to you?" a woman I recognized asked from behind the counter.

"An encounter with a tree," I said and smiled at her.

"And you're walking? I'm sure happy you made it back."

"Not as glad as I am to be back. By the way, this is my wonderful friend, Hope. She's been chauffeuring me back and forth to physical therapy on her days off."

"She must be a really good friend."

"That's for sure," I said, beaming at Hope.

In therapy, Sasha prodded me to practice my new skills at home. "Now that we've gone over stair climbing, I want you upstairs and helping in the kitchen every day." It sounded as if she'd reached the conclusion I might be lazy.

I pushed myself to follow her advice, but the stairs that led from my downstairs room were long and steep.

"I don't want you climbing them when I'm at work," Dave said. "What if you fell?" He didn't have to tell me twice.

I waited for the weekend to make my first trip upstairs. It had been five months since I'd seen the main floor of our house. Dave stood behind me as I began the long, slow methodical climb, carefully leading each time with my left foot. When I reached the top, I looked out and beamed. It was more beautiful than I'd remembered. The warm log walls and view of the mist rising from the mountain across the valley filled me with joy. I was home.

Following Sasha's advice, I cooked Dave scrambled eggs for breakfast. My sense of accomplishment was worth the pain in my shin.

As the two of us sat eating, I looked longingly out our windows. On all sides we were surrounded by oaks, pines, and huckleberry bushes. Yellow finches, titmice, chickadees, and cardinals crowded the bird feeders scrabbling for seeds. It was as if we lived in a giant terrarium.

Our log home overlooked a small mountain near the Appalachians. It was winter and the sun streamed in through the wall of glass doors across from us that led out to the deck. A line from a Joni Mitchell song played in my head.

> And the sun poured in like butterscotch
> And stuck to all my senses
> Oh, won't you stay
> We'll put on the day
> And we'll talk in present tenses.
> (Joni Mitchell, "Chelsea Morning," from the Clouds
> album, 1969.)

On Sunday, I searched through my dresser and closet to find pants that still fit. For a moment, I studied my standing reflection fully nude in the mirror. The skin hung loose on my thighs. I was eating more than two thousand calories a day, but after six months I'd only gained fifteen of the thirty pounds I'd lost. I sat down to try on a pair of my favorite pants. It looked like I was wearing a sack. Digging into the back of the closet, I found another pair I'd saved in a smaller size.

Pain in my right leg brought my treasure hunt to a halt. The tendons and ligaments were still healing. I sat down on my bottom at the top of the stairs and used my arms to inch my way back down. The rest of the day, I had to lean harder on the walker whenever I got up. It was payment for my hour of fun.

Weeks in physical therapy passed, and I traded the walker for a cane. I still moved in a jerky, hesitant sort of manner, but nevertheless, I walked. Though standing was still nearly unbearable, I was willing to take the pain and clumsy gait over life in a wheelchair any day.

Despite my growing mobility, I still hadn't been able to take a shower. My bathroom at home had only a tub and climbing over the side looked daunting. There was a shower stall in Pierce's room. The trouble was I needed help.

Talk about awkward. There were some things my twenty-one-year-old son should not have had to do. But with Dave working long hours, Pierce put a plastic chair in the stall and turned on the water. The shower head put out such a fine mist that after ten minutes, I felt wet but not really clean. I wrapped the shower curtain around my torso to grab the towel Pierce handed me.

A few days later after my last session in physical therapy, Hope suited up to give me my best gift yet. I sat on a bench in the Rehab shower room, trying to wrestle off my skirt and tee. Pushing earplugs into my ears, I prepared for what came next.

It was one of those rare female bonding experiences when you put all modesty aside just long enough to reap the pleasure of becoming perfectly clean. On the way home I basked in the joy of feeling fresher and sweeter smelling than I had in months. After nearly six months of sponge baths, I didn't know clean could feel so good. Gratitude warmed my heart.

When the news got out that I was walking again, friends wrote to express their joy and congratulate me.

Gerald wrote:

Can't wait to see you walk back into Great Foods Manufacturing. Jenny wrote too:

> I can't believe you are walking up and down steps. That is truly the work of the Lord to get you this far! Isn't He awesome! Before long this will all be behind you and you will be back doing all the things you need and want to do. Just keep on trusting in God and having faith. He will continue to see you through.

Perry sent a note too.

> Your steadfast determination to recover from your injuries and not let them cripple you for life is definitely one of the most inspiring stories of survival I've ever witnessed.

And so did Barbara.

> I hope you are staying grounded in your sense of the miracle of living and healing and loving other people, as you have been.

Their encouraging messages pushed me to work even harder. If I did, just maybe I could get strong enough to go back to work by the end of April.

THE TYMPANOPLASTY

As March sped by, the surgery to repair the large, unhealed hole in my ear drum loomed in front of me. Dr. Baker's office had scheduled the tympanoplasty for the last week of the month. A graft, using a piece of my jaw muscle, would patch the hole. I dreaded the thought of it. Any surgery sounded bad, but one on the inside of my ear sounded worse.

When I mentioned how I felt to Dave, he sat down to talk with me. "Let's go over the pros and cons. If you don't have the surgery, you'll always have to wear ear plugs in the shower. You'll never be able to hear very well, and you'll always feel left out of conversations," he noted patiently. "On the plus side, if you have it, you should be able to hear better, and from what Dr. Baker says, you might even feel less dizzy."

I read through the long surgical consent form. It listed all possible risks including, to my dismay, chronic dizziness. At the bottom, it cited potential problems if they left the holes open. Some looked awful, for instance, encephalitis, an infection of the brain.

I'd lost over half my hearing, a problem Dave and Pierce had been quick to point out. When they talked, I often heard something that only rhymed with what they'd said. At other times I could just make out the first few words in the sentence but not the rest. My brain, trying to compensate, filled in the end in a way that often didn't relate to what they actually said.

"We need to go shoot," Dave said to Pierce one night, to which I chimed in, "You need to go shopping?"

"Where on earth did you get that," Pierce said, looking perturbed.

Not surprisingly, more and more, my son and husband left me

out of their conversations and out of the loop. I guess it was easier for them that way. That hurt and left me feeling isolated in my own family. In my worst moments, I felt as if they thought I no longer mattered or that I had nothing of much value to say.

And what about the hearing loss's effect on your ability to work? Dave asked.

That was an issue I hadn't considered. Going back to my nursing job meant the world to me. There was no doubt I had to have the tympanoplasty.

On March twenty-third, Dave had a deadline to meet at work, so Sandi picked me up at seven in the morning to drive me to Regional Med. From Dave's journal, I knew this would be my fourth surgery at that hospital, but the first one I would remember having there. Despite being a veteran surgical patient, the morning of the tympanoplasty, I was a bundle of nerves.

When we reached the surgery center, Sandi gave me a surprise. "You remember my friend, the wonderful nurse anesthetist who used to work with me?"

I nodded. "She was one of the sweetest people I've ever met."

"Well, guess where she works now? I called her yesterday and she's going to be the one to put you to sleep."

"Oh, Sandi, thank you. Now I can relax."

A nurse wheeled me into the surgery suite where Sandi's friend greeted me, smiling. The kindness in her expression made me think of Melanie from Gone with the Wind. She leaned over me and kissed my forehead. "I love you and I'm going to take really good care of you. I've asked God to help me," she said.

I melted in her gaze and floated off to the place beyond thought.

I awoke. Someone was pushing me out of Recovery. They parked me in a small cubicle whose walls spun violently around me. Through it all, I had never witnessed vertigo like this. A nurse bustled in and stopped at my side just long enough to pull out the IV in my arm and apply a dressing.

"Why am I so dizzy?" I asked.

"It's probably just the medication they gave you during surgery."

"I've had fifteen surgeries, and I've never felt like this." My heart raced.

The room lurched violently whenever I turned my head. So severe was its spinning that when I tried to sit up, I fell abruptly on my side. Was this the chronic dizziness the consent form had warned me about?

Sweat poured down my face and my chest tightened.

"Do you need any help getting dressed to go home?" the nurse asked, coming back in.

"I can't sit up," I cried, panicking.

She hoisted me into a sitting position and pulled my shirt over my head, lifting my arm and stuffing it into a sleeve.

"Please," I said. "There's something wrong. Get Dr. Baker."

The petite surgeon soon appeared, peaking around the curtain that closed the front of my stall. She still wore her surgical cap and a harried look. "Don't worry. The vertigo is from all the suturing I did on your left ear drum and the aggressive cleaning to the right one. That will help the smaller hole heal. The dizziness should go away in about six hours."

Then as quickly as she'd appeared, she turned and left. The nurse hoisted me into a wheelchair and pushed me out the door of the hospital into the sunlight. There Sandi sat in her car waiting. She got out and grabbed me under my arms, lifting me into the passenger seat.

Once on the road, she attempted to comfort me with some humor. "Well, I brought you here happy this morning, and now you look miserable."

When I gave her a wretched look, she turned to a different approach.

"All right, you need to embrace the dizziness."

The idea sounded so ludicrous I started laughing, but caught myself. *Embrace the dizziness?* Maybe I'd give it a try. I gave up fighting the vertigo and gave in to it. I turned it over to God.

With that, my body sank deeply into the passenger seat. Immediately, I felt better. I was still dizzy, but the fear had gone.

We reached the house and Sandi helped me get into bed. Just as Dr. Baker had said, in a couple of hours, the vertigo began to subside. A wonderful sense of relief and euphoria took its place. "Thank you, Jesus," I said. "Thank you from the bottom of my heart."

An hour later, Dave walked in from work to find me happy and relaxed on the bed with Delta and Daisy purring softly beside me.

"Well, hey," he said, beaming and looking relieved. "You look like you're feeling pretty good. Well, except for that enormous dressing over your ear. How did it go?"

"Dr. Baker said it went well. I feel great except for not being able to hear with all the stuff she packed in my ears. She won't take it out for a month. That's a long time to have to wait. It's another lesson in patience." I laughed. Dave and I both knew patience had never been my strong suit.

Dave went upstairs to feed the pets and returned an hour later with his dinner and some soup for me. We spent a peaceful evening lying in bed talking. I thanked Jesus again that the dreaded event was over and He'd brought me through. Now I could prepare to return to work.

I wrote to my friends and family:

> I can hardly believe that the time has finally come to go back to work!

My friend, Lynda, in England wrote back:

> Really great to *hear* from you—no pun intended! I'm a bit of a fatalist and believe everything is for a reason, so it'll be interesting to see where this experience takes you. Enjoy the last few weeks of being a lady of leisure!

ROADBLOCKS

Even before the ear surgery, I'd been taking the necessary steps to return to work. My work disability income was running out, and I was walking fairly well, albeit slowly with a pronounced limp and a cane. It felt like time to test the waters.

A couple of days after the tympanoplasty, I decided to pay a visit to my boss. I needed to finalize plans and give her the return-to-work notes from my doctors.

I drove up to her office building and walked in. I found her sitting at her desk, her back to the door. I knocked. She turned, looking startled.

"Oh hey," she said, her smile not reaching her eyes. It was not the warm greeting I'd expected.

Sensing something was amiss, I came right to the point. "I'm still planning to go back to work at the end of April, three weeks from now. I came by to bring you my doctors' medical releases." I handed them to her.

She took them, chewing on her lip and staring down at the papers she held in her hands. Then she glanced up. "Now, don't rush back too soon." Her words dripped with honey and came at me in a burst. She looked back down at the floor.

What on earth is she talking about? I've been out for six months.

I remembered her call in the hospital. "Don't worry about your job. It's secure."

In February I'd emailed her my plans, but now I sensed an obstacle forming in the path back to work.

"I can walk and both doctors have released me to return in April," I said, trying to remain calm.

Then she hit me with a bomb. "I don't want to lose Barbie," she snapped in an urgent tone. "I don't want to lose Barbie." She fidgeted in her chair like she'd been drinking too much coffee.

Barbie? Then it struck me. She meant one of the nurses who'd been filling in for me.

Apparently realizing what she'd said, she softened her tone and composed her face. "I know everyone at Great Foods will be really glad to have you back."

It was too late. The cat was out of the bag. Evidently, my boss wanted Barbie to take my place. All of a sudden, I felt in the way, like she had big plans that didn't include me. My stomach did a flip.

"Just give me your doctor's note, and we'll go from there," she said a little too dismissively.

"I'll definitely be back to work on April twenty-sixth," I said, not backing down. I'd set up those clinics and poured my heart and sweat into them. I wasn't going to let her give my job to someone else that easily.

The corners of her smile wilted.

Truthfully, I'd never quite known what to make of my boss. I'd worked under her but off site for three and a half years, but most of the time was lucky to see her once a month at our department meetings. In her absence, I'd focused all my attention on the workers and supervisors at the plants, considering them the ones I needed to please.

Leaving her office, I pondered her words. Had I read too much into them? I played them back as I drove home. I was used to my intuitions being on target. This time I hoped they were wrong. At least the workers at Great Foods Manufacturing wanted me back. I wasn't so sure about my boss. My body needed more time to heal, but if I wanted to keep my job, something told me I better get back to work.

The next day even worse news threatened to overturn my plans to return to my job. Purely by accident, as I sorted through several hundred work-related emails that had piled up during my absence, I discovered my nursing license had expired. Fresh out of the hospital and struggling to walk, renewing it had completely skipped my mind. All nursing licenses in our state had the same expiration date. They had to be renewed every other year by December thirty-first. In the past, my department had sent reminders. *Funny how this time no one thought to mention something so important.*

In a panic, I called our nursing board, hopeful they'd understand. They didn't.

"No exceptions can be made," the man on the phone barked, after reading me a long checklist I'd have to complete. He obviously didn't care one bit about the accident or my looming deadline to return to work.

"Since your license expired two months ago, sending a check won't be enough. You'll have to complete a notarized application, get fingerprinted, submit passport photos, and provide a sealed copy of your nursing work history before we can consider reinstating you. It could take us up to four weeks to process," he said.

I'd been an RN for thirty years, had never allowed my license to expire, never been sued, or in poor standing, but now, I couldn't set one foot back on my job without their piece of paper. "To do so would invite prosecution," the man on the phone had admonished.

Didn't God want me to go back to nursing? How was that possible? For months, I'd pictured myself walking into the factories, using that image to work even harder. Now, I could only wonder.

Back pain presented another big problem. It hadn't been much of an issue at home, where I could sit or lie down at will. But without those options, how would I manage at work? By late March I decided to do a trial run helping out at the health food store. I'd always loved sharing nutritional tips with the clients there.

On my first day covering the store, after just four hours, my back seared with pain. It hurt so badly I couldn't sit or stand without support, so I laid my head on my arms on top of the desk. When customers strolled in, I had to lean back in the chair, to consult with them on their health problems. Gritting my teeth, I pressed on until six that evening when I drove myself home, exhausted from the pain.

I shuffled into the house and dropped onto the loveseat, my mind churning. What had ever led me to believe I could manage the ten hour shifts at my nursing job? I'd emailed my coworkers that I'd be back soon. But how?

At home, I could lie down whenever my back gave out. When I returned to work I would have to rest in my nursing clinic on the patient's cot during the afternoon break, but how would it look?

Between the pain in my back and legs, my boss's lukewarm reception, and the trouble with my nursing license, I felt defeated. Had the universe conspired against me?

Later that afternoon, Dave found me curled up on the sofa, feeling sorry for myself, "You know you aren't looking at what's going well, only at what's wrong," he said, smiling, after hearing the latest. "Six months ago we didn't know if you would live, let alone walk. Now, look at you." He wandered into his workshop to locate the back brace the back doctor had ordered in Rehab.

"You don't have to wear it. It's just for your comfort," the doctor had said.

The first time they had strapped it on me in the hospital as I sat in the wheel chair, I felt like I couldn't breathe. I never put it on again. When I started therapy to walk, the physical therapists had all agreed that wearing it might keep my back muscles from getting stronger. But today, after only four hours of working, I couldn't sit up. I had to do something.

Dave helped me position the big grey contraption with its metal plates and rods over my torso and cinch it up tight. I considered myself in the mirror and to my dismay I looked like a cyborg in a sci-fi film.

"This will scare the workers or, worse, make my boss think I'm too messed up to work," I whined.

"Well, I was going to make a joke, but seeing that you're about to cry, I won't. Why don't you decorate it with some sequins or silk flowers from the hobby store," he suggested. "Now that would make a statement." Dave knew I loved decorating anything with flowers.

"Or you could just tell everyone at work you're getting suited up for a game of hockey," Pierce added, appearing in the front door from his job at the Police Department. "Those factory guys all love sports."

I looked in the mirror and had to admit silk flowers and a rhinestone or two wouldn't hurt. I noted the brace helped me stand taller as it relieved a little of the pain in my back. But how would it look to my boss? I was supposed to be their wellness nurse. What if she decided I didn't fit the bill?

Despite Dave's and Pierce's support, I couldn't sleep much that night or the next. The back brace only helped with the pain if I cinched it so tightly I could barely breathe. My face broke out in rough red patches from the stress, and in the mornings I had a hard time making myself get out of bed. I couldn't overcome the inertia to exercise or call a friend. No one, I reasoned, wanted to hear from someone so depressed. I felt myself slipping into the doldrums, despite my best efforts to be positive. The steady flow of well-wishers had slowed and without their support, I felt alone and cheerless. Even Jesus seemed far away.

Then it happened. I awoke in my bed in early April, just three weeks before I was scheduled to head back to work. I was still in that drowsy state, fresh from a dream, when it hit me. I realized, as I had so many times before, I had to have hope and a sense of purpose to feel happy again. Hope, though my body was broken and painful. Hope, though fear had lately filled my dreams and threatened my sleep. Hope, though the bills piled high and going back to work looked harder than I'd imagined.

Hope had been that very thing that God had worked through others to bring me in the hospital. He'd brought it as I'd cried out for help from my gurney, then later when I'd prayed in my wheelchair. Now, as I lay in the dark, more answers started to come. Not in a vision from the sky, but in a voice deep within that spoke plainly and thoughtfully and sounded oddly like my own. *Get up and write.*

Though my eyelids were heavy, I stood up and limped over to sit on the loveseat. I grabbed pen and pad and prepared to write. My mind drifted to a book I'd read decades before, Victor Frankel's <u>Man's Search for Meaning</u>. In it, he'd written that while none of us could avoid painful situations, we could always choose how we responded to them. The answer was to find meaning in our ordeals and then move forward with renewed purpose. His message was all the more potent, given that he'd lost his entire family in a Nazi concentration camp like the one where he himself had been kept prisoner.

I started to write.

> God is right here with me in the darkness. He didn't hand me hope and purpose in the hospital, only to snatch them away. They're still with me. Why? Maybe because I choose to have them and because I choose to stay connected with the One who brings them. And God, knowing how much I still need them and hearing my heart's desire, continues to help them grow.

It had been like that at County Hospital, when God first inspired me to record on small scraps of paper everything I'd witnessed and prodded me to extend love to the most unlikely people. Hadn't He done so for the same reason? To give me the hope and sense of purpose I needed to heal?

After coming home, my life had revolved around others taking care of me. It had been more and more about my needs, my feelings, my rehab, and my story. I'd progressed from bed to wheelchair, to cane and fallen into the habit of letting friends and family nurture me and out of the habit of nurturing them. I'd become down right self-centered and the more self-absorbed I became, the less happy.

Now I prayed. "God, what can I do to let go of fear and find purpose again?"

As I asked that question, I found myself on familiar ground. The answer was the same as it had always been before.

Love

How had I forgotten something so simple?

I had to make more of an effort to love others again. If I focused on that, I'd be okay.

Despite my resolve to do so, I still faced some doubts about being able to manage my job.

I wrote to my friend Lynda in England:

> I've worried more about getting back into the mental groove at work than about my physical limitations. The young nurse who's been filling in for me has apparently been dazzling everyone with her energy and charm. That leaves me to wonder if the people at the plants might prefer the younger, more active model to this older one. Guess my insecurities are showing, though I know you won't judge me for them. Thanks for being there to listen and for all your support.

She wrote back:

> What you must constantly remember, though, is that you are literally a walking miracle, which makes you very special—far more than a younger more energetic replacement! I mean, should anyone question the situation, you must remind them there isn't an occupational nurse in the whole state who has a better understanding of what it means to get back to work or who is a better example of how her methods work!!! In other words you are a daily example of your own professionalism and ability to practice what you preach with amazing results. You've already won the gold medal so have nothing to prove to anyone. And I'll keep playing the Euro lottery, just in case. Maybe we can all then give up work.

RETURNING TO GREAT FOODS MANUFACTURING

The next week I worked hard to get my nursing license reinstated. First I drove the hour to human resources to pick up documentation on my work history. Then I detoured to a neighboring town where a nice woman fingerprinted me and took my picture for a passport photo. I placed the thick wad of papers and photos into a mailer and handed it to a clerk at the post office.

"Overnight it, please," I said, knowing I'd done all I could.

The question remained. Would I get my license in time? I was supposed to go back to my job in less than three weeks?

That night I prayed. "God, I don't understand why all of this has been so hard. Don't you want me to go back to nursing?"

The week before I was slated to return to work, Dave drove me to Dr. Baker's. My ears were still full of the packing material she'd inserted after the tympanoplasty. She greeted me with open arms and a warm smile. "Thank you so much for the lovely note," she exclaimed. It struck me that she meant the thank you card I'd sent.

"You did an amazing job repairing my face right after the tree fell. Now I'm hoping you've brought me another miracle with my ear-drums," I said, looking her in the eye.

"We'll soon see," she said as she inserted a little tube into my left ear and got down to the business of suctioning. I heard a high pitched hissing sound as the room began to spin. I grabbed hold of the arm rests. *Why does everything make me dizzy?*

Five minutes later she stopped. "That's it," she announced.

I let out a sigh of relief as the room slowly came to a stop.

"You're free to go in a minute when you feel steady," she said.

"Do you need to hold onto me?" Dave asked, helping me up and handing me my cane.

"No, I'm okay," I replied, surprised and delighted at how steady I felt on my feet. "The whooshing sound is gone too."

"That's great," he said, giving me a hopeful look.

"You know what else?" I laughed. "I can really hear you."

"Wonderful." Dave stared at me and looked happier than he had in weeks.

That evening I didn't have to ask Pierce and Dave to repeat what they said. I laughed and joked as I joined in the conversation. Getting a significant chunk of my hearing back felt like another miracle. I hadn't realized how much I'd retreated into my own world from not being able to hear. Now my thoughts were more in focus, my emotions lighter. I felt more in control.

There was still the problem of finding a more practical way to deal with my back pain. I drove to see Dr. Court, the neurosurgeon who'd inserted foot long stainless steel rods to stabilize it.

"I've got a problem," I said. "I'm supposed to go back to my nursing job next week, but when I did a trial run, my back hurt too much. Is there anything that might help?"

His eyes widened with surprise. "You're going back to work after only seven months? That's amazing. But I'm not surprised you have pain. I had to cut through your thoracic muscles when I inserted the rods. There was no other option." He paused, letting his words sink in. "I could order steroid injections for the pain, but there's a medication I want to try first. I've seen it work for other patients with injuries like yours."

I'd heard of the drug he mentioned. When I got home, I googled it and read the user reviews. Apparently it worked well for a handful of lucky patients, while others suffered with nausea, constipation, and dizziness or worse. But what choice did I have? Armed with the new prescription, I made a plan to try it. After that I would know.

Later that week, back at the health food store, I took my first pill with lunch. Twenty minutes later, it kicked in. Shades of hydromorphone.

By dinner and back at home, I could still sit without hurting. Dave handed me the mail. On top was a small envelope from the Board of Nursing. Holding my breath, I ripped it open. There inside, I saw my license. Now I had everything I needed to start my job.

The next Monday, with emotions running high and my stomach doing flip-flops, I pulled into my parking space at Great Foods Manufacturing. Taking a deep breath, I reminded myself to focus on how much I loved the workers. I grabbed my cane from the passenger side of the car and limped up the walkway. Leah, my friend at the plant, met me in the entranceway, a mop in her hand. She gasped and dropped it on the floor before rushing toward me. Her outstretched hands waved in the air. "Lara!" she yelled.

"Leah!" My eyes filled with tears.

We grabbed each other into a bear hug, wiggling and squealing like two grade school girls for several minutes before Leah stopped to look at me.

"Here, let me help you carry all that stuff. You don't need to be lugging heavy things by yourself." She snatched my back-pack and strode ahead of me through the door of the nurse's office.

I followed, hobbling. The clinic looked just as I left it seven months before. The colorful paintings and posters greeted me from the white walls. I strolled over to the desk and sat in my chair, smiling. It felt good to be back.

Word soon got around of my arrival. Workers, their blue pants and shirts dusty, flooded into my office. It was standing room only. Most expressed the same sentiment as the first one to come in. "I had to see you with my own eyes. I needed to know for sure you were okay. I heard you looked pretty bad in the hospital," he said.

"That's what they tell me."

"I can't believe you made it this far," another said. "You've really inspired me. If you can make it back to work, I can get through my day." He laughed and threw his arms around me and held on as if he didn't want to let go.

"Sorry to get dirt on your scrubs," he apologized. "I hope I'm not hurting your back?"

"No, not a bit," I squeezed him tightly.

While I knew the factory workers were glad to see me, the great outpouring of emotion felt like something more.

"I prayed for you and so did everyone at my church. God must have heard us," one worker said. That message was often repeated. "I think God gave us a miracle," many said.

Basking in so much love felt like a tonic to my spirit. I could feel the heaviness of the previous weeks melting away. *I'm back where I belong.*

Around nine, Barbie walked in smiling. "Oh hey," she greeted me in a friendly voice. "How're you feeling?"

"I'm good." I took another deep breath and reminded myself it wasn't Barbie's fault that my boss seemed to prefer her. I promised to look at her through more loving eyes.

"I'm here to help you and fill you in on what you've missed," she said.

"Sounds good," I said, feeling more positive. *But how will we work together in such a small space?*

When the first worker walked in for help with a medical problem, I turned to Barbie, "I've got this."

I beckoned the man to take a seat next to my desk. Barbie continued to hover nearby, chatting and joking with him as I struggled to concentrate on gathering information.

"I've got this," I repeated, growing annoyed.

When the man left, I swung my chair around to face her. "I know you're here to help me, but I think it would be a lot less confusing for all of us if you'd let me counsel the workers by myself. After, you can tell me what I've missed."

"Okay." Her face registered surprise.

Despite our rocky start, in the next two weeks, I grew to appreciate Barbie. Our different strengths balanced each other well. I would do much worse than Barbie if I needed to share the position with another nurse on a permanent basis. We could probably learn a lot from each other. In any case, we'd be working at different plants. I smiled at the thought.

By the end of the second week, it was time to solo. I took over the hearing testing program in the newer clinic and covered the two ten-hour shifts there on Tuesday and Thursday. Barbie filled in at the older factory across town on Monday and Wednesday. By the weekend, my shin bone burned and throbbed, but with icing and staying off my feet, it felt better by Monday.

Despite the intermittent pain in my legs, before long, I relaxed into my old sense of rhythm at work. Most days, Gerry, who worked down the hall, stopped by to see me. "It's time for you to start thinking about doing a testimony," he said, smiling as I pumped up the blood pressure cuff.

Delivering a testimony meant speaking about what had happened in front of a group, a phobia that had historically rivaled my fear of heights. But would sharing my story help others? If it would, I'd do it.

"I'll put it on my to-do list." I grinned.

Jenny, who'd visited at County Hospital, dropped in to see me too. "Do you have something to cover a paper cut?" I suspected she also came to keep tabs on me. "Keep on trusting in God," she said, gathering her things. "He'll continue to see you through all this and whatever comes next."

"You mean there's going to be more?" I laughed and hugged my friend before she headed back upstairs to her office.

Another regular wandered through the door. I hadn't said a word to him about testimonies when he launched into instructions on how "to be a witness." "People will look to you now as having a special connection with God," he said.

"I never thought of it like that. As I see it, we all carry God's Spirit within us. We just don't always recognize it."

"Your testimony will encourage anyone who's having a hard time or needs faith."

I'd done quite a bit of lecturing over the years at work. But despite doing so, I'd often suffered stage fright before I got started. Most of the time, it diminished once I began talking. Doing a testimony should be no different.

By my third week back, Doris asked me to give a talk on safety to the employees. In the first group meeting, the Plant Supervisor, Robert, called my name. A hush fell over the crowd. Many turned to watch me shuffle to the front of the big room. I turned to face the packed audience, sitting carefully on the stool Robert had left out for me. What looked like a hundred curious faces looked back. Most were smiling.

"Today they've asked me to talk about safety, but before I do, there are a couple of things I want to say. First, I want you to know how incredibly happy I am to be back. It's been wonderful getting to talk with so many of you already. And I know, working together, we're all going to get a lot stronger and healthier this year. Some of us are even going to put on a little weight." Everyone laughed as I pulled on the oversized waist-band on my baggy pants. "More than anything I want to thank you for your generous gifts and especially your prayers. I can assure you I felt the power and love of each and every one as I lay in that hospital bed. They bolstered my sagging spirit and filled me with a sense of peace, love and hope that defied understanding. One thing for sure, I would never have made it without them."

When I finished talking, everyone got to their feet. They clapped and cheered. It was a moment I would never forget and one that would be repeated in the next four employee meetings.

The next week friends and workers continued to flood into the clinics to see me. Just as before, they talked about their medical problems, but now some also shared more personal matters. The accident had apparently broken down whatever barriers existed between us before.

There were other causes for celebration. Business was better than ever. The owners had broken ground on another plant, slated to open in the fall. I would soon be ordering more supplies and furniture for a new clinic. So many employees were pouring in to the nursing office, my days flew by and I felt useful again.

Even outside of work I found opportunities to be of service.

Maggie, my sister-in-law who'd encouraged me in the hospital, honored me by asking for help with a personal problem. Sandi did too. At the factories, workers asked me to pray for members of their family. I felt happy to be on the giving end of my friendships again.

After a month back at work, I wrote my friends and family:

> ...I've had tremendous support from my coworkers. Still it's been hard to get used to this slower, more painful body that doesn't allow me to walk much around the plants.

> Pierce is still pretty happy at the Police Department though I doubt he understood how challenging the job would be. He says, 'You have to be thick-skinned to work there and that's talking about my coworkers.'

> Dave on the other hand never seems to get enough rest. After work he still has all of the shopping and more of the cooking and cleaning than he should have to manage. I try to help him when I can and keep him happy by taking him to our new favorite restaurant for sushi on Saturdays.

PUSHING THROUGH THE PAIN

I'd worked only a month and just settled into my two day a week routine when my boss called. "Barbie's taken a full-time position in a hospital. I have to hire another two day a week nurse. There's no one else to fill in."

A week later, she called again. "I found a nurse, but she can only work one day a week. So I need you to start covering three ten-hour days a week, starting Monday."

"This Monday? So soon?!" I exclaimed. "Could I at least try working a Monday, Wednesday, and Friday schedule? I think I'd have a better chance of managing the extra hours if I can rest my legs in between shifts."

"No, that won't work. The other nurse can only come on Mondays, so you'll have to do two shifts back to back."

I remembered the Thursday and Friday I'd spent at the health food store before coming back to work. My legs and back had taken three days to recover. What if I reinjured them?

Perhaps sensing my reluctance, my boss spoke again. "I really need you to at least try the new schedule. Are you willing to do that?" Her voice was brusque.

"I'll give it a try." What else could I say?

"Okay good. It's settled then. There's a call coming in. Gotta go." The phone clicked in my ear.

So that was that. She'd made up her mind. What if my legs couldn't take it? But I already knew.

"Just tell her to take her job and stick it," Dave said, when I arrived home. "It's not worth you hurting your legs. You've come too far."

I didn't listen to Dave or to my own misgivings. Nor did I pray for guidance. I thought only of my job and how much we needed the income and medical insurance it provided.

The first week on the new schedule wasn't as busy as usual. By the weekend, though, my legs burned and throbbed and had not recovered by the time the new week rolled around. This one looked like it would be a lot harder.

On Monday I trained the new nurse. She looked to be around Pierce's age, and I liked her immediately. That same week, my supervisor at Great Foods Manufacturing scheduled me to do four presentations encouraging the workers to participate in the wellness program. I struggled with a bit more stage fright than usual as I anticipated my lecture. My body felt tired and my legs ached all the time. Why, after everything I'd been through, did I still care what others thought? I'd survived a tree falling and fifteen surgeries. God obviously loved me and wanted me to succeed. Wasn't that enough?

I closed my eyes and whispered, "Jesus, please give me strength and guide my words."

Jenny walked by my door and seeing my pensive expression came in.

"You don't need to be perfect, you know. We all know you're still recovering."

"You're right, but I can't help thinking that my boss wishes I'd just go ahead and work the forty hours each week and cover both plants. If I can only manage the thirty she just gave me, and I'm not perfect in every other area, it's not much of a stretch to think she might let me go." I sighed.

"She'd be crazy to. Even in your present condition you do a far better job than any of the nurses who fill in for you. They've admitted as much."

Once I got started speaking, the presentations went well, but afterward I felt spent. Two months back at work, and despite enjoying spending time with the workers, I was worried. Lately I'd had to double the amount of pain medication I was taking just to get through the shift. Most days I put on a brave face, not wanting anyone to think I couldn't physically manage my job. I pushed through the pain to go out on the plant floors and climb the stairs.

One afternoon I was drawing blood when Jenny laid a CD on my desk. Later, in my car, I played it. The woman on the CD was saying, "People are not looking for you to have it together. They are looking at what happens to you, when you don't." I pulled out the CD and looked at the label. The speaker was a Christian author and lecturer named Beth Moore.

Her message hit home. Lately, I'd often felt worn out from trying to appear stronger than I felt. That was especially true as the pain got worse. I would need to give her words some thought.

By the end of June and two months back at work, they asked me to organize a blood drive at Great Foods Manufacturing. I was thankful to be caught up enough to help with the new project. Blood supplies in the summer were always low as the medical need rose. Dave's voice reverberated in my head. "The first few days after the accident at Regional Med they had to give you eight units to save your life."

I sent out an email appealing to all the workers.

> I can't give blood for a year after receiving eight units last fall, but I'm asking those of you who can to please give for me.

Many answered the call. Some showed up quaking in their boots to give on my behalf.

"I'll go with you and hold your hand if you think it will help," I said. I walked around both plants trying to encourage others. The blood drive turned out to be a huge success. I was feeling pleased when something happened.

I'd just made my last trip to the break room to encourage new donors, when pain in my shin buckled my leg and landed me on the floor. "Get my crutches," I yelled to a friend having coffee.

She ran to the clinic and returned a moment later, holding them out to me.

All weekend, I stayed off my leg.

The following Tuesday, back at work, the pain felt worse than ever. I crutched around the clinic and began to worry in earnest that something might really be wrong. I called Dr. Norton's office.

"Come tomorrow," the receptionist said without hesitation.

By early Wednesday morning, it hurt too much for me to push the clutch pedal, so Pierce drove me to Dr. Norton's. The office looked dark when we arrived. Kenneth unlocked the door and gave me a hug. Then he shook hands with Pierce.

Twenty minutes later, Dr. Norton looked uncharacteristically subdued when he walked into the exam room. I held my breath and waited for him to speak. "You already know how severe the fractures to your tibia were." His words sounded like an apology. He pointed to the x-rays on the computer screen, indicating something next to the metal strut that supported the shin bone. "You have two broken screws. There may be more." He moved his index finger higher on the screen. "Here the tibia has come apart."

He stopped talking. I studied the gap in the shin bone on the screen and the pieces of broken screw. All I heard was the three of us breathing. I'd known something was wrong. Now I knew what.

"Do you think working too many hours made it come apart?"

"It's hard to say."

"Will I need a bone graft?"

He looked stunned, then relieved at my question. "Your choices are either to continue on crutches and hope for the tibia to come together over time or to have a bone graft surgery now. I'll need to rework the hardware while I'm in there."

I sat quietly for a moment more before the nurse in me kicked into gear, and I started asking more questions.

"What are the chances the bone graft will take?"

"Good, given your excellent health."

"How long before I can drive? What about standing? Going back to work?"

"You can drive in two months, and you'll be on crutches for at least three. You can return to work on crutches when you feel strong enough, but no weight bearing till I tell you."

"How soon can you do it?"

"In two weeks."

I took only a moment to think it over. There was no point feeling sorry for myself or worrying about my job. It had to be done. I would do whatever it took to get better. For the first time, it felt like I called the shots, I was in charge.

"Let's get it over with," I said.

As Pierce drove us home, I mulled over what Dr. Norton said. In some respects it would be like healing all over again. With months of not weight bearing on my right leg, how would I get back and forth to work? My mind churned.

Don't think about that now. You'll figure it out after the surgery.

"Darn if Dr. Bolling wasn't right when he said I might need a bone graft," I exclaimed to Pierce, sitting in the driver's seat.

The next two weeks I went to work on crutches and tested the twenty-five workers with hearing tests scheduled for July. Then, so I wouldn't get behind, I tested another twenty who normally had theirs in August. I looked at the calendar. "I'll be back by the third week in August," I vowed.

"How can this be happening to you again?" a sweet young man who came to the clinic asked me. He was the first of many to ask that question.

"I guess I need some fine tuning on my leg," I said, knowing that wasn't exactly true.

It all happened so fast; I couldn't process my feelings. I worked July twenty-seventh, the last day before my surgery. As I crutched out to my car and began driving through the countryside, the pressure in my chest made it hard to breathe. I picked up my cell and called Janelle. Tears streamed down my cheeks and splashed into my lap.

"How will Dave and Pierce cope with driving me back and forth to work? They're still worn out from the last go round," I sobbed. "And what if my boss gets tired of me being out and takes my job?"

I don't remember much of what Janelle said. Mostly she let me cry.

After our conversation, I felt calmer and ready as I could be to face what came next. The bone graft would make my leg stronger. I could go back to work better than before. Still I remembered how much pain a reconstruction surgery involved, and I dreaded it. Even more than the surgery, though, I thought about the next four months on crutches. Doing my job on them would be tough.

That night, Dave announced a surprise. "For your birthday, I'm going to build you a big aquarium across from the bed so you can have something cool to focus on while you're recuperating."

I looked over at him stunned by his thoughtfulness. What had I ever done to deserve such a wonderful husband?

BACK TO COUNTY HOSPITAL

My transporter pushed my stretcher into a room on the Orthopedic floor. Even in my semi-conscious state, I could tell something was wrong. A faint voice kept calling my name, but no matter how hard I strained to answer, I couldn't. Later, Dave filled me in. What was supposed to have been a four-hour surgery had turned out to be eight. Dr. Norton had opened my leg to find a much bigger mess than he'd imagined. Ultimately he pulled out every bit of the old hardware and replaced it with heavier steel struts and screws.

Maybe it was the effect of too much anesthesia, or maybe it related to the rumored pharmaceutical error that had happened in Recovery. But whatever the reason, my floor nurse couldn't arouse me. When I finally opened my eyes, Pierce and Dave were leaning over me.

"Something for pain," I mumbled, but the nurse's face told me she didn't like the reading she was seeing on the blood pressure dial.

"Something for pain," I grumbled again, a little louder.

"I'm sorry, but your blood pressure is still too low," she said, looking worried. My leg had now swelled to twice its normal size, and five long rows of stitches strained to hold the incisions closed. I could also feel a string of sutures on my hip when I reached back to touch the sore area. Dr. Norton had taken some bone tissue from there and implanted it onto my tibia to repair and strengthen the break.

"Please. I've got to have something for pain. I'm hurting so much there can't possibly be any danger of my blood pressure bottoming out," I pleaded, trying to sound more like a nurse.

"I'm really sorry, but it looks like they may have over-medicated you in recovery, and I can't give you anything that might sedate you further."

Sedate me further? I felt so agitated I wanted to scream.

Seeing I couldn't change her mind, I lay perfectly still to avoid jarring the incisions. For the first time since the tree fell, Dave stayed with me on a cot next to my bed. Due to the severe, unrelenting pain, neither one of us got any sleep.

The next morning Dr. Norton came in at seven to check on me.

"What's wrong?" He looked concerned at the sight of my tear-stained face.

"I've had sixteen surgeries and this is by far the worst pain yet. It's not their fault, but the nurses have been afraid to give me any hydromorphone. Can't you order some?"

"Why didn't they give you any? And what was this I heard about something happening in recovery?" He looked puzzled.

"I don't really know, but I'm wide awake now."

Dr. Norton called the nurse. In less than a minute, she rolled in a PCA pump. Soon, I was floating along on a soft cloud of relief. The pump allowed me to help myself to the hydromorphone whenever my leg hurt.

In the aftermath of my lengthy surgery, I also felt nauseated. My nurse gave me the same medication that had made me hallucinate before. I waited to see if anything would happen.

By the fourth dose, I awoke to see demons and ghouls. The big clock that hung across from me was oozing down the wall as if I'd stepped into a Salvador Dali painting.

"Dave, it's happening again," I murmured and pushed the button to call the nurse, who promptly discontinued it. In a few hours, the bizarre images disappeared.

Two days after my surgery, someone awakened me in the middle of the night. In the faded light of my room, I could just make out the hazy form of a man in blue hospital scrubs. As he leaned over to look at my leg, I caught sight of his face. It was Dr. Smith the same doctor who'd shown up months before in the Trauma Unit to stare at my dying ankle graft.

"I remember you," I said, wondering why he'd come.

"I have to take out your drains," he muttered as if he were barely awake.

I looked down at my lower leg and saw that he was referring to the latex tubes that were sticking out from the five long incision lines.

For a brief moment, he glanced up, his eyes wild. He had that haunted look of someone who hadn't slept in days.

Is he okay?

Dr. Smith grabbed hold of the first drain, and yanked.

"Wait!" I yelled, shocked and wincing in pain.

He went right on jerking the others out before I could reach down to stop him. I shouted even louder as blood began oozing from the sutures and running down my leg.

Dave looked on bleary-eyed and helpless from his cot.

"Turn over," Dr. Smith said, dully. "I need to get the one out of your hip."

"No," I said, mustering all my strength. "I'll get the nurse to take it out." I'd been a patient too long to put up with Dr. Smith.

His eyes opened wide. Then, he left.

Shaking, I buzzed my nurse to bring in some dressings.

"Who did this?" she snapped, looking at the bloody mess in the bed, red flaming her cheeks.

I told her. "And please put a note on my chart. I don't ever want him to come near me again."

"I'll be glad to," she said, carefully easing out the last drain.

"Well at least I have a good nurse," I said, smiling gratefully.

After she left, I lay there, feeling proud of myself for standing up to Dr. Smith. What was it I remembered from nursing school? That a passive patient was not always a healthy patient. The implication had been clear. Patients who didn't speak up for themselves were often sorry or worse.

By Saturday, it was three days after the surgery and my birthday. Dr. Norton wrote the order for Dave to take me home. He'd dutifully camped out, lived on hospital food, and worried over me, but now he looked beat.

"Do they really send folks home in this condition?" I asked Dave, who might have wondered which one of us I was talking about.

"It's hard to believe," he said, sounding weary.

As help arrived to wheel me out to the car, I first noticed the transporter's big hoop earrings. It was Delores, the hospital worker who had wheeled me on the stretcher so many times during my stay in the trauma units. She smiled when she saw who it was and leaned over to hug me. With thousands of employees at County Hospital, it wasn't a coincidence that they'd sent Delores that morning.

"I've wanted to thank you for all the times you took a minute to encourage me when I was here last fall." I made a mental note to send her supervisor a letter, telling her how wonderful Delores had been.

"It's good to see you too," she exclaimed. "I've been wondering what happened to you."

At the car, we waved goodbye. Seeing Delores had made me think about another transporter, one who'd given me the gift of faith and hope. *If only I could find her.*

I settled into the front seat, closed my eyes, and slept.

When Dave and I finally made it home, I felt off-balance and foggy from all the meds. How would I get around? I couldn't put weight on my right leg and was much too weak to balance on my left even with crutches. Dave and I struggled to come up with a plan.

My weary husband began rearranging pieces of furniture. He retrieved the bedside commode and walker from where they were stored in his workshop and positioned them next to my bed. In an effort to clear the remaining clutter, he grabbed some of the folders I'd brought home from work and was halfway to the stairs, when I shouted after him.

"Hey, those are some educational articles I'm writing for the workers at Great Foods." Storing my work folders upstairs hadn't been part of our plan. "Why are you doing things without consulting me?" I cried.

He came back and settled on the bed. "Sorry, I'm just so incredibly tired and I've still got to drive over to Regional Med to pick up the injectable drug Dr. Norton ordered to prevent clots."

Right on cue, Pierce walked in the front door. "How did it go at the hospital?"

"Okay, but your dad's wiped out. Could you drive him over to Regional Med to pick up my medication?"

"Sure. That'll give us a chance to talk," Pierce said.

"Thanks," Dave said, nodding at our son.

After they left, I lay back limp on the bed. Tears poured from my eyes and streamed down my face. The grief and pain felt never ending. This had been by far the worst surgery yet. I blew my nose into a tissue and settled more deeply into the pillows.

Despite my tears, it felt good to be home. Marley the big white dog and Delta the cat joined me on the bed. My paintings and photos smiled down at me from the walls. "Happy Birthday, Lara," I whispered, sighing. The irony wasn't lost on me.

Later that afternoon, I began to take stock of my blessings. I thanked God for seeing me through what I dearly hoped would be my last surgery. Before I forgot, I asked Him to help me manage at home when Dave and Pierce headed back to work on Monday.

Then, I called the only friend who might be able to come.

A DIFFICULT RECOVERY

On Monday, Sandi strolled in at ten in the morning, carrying a picnic basket. She pulled out all the fixings for most any kind of sandwich I might like. I ate hungrily for the first time in five days. The anesthesia and narcotics had once again taken their toll on my appetite.

On Tuesday, Sandi cleaned the bathroom and swept the floor in my room. Like Jenny, she was a friend who put her spiritual convictions into action. I admired and loved her more than I could put into words. Each day before she left, we prayed, and after she'd gone, I thanked God for giving me such a beautiful friend.

The next few days my emotions ran the gamut. I struggled with the idea of going back to work while still dependent on crutches and so cloudy in my thoughts I felt worn down and off balance in every possible way.

In the day or two ahead of the surgery, it had occurred to me Jesus might want to use the recovery period to burn out any lasting traces of fear and insecurity from my being. He would use it to help me trust Him even more. Now, I held onto that thought.

For the next two weeks, though dizzy and weak, I made myself stand on my left foot and lean over the walker to hop my way to the bathroom. I refused to use the bed-side commode. Dave had cleaned up after me enough.

Confined to the bed and walker, I stayed in touch with the outside world the only way I could, by writing notes to friends about my progress. Writing them kept me busy. It also gave me some small measure of purpose and control. The many messages of encouragement I got back, along with my determination, helped fuel my positive attitude.

On July thirty-first, I wrote a note to family and friends:

It's my first day home after surgery. This has been really rough, as we all thought "reworking" the hardware didn't sound so bad. As it turned out, my wonderful trauma surgeon ended up doing an eight-hour surgery to replace the original hardware with much heavier duty struts and screws. He also did a bone graft. Thank God, Dave was with me for the four days in the hospital.

Jenny wrote back to encourage me:

I know that what you are experiencing is really hard. But God is really good!! He knows exactly what you are going through and knows exactly how to get you to where you need to be. Beth Moore says, 'There is so much purification in persecution' and that is so true. God loves you. Hang in there...

'For God has not given us a spirit of fear, but of power and of love and of a sound mind.' (2 Timothy 1:7 NKJV)'

'...His understanding is unsearchable. He gives power to the weak and to those who have no might He increases strength. Even the youths shall faint and be weary and the young men shall utterly fail. BUT those who wait on the Lord shall renew their strength; they shall mount up with wings like eagles, they shall run and not be weary, they shall walk and not faint.' (Isaiah 40:28-31 NKJV)'

I love those passages. They are really powerful! To think that the Creator of the whole universe and everything in existence is so big... and yet merciful enough that he cares for each one of us. Love, Jenny

After I read and reread the note from Jenny, particularly the part about mounting up with wings like eagles, I felt stronger. I reread the quote by Beth Moore. "There is so much purification in persecution." I wanted to believe she was right.

Five days later, I wrote friends again, this time with a different message:

I'm feeling a great deal better today! The pain and massive swelling of my leg have subsided and my spirit is a good bit brighter, too. I feel full of hope for a full recovery for the first time since waking up after the surgery last Wednesday. Through all this, God's love has been with me, bolstering my spirit especially through the support of loving friends like you. This has been no small feat and seems to be how He works to help all of us.

Let me know if there is something I can do for you. If sometime you might need a listening ear or a prayer spoken on your behalf, I am here. I would love nothing more than to feel useful during these long days of recovery.

Lynda wrote back from England:

You are a very, very remarkable woman and certainly an inspiration to us mere mortals.

I wrote back, laughing at her words:

Thank you for the lovely compliments. It might be tempting to let you go on thinking that I'm remarkable, but I know better. Most of the time I'm only doing what I have to do to make it through whatever's happening at the moment, so I can get back to making a living. So you see, I'm not so remarkable after all, though I love the accolades and thank you for seeing me in such a positive light.

I felt more blessed and comforted with each new message. The love and validation from their words warmed and strengthened me. I traded my walker for crutches and began to exercise again, first with hand weights in the mornings and then pedaling every night. I ate more and prayed to calm and motivate myself. I began to figure out how I would manage my job while maneuvering about on crutches. With a few adjustments, maybe I could make it work.

Sometimes on difficult days, I prayed asking God where He could possibly be going with my journey. On one of those days, I also called to talk with Jenny.

"It is perfectly fine to have days when we doubt," she said. "Lord knows I have them all the time. It's when we are the weakest that we tend to lean on God the most. That's a good thing, right?"

It was good to hear Jenny say at my weakest I would have to lean on God the most. Making a positive out of a negative was her gift.

In the week before my scheduled return to work, a friend at the factory sent me a quote in an email that spoke to me. Unfortunately, it didn't list the author.

Those who submit to the leading of God's Spirit—who face their afflictions confident that the Lord is producing something in them—emerge from their crucible with a strong faith. And they testify that the Spirit taught them more during their suffering than when all was well in their lives.

Powerful.

THE BOTTOM DROPS OUT

The week before I planned to return to work, I lay awake trying to figure out how I would manage my job while still dependent on crutches. How would I carry supplies? How would I balance on one foot to free my hands to clean a wound or wash chemicals out of a worker's eye?

The prospect of standing solely on my left foot troubled me. It had been all but torn off in the accident and my ankle still hurt.

At last, satisfied with my plan, I settled back on my bed for a rest. I would use crutches and my wheelchair when I returned. Adding the latter to the mix would leave my hands free and give my ankle a break. Anyway, I'd only need the wheelchair for treating complex injuries until my bone graft healed.

Despite my plan, I had a nagging feeling that I couldn't shake. What if my employer didn't go for their wellness nurse working from a wheelchair? What if they decided my thin frame and crutching gait spoiled their cool corporate image? I lay pondering the situation as I exercised my legs on the bed.

I picked up the cell and phoned Janelle. My call found her at home, cooking.

"What do you think? Am I crazy to worry?" I shifted uneasily on the bed, wanting her to reassure me.

"I think with your experience and motivation, they should be glad to have you back." She sounded confident.

"Thanks," I said, not quite convinced.

Later, I ran it past Jenny who agreed with Janelle. Still the feeling didn't go away.

Three weeks after my surgery, and only six days before I planned to return to my job, I faxed the medical note Dr. Norton had written, releasing me back to work on crutches. Later that afternoon, the phone rang. Caller ID told me it was my boss.

"We have some bad news," she started. That "we" included her boss, who was also on the line. I held my breath.

They skipped the pleasantries. "We need to terminate you," she announced, her voice dull.

My heart plummeted to the floor. *Terminate you.* The words echoed in my head, sounding lethal.

I really didn't have to hear the rest of her speech. Struggling to speak, the words caught in my throat. "The bone graft my surgeon just did has resolved the problem with my leg. I'm sure it will be stronger once it heals." I had to make them understand.

"Maybe so, but we need a nurse right away to cover the full forty hours in the nursing clinics," she replied. "You've already told us you can barely do thirty. And you can't lift seventy-five pounds or walk and stand for prolonged periods. The job description requires both." She delivered the message deadpan with no hint of remorse.

"That description relates to hospital nurses, not to those of us working in factories," I snapped. "I don't ever have to lift anything heavy there." *What's she up to, bringing up standards that don't apply?*

"Well how would you do CPR in an emergency?" her boss countered.

I tried to think, but she was putting me on the defensive.

Then the answer came. "I've trained over forty workers in both plants to serve on my medical team. If someone has a heart attack, as the nurse I'd be running the code and doing rescue breathing, not chest compressions."

She went right on as if she hadn't heard my words. "We don't see how you could handle emergencies in your condition," she repeated.

"Why are you doing this?" I asked. "You've been telling me for years what an excellent job I've been doing. I have it in writing. Now you want to take it away on a technicality?" My cheeks burned.

"We all know you've done good work. That's not in question.

Everyone at Great Foods Manufacturing agrees too. Terminating you has nothing to do with your performance, and it's nothing personal. It's what Human Resources recommended. It's just business," she added.

"Nothing personal? You're taking over half my family's income and all our medical benefits. What insurance company will cover me if I lose my job? And who will hire me? You're throwing my family to the wolves." I nearly spat my words.

"You might be able to get COBRA. Talk to Human Resources," she said, referring to the medical insurance employees could buy when they lost their jobs. My boss had stopped talking.

"COBRA's no help. Last time I checked it cost over a thousand dollars a month for a family," I countered, trying hard to control my voice. My insides were shaking.

"I really don't know much about it," she said, sounding like she wanted the conversation to end. "Just talk to HR."

"How do you expect us to pay our bills?" I cried and felt sick.

"Maybe you can get unemployment."

Silence.

They'd made up their minds. It was useless to say more. The ax they wielded had fallen.

I hung up on them and sat immobilized in my wheelchair, staring at the computer screen without seeing. Panic seized me. I was drowning in fear.

Jesus, what can I do?

I forced myself to think. I'd done a good job my four years at Great Foods Manufacturing. After my return to work, more workers than ever before had poured into the clinics seeking counsel on health matters and other more personal ones. Many seemed motivated to lose weight and lower their blood pressures, some for the first time. Their presence suggested they'd trusted me, that I was doing something right. Thinking about that made me feel good about myself. It wasn't Great Foods Manufacturing's fault that my employer had fired me and yanked me out of the clinics in their factories. It wasn't my fault either.

Several of my nursing colleagues had also offered high praise. One was particularly complimentary. "When you were in the hospital, I went through your work files, trying to figure out where to start filling in. I was really impressed with all the wellness articles and programs you'd written," she said. "How did you ever find the time?"

"I wrote most of them at home," I replied.

"Really? On your own time?" She raised her eyebrows. "And you posted your home phone on the clinic doors? Did workers call you after hours?"

"Sometimes. But usually only when they'd been injured."

"And did your boss pay you for that time?" she asked, looking doubtful.

"No. I didn't ask her to."

"Well, don't look at me," she said, her voice rising. "I won't work for free."

"I didn't do it for my boss," I said. "Taking calls on the weekends just made it easier for me to keep an eye on the workers who got injured. And I could concentrate better when I wrote articles at home. Anyway, I enjoyed doing those things. I thought they mattered."

She looked at me like I'd lost my mind. "Well, anyway, they were lucky to have you."

Coming back to the present, I shook my head and sighed. My work performance had apparently impressed a few employees and nurses. But to those who hired and fired, my efforts had mattered little.

A dark cloud formed over my head and threatened to stay. I'd languished for weeks in the hospital, suffering through sixteen surgeries and rehabilitation. I'd struggled through long months of recovery at home, broken screws, tornados, vertigo, hearing loss, and fights with insurance companies. None of those trials compared with how terrible I felt about losing my job.

There was no doubt in my mind that my bosses knew firsthand the competent and committed employee I'd been. Now, it seemed they couldn't find it in her hearts to go to bat for me. That angered me most of all.

I wondered if Barbie, the nurse who'd filled in full time, had wanted my job. Later, I found out they gave it to her. By terminating a nurse with twenty-five years' experience and replacing her with one a year out of school, my employer had found a cheaper deal. For four years they'd demanded loyalty from me, but in the end, gave none in return.

That night I lay in bed and talked to Dave. "I can't believe they did this to us, after all we've been through," I cried. A tear rolled down my cheek.

Dave looked concerned. "They were despicable to do it. But truthfully I was more worried about you going back to work. I couldn't have stood it if some other terrible thing had happened to you. Now your legs will get a chance to heal."

"You're not worried about the money?"

"Well, I know we'll have to tighten our belts. No going out to eat or new clothes. But my boss gave me a little raise today." The corners of his eyes creased with his smile.

"Really? You didn't tell me."

"Well, it was going to be a surprise. So don't worry. I just want you to be happy and get stronger. You've been through enough, and you're still way too thin."

"I'm glad you're not upset," I said, at least feeling good about that.

"No I'm not upset. I'm relieved."

We turned out the lights. Soon Dave was breathing heavily on his side of the bed. He needed the rest.

I lay awake, my mind still churning and my chest and stomach tightly tied in a knot. I ran figures in my head and calculated to determine if we'd have enough to pay our bills. Depending on how much they charged for COBRA health insurance, we might just make it. At least for a while.

I turned to Jesus to find some peace, but felt disconnected. I started praying anyway. "Thank you for Dave's raise and for all the good people you've brought to help me." I began reciting their names out loud. My husband's and son's were at the top of the list. That process went on for quite a while. It comforted me to see how many

I could still name. Warmth spread slowly through my chest. As I continued to pray, it expanded to fill my whole body with a reassuring peace. I relaxed into the mattress. "Thank you," I said again, "for always being there."

By the time I finished, I could breathe a little easier. I reviewed what had happened and what I could do to improve my situation. I couldn't change what my bosses had done, but I could get back to taking better care of myself. I could exercise more, eat a healthier diet, reach out to help friends and family, make time to talk with and listen to God, and get back to writing my story. That was where I'd start. To live well would be the best antidote for being wronged. I would give it a try.

I wrote to my friends to vent:

> Late yesterday afternoon, just after faxing a medical release to my bosses, they called to inform me they'd taken my job! I guess I shouldn't have told them I'd be returning to work on crutches and in a wheelchair!

> Well, despite having premonitions this might happen, I can tell you being 'terminated' certainly knocked the wind out of my sails. I felt and still feel completely devastated though I doubt the full weight of my loss has hit me.

> Then last night as I was praying, I remembered an old quote. "Living well is the best revenge," by George Herbert, an English poet. I hadn't thought of that line in twenty-five years. Back then I'd been slogging through a divorce when a friend sent it to cheer me. It spoke to the anger I'd felt then and now...but also to the hope. So I'm starting again with a new to-do list.

WITH A LITTLE HELP FROM MY FRIENDS

"The LORD is close to the brokenhearted and saves those who are crushed in spirit." (Psalm 34:18 NIV)

When I sent my message, an outpouring of love, concern and outrage came flooding swiftly back. In my anguish, I had cried out to God for help and once again He answered by sending the love of friends. I welcomed the break from my fear and anger.

Hope called. "I've experienced traumas in my life, and at the times, I felt afraid, overwhelmed, and hopeless," she said, slowly. Then more quickly, "I allowed myself to grovel in all that for a while but ultimately, I pulled myself up with the help of family and friends. Lara, the hard part is behind you. You can do anything! God uses people to answer prayers and the people are already in place, you just don't know who they all are yet."

Barbara wrote:

> I've read your letter over and over, and just find your news so painful and your courage so admirable that I am stymied about what to say. I held you in the light today, very intently, in our Quaker Meeting, where I was sitting in a room of about seventy strong Friends. I imagined all the love in the room focusing on you at the same time, in a sort of magnifying glass effect that would just clear up any little tangles. Anyhow, you were for sure getting MY love during that time.

I considered what Barbara wrote and felt the healing power of her love.

Many others wrote to say they felt utterly outraged and shocked that anyone who knew me could do such a thing while rationalizing with comments like, "It's just business."

"Have those corporations taken over their very souls?" one wrote. Lynda wrote:

> I guess the biggest hurt is how one human can treat another in this way. Even if the outcome could not have been changed, the way it was dealt with could. After all your years of loyal service and recent efforts, at the very least they should have visited you at home and told you face to face and maybe offered support in some other way.

I couldn't have agreed more. The impersonal manner in which my bosses had delivered their messages felt as cold and harsh as if their hearts had turned to stone. Neither had my employer offered any severance nor other compensation for my loss. Their thoughtlessness was beyond belief. I got mad all over again thinking about it.

Yet each new message and call helped cushion the blow.

Hope called again, "I'm so glad to hear you felt ANGER and so glad you awakened this morning with goals. Someday, I'll tell you what has happened to me in my life and how I've come to know that the hardships I faced have made me the person I am today. No regrets that I could do anything about."

And Lynda wrote again, perhaps commenting most graphically and with her usual biting wit:

> You are quite an amazing person but do remember that you are only human—and it's okay to feel angry and make a little doll and stick pins in it!!!!

Despite the pain I had to laugh at my English friend's outrageous suggestion. Her indignation on my behalf felt like a tonic for my sagging spirit.

She wrote again, this time with a more serious message:

> What about your human rights under your Constitution
> or maybe your trade union? They wouldn't be allowed
> to do that to you over here.

I shared her letter with Dave, who laughed, though somewhat bitterly. "Tell Lynda most of the protective agencies for workers here, particularly in the past twenty years, have lost their power and funding to legally empower your claims in any way that would be useful," he said. Dave had always made a point of staying informed.

Another friend emailed:

> What about your rights under the Equal Employment
> Opportunity Commission (EEOC). Don't they protect
> the rights of women over fifty?

"Not a bad idea," I said, speaking to Dave.

I called the EEOC. A nice man informed me I was welcome to file a complaint against my employer. "You have that right since they made no apparent attempt to accommodate your physical limitations in any way."

"What would that accomplish?" I asked.

"Our attorneys would make every effort to force them to give you back your job."

"Really?" I let that settle in for a moment. But would I want to work under someone who'd been told to take me back against their will? I could envision a few problems with that scenario. Still the EEOC did seem the right agency for handling situations like mine. I'd have to give their proposal more thought.

Others mentioned Social Security Disability. That sounded like one of the few places where I might get some help financially until I felt strong enough to get back to work. But *disability*? Despite my struggle to walk, I'd never thought of myself as disabled. I wanted to work, not retire.

"It's probably the only way you'll ever qualify for medical coverage once the COBRA runs out," Dave said. From what I understood about the way insurance companies operated, I had to agree. I felt backed into a corner.

At Dave's request, I called an attorney who specialized in disability. Her receptionist set me up for her earliest appointment which wasn't for a month. "It could take a year or two to get approved," she said. "Social Security Disability is swamped. Lots of those who've lost their jobs and can't get new ones are applying for it. That's one reason it's taking so long."

"So much for government assistance for the disabled," I said, feeling discouraged. I'd have to wait and see what the attorney said.

The fear monster continued to rear its ugly head at least a dozen times a day. Periodically, I'd look up and thank heavens another email or letter would arrive, making me feel calmer, cherished and loved. I couldn't believe how much my friends and family still believed in me, when I felt so defeated.

Many who wrote voiced the belief that how we treated others came back to us.

"I believe you reap what you sow, so their time will come," one wrote.

"What goes around, comes around," wrote another.

A few just described those who had done this to me as "evil" and left it at that. Others talked about a new chapter opening in my life.

"When one door is closed, God is faithful to open another," one wrote.

Over dinner, Pierce put his own twist on it. "Whenever God closes a door, you need to get a crowbar and pry that sucker open," he said with a smirk.

I laughed at his offbeat humor, though the crowbar approach had never worked too well for me.

Each person who wrote or called had a slightly different take on my plight. A college friend wrote, "This has all the earmarks of a spiritual battle."

That sounded about right, as if some terrible force in the universe had taken up arms against me. I wanted to know more.

My friend elaborated:

> I'm just saying that you and Dave have been chosen to
> wake up and realize that you are important. The story
> of Job is another example.

His comments left me more confused than before, but curious. Apparently, he believed that when catastrophic events happened, they often had something to do with God trying to get our attention for some higher purpose. Not knowing much about Job, I'd already begun to relate to his suffering. Now I wanted to see how he'd dealt with his struggles.

I found that God had removed Job's protection, allowing Satan to take his wealth, his children, and his physical health in order to tempt him to curse God. Despite Job's difficult circumstances, he never did. And although he protested his plight and pleaded for an explanation from God, he stopped short of ever accusing Him of injustice.

After reading about Job's trials, I sincerely hoped my own would ultimately be less catastrophic.

A few days later, I got a note from Perry. Rather than pointing the finger at God or Satan for what had happened, Perry, like Dave, felt my employer was mostly to blame. He wrote:

> If your employer had cared more about you personally
> and less about their own image and liability, you
> would still have a job. End of discussion.

> Lara, in your letter, I expected a paragraph or two
> expressing the positives surrounding your situation
> because you are a positive person. You could have
> been angry, grown bitter and given up by now, but

that's not you. You are a strong, intelligent person who
doesn't know how to give up, a Wonder Woman and
a true inspiration to us all.

Though I felt like anything but a Wonder Woman, it sure made
me feel good when Perry got wound up on my behalf. Quite a few
others wrote to say God had something in mind for me. Given the
loss of my job, I didn't see what that could be.

My friend Liz who'd often visited me in Rehab wrote:

I know this is going to be a hard adjustment, but you
can and will do it! We don't know what the future
holds, but from your experiences this past year, you
have been strengthened in your faith and love for God.
He brought you through all your injuries, hospital
stays, surgeries, etc. He will remain with you now.
What you write may have a much bigger impact on
more people's lives than anything you could ever do
as a nurse (and you are a wonderful nurse).

Later that same day I had a call from Ann, my mother-in-law.
"Are you feeling forsaken?" she asked tenuously, instead of saying
hello.

I knew she was referring to her favorite Bible verse, the one she'd
quoted so often in the hospital.

"Not really," I said. "I don't think God had anything to do with
what my employer did."

We talked a bit longer and were saying our goodbyes when she
added, "And don't forget to look for a surprise in your life."

I guessed she was telling me that blessings could still be found
in unexpected people, places and situations. Her message sounded
hopeful and from my experience, completely true.

With the arrival of each new letter and email, I felt God's Spirit
comforting and supporting me.

Maggie, my sister-in-law, wrote:

Wow. This was a shock! However, I do believe that 'all things work together for good for those who love God, who are called according to his purpose' (Romans 8:28 NET), so I think God has something better up His sleeve and you will be ready for it. He never deprives his kids of what they need, but drives them to better things. He loves you and you can rest in that truth and His provision for you. Keep me posted.

And Lynda wrote:

I feel you are being steered on a journey that you will just have to trust will be better for you…

Many were upset by what had happened to me. Jenny wrote:
I have been so very upset about your circumstances. I think it is just terrible that you lost your job. It has really knocked the wind out of me, too. I will miss you so much not being here at the plant! I do know, without a doubt, that God has an even better plan for your life…

Another woman at the factory sent me a card which said:

I know in all my being that you of all people are meant for a higher calling than we average folk. Listen to God's voice.

Once again everyone sounded so sure that God had a blueprint for my life. But in light of losing my job, I didn't see one. Beyond writing my story, I could think of nothing that might suggest a new beginning. More than one person had told me that publishing anything in the present economy would be incredibly difficult. Yet despite their misgivings, something spurred me on most days to sit at the computer and do my best to put that which had been nearly inexpressible into words. I believed it was important to share the story of a former agnostic who'd found faith and strength in God after suffering doubt and fear most of her life. Maybe it would give others hope.

The words Liz said might have empowered me most. We'd been talking on the phone for quite a while when she said, "Lara, you already know you're not alone."

It was a statement of fact, not a question. I took a moment to reflect on what she'd said. I had learned in the hospital that Jesus' Spirit was alive within me, inseparable. Knowing that one thing had made all the difference. It had given me the sense of security I'd longed for and stopped me from despairing. As a former world-class worrier, that was saying something. God had performed another miracle.

BARGAINING WITH GOD

The next morning I awoke with a very strange thought. *Could losing my job be another gift?* It had been a week since they'd terminated me. I didn't feel remotely happy, but for the moment, I felt open to some brighter possibilities. For the first time in years, my life was completely unencumbered by schedules, work-related pressures, and a to-do list the length of my arm.

They'd cut off my income. That thought alone would normally have induced panic in me. But I made up my mind, at least for the moment I'd make the most of my quiet time and see what came up. That would involve turning our financial needs over to God, something I'd never been able to do.

Messages of support continued to stream in, even from people who'd been out of my life for a long while. Sometimes they needed some reassurance in return.

My cousin, with whom I felt a particularly strong connection, wrote me a note from Afghanistan:

> Lara, Remember when you are feeling sad just how loved you are. It is rare to find that sort of giving love over here. It is a feature common to our landscape and absent from this one. All good love from our hearts to yours, and we'll see you soon for a good laugh.

I wrote him back:

> You are right, dear cousin. I have been so richly blessed with love. It has been that single thing, without

a doubt, that has carried me through every peak and valley on this journey so far. And not just receiving love, but the pleasure of giving it as well. For me the love of friends and family have been absolute proof_ that God loves me and wants me to recover for some purpose. Having said all that, I still have to remind myself to focus on the day right in front of me and not look too far ahead or back at what I've lost.

Just remember, that God loves you, too, and is always with you. He will send His Holy Spirit to fill your heart with just what you need in that barren place. I'm so glad that we're reconnected. Praying for you and sending you love.

"We all just need to circle the wagons," Hope said, after I phoned her. "We missed celebrating your birthday, so we'll have to do that too." Somehow she always seemed to understand when I needed her most.

That Saturday, and a week after losing my job, Hope and her husband, along with Mary, another nursing friend who'd been filling in for me at the plants, joined Dave and me for lunch at our favorite sushi restaurant in town.

"Happy birthday," Hope said as she stepped out of her car.

"Thanks," I said, half-heartedly.

"Lots of workers have asked about you, Lara," Mary said. "They're really upset that your boss won't let you come back."

"More like, they're furious," Hope said. "But not as mad as we are." She nodded at Mary.

"I know what you mean," I said. "But let's not spoil our time together talking about all that."

We traded a few stories about what else had been going on at work and laughed about them. Before long, our time together had ended.

"Let's promise to get together every month," said Hope, hugging me goodbye.

"Yes, let's," I said, smiling and hugging her in return.

With our luncheon over and my friends heading home, despite our promises, it would be quite a while before I saw them again. With few exceptions, most of my friends lived forty five minutes to an hour away, one downside of living in a rural area. The distance would make it hard to get together very often. That thought made me sad all over again. I'd known losing my job would impact our finances. Now it struck me that it would also limit seeing friends.

"I just wonder why God is allowing me to be stripped of so much," I asked Jenny when she called.

"Maybe He's moving things out of your way to work with you," she answered.

There was no denying it. God had been moving a lot of what I enjoyed out of my life. If Jenny was right, what would He want me to work on next?

My emotions continued to rise and fall as my first week being unemployed came to a close. One moment I felt at peace only to find I couldn't breathe the next. An invisible band encircled my chest, constricting the flow of air into my lungs.

Mornings were hardest. Sensing there was no real reason to get up, I slept later than usual. My resolve to exercise and pray also met with resistance. I made out a list at night to help keep me on track the next morning.

Afternoons were a little easier. By that time of day, the anger pushed me to call attorneys for advice, only to find the ones on TV didn't handle cases like mine. Most limited their practices to clients who'd suffered auto wrecks or work-related injuries. Apparently, being smashed by a tree in the woods didn't count. An application from the EEOC arrived in the mail. Faced with the prospect of forcing Regional Medical to rehire me, I couldn't bring myself to fill it out.

I'd heard my state called a "Right to Work" state. Ironically, that seemed to mean that a company could fire their employees for any reason. By using an RN hospital job description to terminate me, my boss had done an excellent job of dotting her I's and crossing her Ts.

Right then I swore I'd stay positive. I refused to go through life as a victim. Becoming a victim would make everything Jesus had already done to help me a tragic waste. Besides, my right leg still had a lot of healing left to do.

In the hospital, I'd understood that if I wanted to live, I had to hold fast to hope. Without it, I just wouldn't make it. Now the situation looked no different. My newly rebuilt leg was extremely fragile and my body, terribly weak. If I gave in to despair, the bone graft might not take.

Despite my best efforts, spiritual doubts crept into my mind. As a child, a close relative had once told me that people made up the notion of God so they'd have a crutch to lean on when they felt scared. Even then, I'd wanted to believe otherwise, to know God was real. When I'd felt Jesus' Spirit awaken within me in the hospital, feeling as tangible as anything I'd ever witnessed, I knew my wish had come true. Prayer had worked and God was indeed, real. Now, more than ever, I needed to hold onto that conviction.

The next week, a pall still hung over me. My cell rang. It was Sandi. "Why don't you come eat lunch with my friend and me on Wednesday? You'll like her and it'll do you good to get out."

I hesitated. In my depressed state, it was difficult enough just being with myself. Hanging out with someone I hardly knew would be harder.

"Okay," I finally said, knowing I should go.

On Wednesday, Sandi pulled up in her little blue convertible and drove us to the restaurant to meet her friend. At lunch, the two women did their best to cheer me up, but my heart felt encased in lead. "You should apply for disability," the friend said. "With injuries like yours you shouldn't have any problem qualifying."

"Maybe so," I said, not feeling at all optimistic.

"What was that you were telling me about plans to volunteer at the health food store?" Sandi asked, changing the subject.

"The owner got excited when she heard I wouldn't be going back to my nursing job. She wants me to come help educate her customers. And she doesn't care that I'd be doing it from a wheelchair." I managed a smile.

"Sounds perfect, but how will you get there?"

"Pierce will have to take me and Dave can pick me up."

Buoyed by the prospect of teaching again, I started to feel happier.

The next Saturday, Dave, Pierce and I drove back to town for some more sushi. I had gone over our budget with a fine-toothed comb, slashing anything I could to make it work. The last thing I wanted to give up was my Saturday lunch dates with Dave, though truthfully, I doubted we could afford them. Our income had dropped by over seventy five percent when I factored in the increased cost of our health insurance. Despite that thought, the three of us laughed and joked over lunch as Pierce entertained us with more stories from the police academy.

"Would you care for some dessert?" the waitress interrupted when we'd finished eating.

"I'll have some chocolate ice cream," I said.

"Me too," said Pierce, grinning.

When she brought it over, Dave looked at it longingly. "Hey, I guess I'll have some too."

"Are you sure that's a good idea?" I asked, raising my eyebrows.

"I know I'm allergic to it, but maybe it won't bother me this once."

I wasn't convinced. I was already wishing Pierce and I hadn't ordered any.

Back home, Dave disappeared into his workshop to add some final touches on my new aquarium, and Pierce left to go target shooting with a few friends. I had just settled into a call with Janelle when Dave stumbled into our room, looking as white as chalk and bent double.

"I've got to go," I said and turning to Dave, "What's wrong?"

"My side is killing me. It must have been the ice cream." He lay down on our bed.

On automatic pilot, I began assessing the situation.

Skin, pale and hot. Temp, 100.6. Blood pressure, 150/96. "Are you nauseated?"

"Yes, very," Dave groaned and closed his eyes.

Dave had gotten sick many times from drinking milk and eating ice cream over the years, but this was no ordinary dairy reaction. When I gently pressed on Dave's side and let up, he nearly jumped off the bed. "Don't," he yelled.

His abdomen felt as hard as a wooden board. *Rebound tenderness in the lower right quadrant.*

"Would you feel better lying on your side?"

"No, I can't. It hurts too much." Without warning, Dave vomited with great force over the side of the bed.

My breath caught as I recognized the classic signs of appendicitis. *Should I call an ambulance?* The thought of going back to the hospital made me feel sick. It had barely been a month since my eight-hour surgery, and I still felt weak and off balance on crutches. Even worse was the thought of Dave undergoing emergency surgery. But if it turned out to be appendicitis and he didn't get treatment...

"I'm not going to the hospital?" Dave protested, reading my mind.

"Well you might have to if you don't start looking a whole lot better."

"No, I'm not going. They'll do surgery on me without giving me a chance to improve on my own."

I picked up my cell. It was nearly midnight. "Pierce, could you come home? Your dad's really sick and you might have to take us to the hospital," I said, knowing I couldn't drive.

"I'll be there in ten minutes." His voice sounded tight.

Dave shuffled quickly to the bathroom to vomit again.

With Dave in the bathroom, I prayed. "Jesus, don't let anything happen to my husband." Hot tears poured from my eyes. Fear suffocated me. "And don't make him go back to the hospital. He can't take much more of it," I stammered. "If you really want him to trust you, you've got to help him." I was ranting.

My prayer boiled with anger and fear and went on that way for a good five minutes. I wasn't being the least bit fair, respectful, or trusting, but I didn't care. As I played it back, my employer wasn't the only thing that had angered me. No denying it. After all the blessings and trials, I was also mad at God. *If anything happens to Dave… …* My body quaked with fear.

I was still lost in thought when Pierce burst in.

"What's going on," he asked, puffing.

"Your dad ate ice cream and his intestines are inflamed. He might even have an appendicitis."

"What do you want me to do?"

"For the moment, just pray," I said. "He doesn't want to go to the hospital, but if he's not better in ten minutes we'll have to take him."

"Okay." Pierce ran upstairs to change his clothes.

Sitting down on the love seat, I took a deep breath and closed my eyes. "Jesus, tell me what to do. I'll do whatever you want." My breathing slowed and as it did, peace began to fill my heart.

I got up and moved over to sit with Dave who'd gotten back into bed and was dry-heaving again. I mopped his brow with a cool cloth and waited for a sign, feeling in my bones one was coming. For a few minutes, nothing happened. I waited a few minutes more.

Then, Dave's knitted brow smoothed. I placed my hand on his abdomen. Slowly, the tightness was easing. Like a too-taught rubber band that had been released, his muscles relaxed.

He opened his eyes. "I think I'm feeling a little better," he said, color returning to his cheeks. Then he slept.

I awoke him twice during the night to check on him. "How're you feeling?" I asked each time.

"Better," was all he said.

The next morning, Dave's temp read 99. The pain had all but gone, though when I pressed on it, the right side still felt sore. I gave Dave some goldenseal and colloidal silver for good measure, knowing he was allergic to most antibiotics. We had long since come to believe in the healing power of God's restorative plants, the herbs. "Jesus, thank you for guiding me and calming my fears," I whispered. "And thank you for helping Dave." It hadn't been my threats and ranting prayer that had saved him. God had done that all on His own.

By Monday, Dave only hurt a little when he walked. All other symptoms had gone. I continued to give him the goldenseal. Despite his improvement, I silently swore to take him to the hospital if the pain returned.

I'd put him on clear liquids, but now with his appetite returning, I started him back on a dinner of chicken and rice. Then we waited again.

"I feel fine," he said an hour later. "And don't worry; I'm never eating ice cream again."

"I know that's right," I said, teasing.

Over the next couple of days Dave continued to improve. Jesus had answered my prayer. He had healed my husband.

"Maybe God's showing you that He can provide everything for you, that He's the only one you really need," Jenny said, calling from her office. "You need to have faith. I think that's really what He wants. Remember, 'Ask, and it will be given to you; seek, and you will find; knock, and it will be opened to you. For everyone who asks receives, and he who seeks finds, and to him who knocks, it will be opened.'" (Matthew 7:7-8 NIV)

What Jenny said felt right. In confirmation, my heart warmed. I thought of a quote by Ralph Waldo Emerson that spoke to me. "The wise man in the storm prays to God, not for safety from danger, but for deliverance from fear."

Once again it turned out that having hope was not really about counting on God to eliminate our difficulties. It was about believing that He would give us exactly what we needed to get through them.

DAVE GETS A MESSAGE

A wave of relief washed over me whenever I reflected on Dave's miraculous recovery. But despite my gratitude to God for healing him and the reassurance from Jenny, by the start of the next week, I felt wrung out. Worse, I couldn't focus to pray. The outrage relating to my unfair treatment from my employer now joined forces with fear over Dave's close call. Together, they disrupted my thoughts and lodged like a pile of lead in the pit of my stomach. Anxious dreams awakened me in the middle of the night and jolted me out of bed in the early morning.

By afternoon, fear took a backseat to fury. It stimulated me like too much caffeine, driving me to contact more government agencies and lawyers and write diatribes to friends. It consumed me to the point that two weeks after my termination, I hardly recognized myself. Where had my compassion gone? My faith? I had taken pride in thinking I had become both more loving and trusting in God. Now, the thought that I'd lost the best parts of myself sickened me.

Dave raised his eyebrows as his typically upbeat wife launched into yet another tirade when he walked in the door from work. "Are you okay?" he asked for the second time that week.

"No, but I will be." I didn't want him to worry.

By the middle of the week, I felt numb. Pierce drove me to Great Foods Manufacturing. where I'd arranged to pick up my belongings. Quite a few of my paintings and prints still hung on the clinic walls. There were also file boxes filled with articles and presentations I'd written. Somehow we had to squeeze all of it into Pierce's sports car.

Even the thought of seeing friends didn't cheer me. What would I say? I was feeling far more like a victim, a hollow shell, than the upbeat nurse who'd worked to motivate their coworkers to get in shape. As Pierce pulled into the parking lot, I gathered what courage I had to face them.

Mary, who'd been left to train my replacement, looked like she wanted to cry as she met us at the car. She handed over the first of many file boxes to Pierce.

"It looks like you've worn yourself out getting all my things together," I said. "If you show Pierce where to go, he'll get the rest of the paintings."

"I don't feel one bit good about what they've done to you," she declared, shaking her head and walking toward the building with my son.

I was just about to agree when Jenny, Leah, and another work friend appeared from inside the factory. So did the plant supervisor's wife, Dottie. They enfolded me in a big group hug. In that moment, the awesome power of their love knocked something loose in me and the flood gates broke. I cried as they stood there holding me.

When they let go, I sensed something I hadn't for several weeks, that lovely state of peace, lately held hostage by my anger and fear.

The four of them beamed at me as I balanced on one foot leaning against Pierce's car. Then Dottie presented me with some large sacks. "Here," she said. "Meat from our freezer. Robert and I want you and your family to have these." She smiled and handed them to Pierce.

"But this must be everything you had. Did you save anything for yourselves?" I asked, overwhelmed.

"Don't worry. We bought a whole cow this year, and anyway, it's just the two of us at home these days."

"Well, if you're sure...thank you," I said, hesitating.

Pierce loaded the bags into his trunk. Sacks of beans, rice, grits, and nuts followed. There must have been enough food to feed our family for a year.

"Wow," I said. "I don't know what to say."

"We're just so glad to be able to help," Dottie said. "You know my husband and I think a lot of you. You were always there for him and so many others at work."

"The feeling is mutual," I said, smiling.

Jenny and our other friend handed me a card. I opened it. "Please know that we love you very much and you are always in our prayers. We believe that God has a lot more in store for you." Inside, I found seventy five-dollars.

"This is too much," I whispered to the two women, feeling uncomfortable all over again. "I know you two don't have this kind of money."

"Don't worry. They gave us a little extra this week," Jenny said.

I held out my arms to embrace them again. It struck me that every one of my friends from work perfectly embodied Jesus' generous spirit. I vowed to be more like them. Another happy thought crossed my mind.

"Hey, as soon as I can drive, I want to come visit your churches and thank the people there for praying for me," I said. "I know their prayers really made a difference."

They all agreed it was a wonderful idea.

As Pierce and I drove away, for the first time in days, I felt happy.

"That was really nice of Dottie and Robert to give us so much food. Dad will be thrilled," Pierce exclaimed.

"I'm completely blown away myself. Thank you, Jesus, for blessing me with such wonderful friends. What would we do without them?"

That night as I sat holding the bone stimulator to my leg to encourage healing of the bone graft, I picked up a book and began reading where I'd left off months before. It was saying that although we weren't always responsible for what experiences happened to us, we were responsible for how we reacted to them. We could give up, or we could turn the situations over to God, allowing Him to use them for our highest good by transforming us into becoming more like Jesus.

The part about God using our experiences to transform us caught my attention. Hearing that He was using everything that had happened to mold me into someone wonderful felt amazing. If God really had a plan for my life I felt sure it would be just like that, to make me into a better person. For the moment, I began to see everything, from the tree falling to my leg coming apart and the loss of my job, in a little different light.

The understanding that God was using my trials to make me more like Jesus comforted me. It filled me with a renewed sense of peace. I'd long since believed that God's allowing the tree to fall on me and then doing all He could to help me survive suggested He thought I was special in some odd way. Why else would he have entrusted me with such a unique experience?

Despite those happy perceptions, by the next Sunday when a second illness struck Dave and our computer died, I concluded my college friend had been right. The universe did have the two of us ensnared in a battle. I found myself questioning God all over again.

I could see by his face, Dave was suffering again. He looked ashen and miserable. His forehead burned to my touch, and his whole head throbbed with pain. Taking his blood pressure using my old cuff, I discovered the valve leaked air. To my shock the dial read a whopping 170/120 when it should have read less than 120/80. *That can't be right.* I hastened to recheck it, but when I pumped it up again, the valve blew out with a loud popping sound. In frustration, I threw the cuff on the floor.

"Why is this happening, God?" I cried. "Why are you allowing Dave to be sick again? What are you trying to tell us?" *And why do these things always happen on a Sunday?*

I was fighting the impulse to protest further when a frightening thought hit me.

What if God planned to strip me of all I loved to mold me into a more Christ-like person? What if He took everything?

That notion stopped me in my tracks. But did it ring true?

I believed God loved His children as much as I loved my son. I doubted that taking everything that really mattered to me was what he had in mind.

I went to work locating all the herbs and other nutritional supplements in the house that might possibly lower Dave's blood pressure and alleviate his headache, before he could see the doctor on Monday. I found some magnesium, l-arginine, Coq10, and garlic capsules for the blood pressure and offered those to him as well as some chamomile and kava kava to help him relax. He didn't hesitate for a second before gulping them all down with a big glass of water. Then I sat down on my love seat to wait for them to take effect and pray to Jesus, who I reminded myself had never let me down.

An hour later, Pierce ran down the steps to my room. "Hey Mom, here's a blood pressure cuff I found in the pantry."

"Great. I forgot about that one." I wrapped the cuff around Dave's arm and pumped it up. *Jesus, please let it be lower.*

"It's 120/88 or just a little high," I said, sighing with relief.

"My headache's feeling better too," Dave said, the color returning to his cheeks.

In another two hours, the headache, fever and sore throat had all but gone. "I'm feeling a lot better, but what the heck was all that about?"

We'd often witnessed the healing power of herbs, vitamins, and minerals, but neither one of us had ever seen anything work quite this fast before. I stared back at him in wonder.

"I think God is trying to tell you something," I said, trying to gauge his reaction.

"Really?" Dave looked more receptive to the God talk than usual.

"I think so, but I'm sure you have to be the one to decide what the message is."

"Why can't God just say it so I can understand?" he said, sounding perturbed.

"Maybe He's just telling you He loves you and you can count on Him to be with you."

I thought I'd better leave it at that.

A week later, I called Ann. "I'm afraid I've been awfully hard on God these past few weeks."

To my surprise she didn't sound taken aback. "God understands when we question or get angry with Him. He wants us to come to Him when we need something."

"I kind of figured He could take it," I said, chuckling. "Lately, I've felt good knowing that He's using all these trials to polish my rough edges. I must have a lot of them because He definitely has me in His accelerated learning program. Maybe He thought I had some catching up to do."

"Don't we all," Ann said with a laugh.

"Maybe it's just my way of consoling myself or maybe it's a little too much ego, but as odd as it may sound, I think He must feel I'm pretty important to be working so hard on me."

"I've been wondering all year why He'd given you so much to deal with," Ann said.

"Well, more than some and less than so many others. You know as well as I do, there's always someone a lot worse off. In the meantime, I'm hanging onto the idea that He thinks I'm special."

MORE GOVERNMENT AGENCIES

"You can at least get unemployment, right?" It was my brother, Josh, on the phone. I'd heard that question a dozen times before.

"I guess so," I said. "I've been working for almost thirty years, but even so Dave doesn't think they'll give it to me."

"Really, why not?"

"I'm not sure."

That night my husband filled me in after he'd reviewed the Department of Labor's website. "They'll place all kinds of demands on you that you can't realistically meet."

"Maybe so, but we need the money, and I won't know for sure unless I go down to their office and talk to them."

"Well, I see I'm not going to change your mind," Dave teased.

On Wednesday, Sandi drove me to the unemployment office. I crutched slowly to the counter and attempted to balance on one foot as I signed in. I felt dizzy. Then I sat down to wait.

Decades earlier, I'd applied for unemployment after an employer filed for bankruptcy. I'd spoken with a nice counselor who smiled at me across her desk and asked a few questions. Within a week, I'd received my first check.

On this day, things were different. A tired-looking woman herded about twelve of us into a small room. "Take a seat at a computer," she said. She gave us instructions on how to complete the questionnaire on the screen.

I looked at the computer. The first question was the one Dave had warned me about. It asked if I were ready, willing, and able to work forty hours a week. There didn't seem to be any option listed for an applicant who was at home recovering from surgery or needed to work part-time for medical reasons. Surely I'd missed it. I raised my hand. The woman came over.

"If I put down that I can't work full-time right now will that exempt me from benefits?

"Yes, it will. This part of the government isn't concerned with your injuries or medical limitations." She looked down at my crutches.

So that was that. Dave had been right. If I wanted to get unemployment I had to suck it up and commit to the prospect of going back to work full-time right away even if I was still dizzy, weak, foggy, and on crutches. At least they hadn't specified what kind of work. *How about a nursing job at home where I can sit on the sofa with my legs elevated reviewing medical charts on my computer?* I chuckled. Someone had once mentioned that insurance companies sometimes offered positions like that to nurses. I'd have to go online and see.

Truthfully I suspected my back wouldn't tolerate sitting all day either, but I would give it a try if that's what it took to get unemployment.

I already knew what Dave would say when he came home from work.

"I know you want to go back to work, but have you lost your mind? Do you want to hurt yourself again?" he said over supper, glaring at me.

"I guess I'm counting on the Department of Labor to do what's right and give me benefits anyway. That would buy me time to heal and let me see what I'll be capable of doing in a few months."

"Whether they should or not, that's not how it works," Dave said patiently.

A week later I was sitting in my wheelchair writing at the computer when I got a call.

"I see no evidence whatsoever that you're serious about looking for work," a woman from the unemployment office snapped.

"What do you mean? I've been researching insurance nursing jobs on line," I said, taken aback.

"I see no evidence," she repeated disdainfully.

"What kind of evidence are you looking for?" My chest tightened.

"You didn't even bother to sign up for our classes on writing a resume or interviewing for a job."

"I have a good resume and communication skills, so I didn't think it was necessary," I said, feeling wary. "But if you think it will help me get unemployment, I'll do it."

I don't recall the rest of what she said, but her accusatory tone told me all I needed to know. She hadn't called to help. Was it her job to harass applicants who'd been terminated for "health reasons" rather than for the usual "lack of work?"

My thoughts were in turmoil. It had been hard enough just getting to the unemployment office to fill out the application. How would I get back and forth for classes? I could never ask Sandi or Hope to take me when they'd already done so much. Sensing it wouldn't help to discuss it further, I stopped talking.

That evening I talked to Dave over dinner. "You were right. I've just been kidding myself into thinking I could satisfy their requirements. But it isn't fair." Once again, something was blocking my way forward.

"It isn't, but you need to let it go and give yourself a chance to get stronger," Dave said gently. "That matters more than the money."

"Sandi and Hillary both suggested I should look for a part-time job. They seem to think I could handle one."

"Well, I don't agree. That's the worst idea I've heard yet. And how would they know? They haven't watched you wince in pain or get dizzy every time you get up on crutches, have they? They obviously don't understand how fragile your legs and back still are. Don't let anyone pressure you or make you feel guilty." Dave's voice was getting loud.

"I'm sure they were just trying to help," I said, feeling the fear beneath his anger.

"I'm sure they were. I think part of the problem is that you don't tell people what's really going on. You're always telling them you're fine. Well, you aren't fine. And I'm not either. We may be better after a few months of rest and healing, but we aren't now. Hey, I saw you

under that tree. You were squashed flat like a possum on the road."
Dave raised an eyebrow and gave me a pointed look.

I laughed in spite of myself. Dave's quirky sense of humor got
me every time.

"By the way, your new aquarium is about ready. I just need to
buy you some cute fish. Then you'll have something entertaining to
look at while you're getting better," Dave added.

"I can't wait," I said, feeling loved.

With Dave's encouragement, I reluctantly stopped pursuing
unemployment and a new job. Though my spirit was ready and
willing to go back to work, my legs, back and ankle-- fastened
together with so many screws, bolts, struts, and rods--were not. I
began to understand how much God wanted me to take some time
to heal. He had sent me another message, just not the one I wanted
to hear.

A week later, I got a letter from the unemployment office
announcing my request for benefits had been declined. It was
probably for the best, but their pronouncement still hit me hard. I felt
angry at a system that had failed to support those of us who wanted
to work but couldn't.

I reflected on something Jesus had said. "Assuredly, I say to you,
inasmuch as you did it to one of the least of these, My brethren, you
did it to Me." (Matthew 25:40 NKJV)

What would the woman on the phone have said about that?

FAMILY CONFLICTS

Money worries gnawed holes in my confidence and upended my normally happy state of mind. I'm ashamed to admit, I sometimes snapped at my husband, especially when he lost his temper. He often snapped back.

One Saturday after that happened, remorse hit me like a dump truck. *What the heck's wrong with me? I've been so caught up in my own feelings I haven't even considered Dave's. I have to tell him.*

I crutched into his work shop. "Please forgive me. I shouldn't have snapped at you like that. It's just that sometimes when you lose your temper I feel like you want me to notice how overwhelmed you are and fix the problem. Then, I want to fix it but I can't."

"Well, I don't."

"Not even a little?"

"Nope."

"Okay, maybe I'm wrong on that one, but how about this. It's been hard for you to see me so torn up about losing my nursing career?"

"You're right on that one."

"I know it's easy to say, but try not to worry about me. I'll be okay." I said.

"You promise?"

"I promise. Hey, God has gotten me through a whole lot worse," I teased.

"That's for sure," Dave said, his voice softening.

We sat in silence for a moment before he spoke again. "You know, you're still beautiful to me, and I love you more than anything."

Despite my hobbling gait, unsightly scars, infantile outbursts, and aggravation over losing my job, Dave still loved me. If there was ever a hint that he no longer found me attractive, I never saw it. In large part, I owed what positive self-esteem I had left to him. His attitude had made all the difference. I silently thanked God for the gift of Dave.

"It means everything to hear you say that. I never would have made it through any of this without you." I swallowed before I continued. "But I can tell you're sick and tired of the endless chores and it breaks my heart not to be able to help you."

"I am, but I'm not sick and tired of you."

"Hey, it won't be too long before I can do my part again," I said, smiling. "It'll get easier."

"I know."

Knowing Dave still loved and valued me made the world feel brighter.

When we were done talking, I sat down, thinking. I couldn't be kind to strangers but short with my family and still feel good about myself. I'd never liked seeing that kind of hypocrisy in others, but now I saw it plainly in myself. Taking out my feelings on the one who had done the most for me felt awful. I promised myself I'd do better. I'd start by cutting Dave some slack. With a little effort, I could.

A more serious issue preyed on my mind. After dinner, Dave and I sat downstairs reading on our bed when I brought it up.

"I've been wondering about something."

"What's that?" he asked slowly. He raised one eyebrow and looked at me sideways.

"Well, lately you seem pretty uncomfortable when I bring up Jesus. I know we didn't talk much about Him before the accident. Does my talking about him now bother you?"

"Why would you think that?" Dave frowned and stiffened in his chair.

"Well, lately you've been quick to point out whenever self-proclaimed Christians don't act like you think they should. Are you trying to make a point?"

Dave didn't answer. I could only guess what his silence meant.

"It's even crossed my mind you might be worried I'll turn against you?" I said slowly. "If that's so, you don't have to worry."

"That doesn't concern me. Just don't try to convert me." He sounded adamant.

"I won't. In fact, I probably wouldn't believe in Jesus myself if I hadn't experienced His Spirit firsthand. You just seem so stressed lately. I thought you could use some extra comfort."

"I can't see how turning to Jesus would help. I guess I still tend to associate him with the bad things people do in His name."

"You know those bad things have nothing to do with Him," I said, understanding. "Jesus is all about love. Anyway, there's no point in judging Him by what some of his followers do."

"Sometimes it's hard for me to separate the two."

"You know, Dave, Sandi once said if anyone based their faith on what the other church goers did, they'd never become a Christian. It sounded like she spoke from experience," I teased. "Anyway, we don't really have much control over what other people do. We can only keep trying to be the best we can."

"You're right," he said, looking more relaxed, "but still don't try to convert me. That's not going to work."

"Okay, it's a deal," I said gently.

Dave was my lover and best friend. He'd worked himself to a nub on the job, returning home only to cook, clean, wash, repair the cars, feed the pets and care for me. The stress had turned his hair white and deepened the character lines in his face. Worse, he didn't trust God to help him one bit. It broke my heart to watch him struggling alone.

Maybe what I'd said would help. Maybe it wouldn't. But whether it did or not, I had to let it go. I had to turn him over to God for safe keeping. "Take care of my husband," I whispered.

STRUGGLING IN THE NET OF LIFE

By the third week in September, a month after losing my job, I still worried Dave and I wouldn't have enough to pay our bills. Yet, time and time again, Jesus had shown me His Spirit was with me and willing to provide whatever I needed to get through this.

In an effort to keep my mind off my fear, I pushed myself increasingly to write, exercise and reach out to people I loved. When I talked to Jesus, despite worries over money, I sometimes felt the peace I'd experienced so often before. It was only there I found solace.

One afternoon, Hope phoned. "Do you remember the safety manager at that plant near your house where you gave flu shots last year?"

"Sure," I said. "She's the one who asked me if I would be interested in working there."

"That's the one. I saw her this morning, and she asked why you weren't giving their shots this year. I told her the whole story. She wants you to call her right away. I think she has some information for you."

I took Hope's advice and called.

"Hey it's good to hear from you," the safety manager said. "I know an excellent attorney who handles worker's compensation cases. I know the tree falling on you wasn't work-related, but the aggravation of your injuries certainly was. I think you have a good case."

That night I discussed it with Dave.

"You're not even close to being over your last surgery," he said, sounding weary. "The last thing we need is a legal battle."

All through September the bills continued to pile up, so Dave and I reluctantly decided to see what the attorney had to say.

The waiting room welcomed us with its dark paneling and imposing mahogany furniture. The attorney, a man who looked to be in his early thirties, invited us in. He motioned for us to sit at the far end of an enormous conference table and tell him everything that had happened.

We did our best to fill him in.

"You have a good worker's compensation case since going back to work definitely made your injuries worse," he said, "and I'd be glad to represent you."

An hour and a half later, Dave and I were gathering our notes to leave when the attorney added with a note of warning, "If you decide to go through with this, you need to know your employer's lawyers will fight hard. They'll try to drag you through the mud and make you look bad. Think about whether you want to subject yourselves to that much stress right now. You've already been through a lot. If you do decide to go through with it, make sure your trauma surgeons are on board. You can't win without their support."

"This is sounding worse by the minute," I lamented as Dave and I made our way along the sidewalk back to the car, a wave of dread passing over me.

Dave nodded, sighing.

As it happened, I had an appointment that afternoon for a checkup with Dr. Bolling. I was already leaning against pursuing any legal action and felt awkward about bringing it up to him. What if he thought I was out to milk the system or worse that I was choosing the easy way out? I didn't want it to change his good opinion of me.

Thirty minutes later, Dr. Bolling walked into the examining room, smiling and reaching out his arms to hug me. Then, seeing Dave, he grabbed his hand and shook it heartily. We were filling him in on what the lawyer said when he made an interesting comment. "While your spirit of determination certainly helped you survive and recover, ironically it sent you back to work way too early, causing your leg to come apart and you to lose your job. We really need a better system that makes it possible for severely injured workers to wait at least a year to fully recover before going back to work."

"I couldn't agree more, but not many employers are willing to hold a position that long. I doubt mine would have." I gave him a wry smile.

"Too bad," Dr. Bolling added. "If you need me to write a letter to go with an application for social security disability, just say the word. It would be appropriate for you right now. That program was originally designed for patients in your situation. And you can always go off it later if you're able to work again. Right now, you can't. I'd also be glad to support you if you decide to go the worker's compensation route. I was angry when you wrote me that your employer had taken your job just as you were on the road to recovery. I think they made a big mistake. Anyway, you know how much I love a good fight." His boyish face bore a fierce expression.

"Thank you," I said. "You've always been willing to do whatever I needed. That means more than you know. I really don't want to go the disability or the worker's comp route, but they have me backed into a corner. Thank goodness for the generosity of friends and family, but we sure don't want to have to rely on them to pay our bills."

"That's for sure," Dave added.

"Just remember more important than disability or worker's comp, I believe there is something positive in store for you—the book you're writing or something else," Dr. Bolling said, smiling.

I nodded, not quite believing it was true. "Hey, let me know if down the road you need a good part-time nurse." I gave him a weak smile.

"You can count on it."

Dave pushed my wheelchair out into the sunshine, and we got into the car. I was feeling grateful for Dr. Bolling's support and thinking about his assertion that we needed a better system for injured workers when a grey cloud passed over the sun, and I shivered. Every legal option we'd explored seemed to have a downside.

"Why do all these choices look so hard? Dr. Bolling's right.

There's got to be something more positive in store for us. We just can't see it yet," I said more gloomily than I intended.

"I know you're worried about us not having enough money, but don't be. I'll do my best to take care of you."

Though downcast, Dave's words melted my heart. It hadn't been that long since his own career had been downsized, and he'd had to scramble to start a new one. It struck me how much courage that must have taken.

"Thank you," I said, tears burning my eyes. I reached over and grabbed his hand giving it a squeeze. "Guess I still get furious when I think of how much loyalty my employer demanded from their employees while giving so little in return. Then I remember how Jesus fed the poor, healed the sick and lame, asking for nothing back. I try to reconcile that picture with what my company did to me. Isn't extending support to those in need, even to the ones who can only go back to work, relying on crutches and a wheelchair, exactly what it means to be a Christian?"

"It is to me," Dave said. "I may not have as much faith as you do in Jesus, but I grew up in my parents' church reading the Bible. Jesus' support for the needy was well documented. And He didn't just teach His message through words; He demonstrated it over and over by what He did."

"That's what attracted me to Jesus and so many of his followers in the first place," I fumed.

We rode for miles in silence, my thoughts dark and churning, before I spoke again. "I thought it couldn't get any worse after the tree fell and my world was shattered. But that just happened to my body. Now, I see what being shattered really means. My life will never be the same."

Dave glanced over at me, solemn.

Jesus, why did you let them take my job? A lone tear started down my cheek. As a factory nurse, I'd understood what had to be done and how to do it. In helping the workers, I'd found a sense of purpose and felt good about myself. Now, I just felt scared.

But scared of what? Was it really just about not having enough money to pay the bills... or something else?

I paused a few minutes to consider the question.

With Dave's income and my budgeting skills, we wouldn't starve. And with the house and cars paid off, we'd always have a roof over our heads and a way to get where we needed to go.

So if it wasn't the fear of having enough money, what then? That God had grown weary of helping me? Not likely, after everything He'd done to bring me back to life and convince me He was real.

Then it hit me. The prospect of having to start over in my present condition, not poverty or losing God's favor was what frightened me most. I trusted God, just not myself.

When the tree had struck my head, rendering me unconscious, I'd suffered a severe concussion, and undergone sixteen lengthy surgeries. After the most recent, an eight hour anesthesia laden ordeal, I'd been driven back into the fog. My mind, like the proverbial monkey tied to a pole but jumping in slow motion, now lurched from one thought to the next barely able to bring them into sharp focus. It had been hard enough to return to a job I already knew. I'd surprised myself then. Now, I would be forced to swim into uncharted waters. But could I?

STARTING OVER

Tears were starting again by the time Dave pulled into our driveway and wheeled me into the house. I averted my gaze to hide them.

"I'm going upstairs to cook dinner," he said.

"Okay, I'll be up in a few minutes."

Dave nodded as he ascended the stairs.

Using my crutches, I stood on my left leg, pivoted, and dropped onto the loveseat. It had been several days since I'd really spoken to Jesus. "Can't get any guidance if I don't spend time with you, can I?" I whispered.

Taking a deep breath, I closed my eyes and opened my hands, turning them upward, waiting to feel Jesus' presence. I sat for a few minutes allowing my heart to open before I felt the first hint of warmth forming in my chest.

"Thank you for being with me." A lone tear slid down my face. "I can never thank you enough for saving my life…but how can I start over when I still can't think clearly?'

A fan whirred from across the room.

You already know. I felt rather than heard the message.

I started to go over what I knew from experience. *Jesus and the Holy Spirit are real. They're right here with me, part of me. In the worst situations, They bring me peace. Not just any peace, but one so full of love, joy, and hope, it leaves me wanting for nothing. They will continue to give me exactly what I need to draw me closer to Them and create something new and positive in my life. Even here in the fog, Jesus and the Holy Spirit are with me- loving and guiding me. I'm not alone.*

I stopped reviewing and opened my eyes. Just this week Jesus had sent so many wonderful people to help me. There was my precious friend, Hope, the Safety Manager, a straight talking lawyer, my dear Dr. Bolling, and…

I glanced up to see my husband slowly descending the stairs.

"I don't want to interrupt you but dinner's ready."

"I was wrong to think God might have grown tired of helping me," I said.

"I don't know about God, but *I've* been right here since the tree fell on you."

I stared at Dave, perhaps seeing him clearly for the first time in days. His sad eyes spoke volumes about my neglect.

"More than anyone," I said. Blinded by worry, I'd barely noticed the one person who'd stood by me through it all. I remembered something he'd told me about what happened that terrible night in the woods. Overwhelmed at the sight of my grotesque injuries and the woman he loved drenched from head to toe in blood, my husband had struggled to determine what he could do. Suddenly, in a moment of total clarity, he knew. He had to keep me from moving. So, while I'd fought to sit up, he held me down.

A light went on. "If it hadn't been for you, I would have been paralyzed. I'd be in a wheel chair," I said. "Dr. Court told me if they'd moved me before he inserted the rods to stabilize my spinal fractures, my back would have folded like a piece of paper." I shuddered at the thought. "I think God must have been guiding you, telling you what you needed to do to protect me. I'm just grateful, you were listening."

The late afternoon sun was flickering through the window and illuminating Dave's handsome face. Strength shown in his pale blue eyes as the corners of his mouth curled into the beginning of a smile.

"Let's not go upstairs just yet," I said.

"No?" He came over and settled down next to me. I leaned into him, resting my head on his chest. He reached around me pulling me closer. I could hear his heart beating slowly. "I love you," I said, tilting my face up and kissing him on the cheek.

"I love you, too," he whispered, stroking my arm.

We'd taken on the impossible before. With God's help, maybe we could do it again working together.

WHOMP DAY

It was Saturday in late September and about a month after they'd taken my job when Pierce had an idea. "Hey, why don't we all go out to our favorite Italian place and celebrate 'Whomp Day.' It'll be my treat."

"Whomp Day?" I said.

"You know, *Whomp,* as in the anniversary of the day the tree fell on you. It's September 26th. We've made it through a whole year."

"So it is," Dave said, looking surprised.

"Yup, time flies…," Pierce gave us a half smile.

Pierce drove us to the restaurant where the hostess seated us in a corner booth. He ordered wine with our dinners and made a toast. "To the three of us!" He raised his glass. "To a better year ahead."

I clinked my glass against the others. "To a better year," I said. "I'm glad we're marking our passage through that dark time. We did it. We survived." Dave and Pierce nodded and smiled, but my own chest was growing tighter. Something was weighing me down.

As Pierce and Dave talked about their own interests, my mind drifted back to legal matters. The prospect of pursuing a Worker's Compensation claim against my employer was creating a knot in my stomach. In the moments I'd been able to turn things over to God, I'd found some relief, but when I contemplated legal action, the knot tightened. Now I prayed silently for guidance.

Letting the Holy Spirit and my feelings direct me, over dinner I came to a decision.

"I've made up my mind," I said, sipping my merlot.

Both raising an eyebrow, Pierce and Dave looked over at me.

"If it's all the same with you, I've decided not to go ahead with the worker's comp claim. It'll just stress us out and keep me fixated on what I've lost. It's not the positive focus any of us need." I looked fondly at my husband and son sitting across the table. "Anyway, what's more important than our peace of mind?"

"I'm so happy to hear you say that," Dave said, sighing. "I doubt Pierce or I could stand a legal battle. After the two-month ordeal in the hospital and everything since, I don't have the strength to take on a fight."

"Me either," said Pierce. "Just working at the Police Department's enough."

"I kind of thought that might be the case, so I'm going to go ahead and apply for disability instead. We just don't know when I'll be able to go back to work. I'm going to see that attorney tomorrow to see what she has to say."

"Good," Dave said, looking relieved.

The next morning, Pierce drove me the forty miles to my appointment.

"Hi, I'm Rachel," the attorney said and invited us into her office. "Won't you have a seat?"

I crutched over to the easy chair in front of her desk and flopped down. Pierce took my crutches and handed her the synopsis I'd written. It documented my injuries and surgeries as well as my triumphant return to work and subsequent termination.

The attorney shook her head as she read. Then taking off her glasses, she looked up. "This is unbelievable. I've been doing this kind of work for thirty years, and I've never seen injuries this bad. You don't need to retain me to get disability. I'm going to type a cover letter to go with your outline, and my secretary will help you file the application today. There's no charge for either. I hope you won't have to wait too long before they approve you. The system is so backlogged it could take the better part of a year. Call me if for some crazy reason they deny you. You can hire me then."

"I'm really hoping I can go back to work when my leg heals," I said quietly.

She studied my face for a minute. "I can tell you're a strong woman, but you deserve to enjoy your life," she said. "You've worked long enough."

"Thank you," I said, stunned by her compassion. "Thank you for your honesty and your willingness to help."

Just when I felt sure the legal system was completely broken, along came an attorney like Rachel.

QUIETING THE MIND

A few days later, Sandi picked me up and we drove north for an appointment with Dr. Norton. It had been two months since the eight-hour surgery to reconstruct my right leg again, and was time to check on the status of my bone graft.

Despite the sunny fall day, in the waiting room, I fidgeted in my seat. It was hard to relax knowing from experience that some grafts didn't take. What if mine was one of them?

Sandi scrutinized me from where she sat across from me.

Anxious thoughts were making it hard to pray. I closed my eyes and focused on my breath. It was a technique I'd learned years before to relax.

Ten minutes later, I opened them and smiled at my friend. "Much better," I said.

"It's good to keep your focus in the present. That's where you'll find Jesus and His peace."

Her comment struck a chord. Experience had taught me if I settled into the moment, that simple act brought greater clarity and peace. It worked in much the same way as had watching the parade of people who'd passed outside my Trauma room door. Observing them had been like watching a movie, keeping my focus in the present and me calm.

The x-ray tech called me back and took some pictures of my leg. A few minutes later Dr. Norton bustled in, smiling and shaking my hand, before he sat down to study them.

I held my breath and waited for the news.

"The bone graft is doing well," he announced, looking pleased, "but you'll still need to stay on crutches for at least another month, while it continues to heal."

"Yes!" I shouted. The news was an answer to prayer. It meant however slow and awkward my gait or painful the process, I would walk.

Back at home and remembering Sandi's advice, I did my best to quiet my mind each day before I prayed. Doing so helped me connect with God's Spirit more quickly and deeply. After praying, I took a moment to listen. A customer in the health food store may have said it best. "When we pray, we talk to God, when we quiet our minds, we listen. There's a time and a place for both."

For a long time I'd ignored the second half of that equation. I'd talked, but forgotten to listen. No wonder God had had so much trouble getting my attention.

THE STAGE OF ANGER

Late in October, a month after Whomp Day and two months after losing my job, I still walked with crutches and balanced on an emotional tightwire.

Why did I feel so bad?

Jesus had given me hope and strength, but I felt pain. No matter how hard I tried to focus on the good, I couldn't pretend that losing my job and so much of my mobility wasn't agony. I had to take the time to grieve.

What I hadn't bargained on was my original loss being joined by so many others. It wasn't just the loss of my mobility, but the loss of my income, mental clarity, physical comfort, independence, ability to provide for Pierce's education, and self-confidence. It was the loss of my ability to take care of our home, mow the lawn, paint, change a light bulb, shop, walk the dog, and feed the birds. If those weren't enough, I saw losses mounting up for Dave and Pierce, too. My husband, often in pain from years of heavy lifting at work, struggled to do his job as well as the household chores I'd always handled before. My son who rarely complained, now grumbled about feeling tired and a pain in his gut that didn't go away. No wonder my well of sadness felt like a bottomless pit.

I'd counted on my new faith to speed up the process of moving on. It hadn't. While I could feel Jesus' spirit working overtime behind the scenes to keep me from despairing and bolstering my spirit, there were many times when the emotional pain threatened to overwhelm me. Would it?

Dr. Kubler-Ross, who originally described "the stages of grief" as denial, anger, bargaining, depression, acceptance, was right. Those of us who suffered loss didn't always travel through those stages in order. Nor did we visit them once and move on.

There was one in particular that continued to plague me. Anger. While the anger motivated me better than the fear, it was not a happy place to be. It drove me, like an amphetamine, just not in the direction I wanted to go.

It gnawed at me and made me want to run screaming through the house. Though it felt good to let it out, it also unnerved me. Shouldn't I be doing better than this? Was I going crazy? Losing control? I reflected on all Jesus had done to help me survive and wondered if I was letting Him down.

That thought made me feel even worse.

Granted, friends had pushed me to express my outrage, suggesting I rightfully deserved to be mad at my former employer. "Get an attorney and take legal action," many had prodded, their words sounding far more furious than my own.

But I'd made up my mind. I wasn't going to take the vengeful path, believing that in the process of giving anger too much of a voice, I might get sucked down by it.

Truthfully, more than once in the fall of 2010, I'd gotten mired in resentment and felt defeated. During that period, when people tried to tell me how lucky I was not to be worse off or how I needed to stay positive, it riled me. I knew they meant well, but their words seemed to be suggesting I just needed to quit whining and move on.

When they discounted my feelings or pushed me to feel better than I actually did, that only left me less willing to share my true emotions the next time we spoke.

I was praying one afternoon when it came to me. I didn't really want to give up the anger. It energized and motivated me in a way that the sadness never had. It kept my panic in check. It felt good.

I sensed some other feelings lurking just beneath the anger. Fear, hurt, envy, and pain.

Letting myself feel all of them made me remember Mrs. Marcus, a friend of my parents when I was in high school. I'd thought the world of and admired her, so it made me sad when my mom wrote me at college to tell me she'd lost her husband. "She's really having a tough time getting over it," she'd said.

A year later and at home for a visit, I asked my mother about Mrs. Marcus.

"She's still not over it though it's been over a year," Mom said.

As young as I was, I understood. "Mrs. Marcus still needs to grieve. She didn't just lose a husband, she lost her soul mate. She might need a little more time to get over losing someone so special."

Two more years went by, and I finished college and came home. Though I hadn't been in touch with her, I had the impulse to go visit Mrs. Marcus.

"You know it's the strangest thing," Mom said. "She moved to New York City, went back to college, finished a master's degree, started a whole new career, and got married. Everyone says she's never been happier."

"It doesn't surprise me. Good for her," I said, smiling to myself.

If ever there was someone who was a testament to the value of grieving fully, it was Mrs. Marcus. Knowing how much her life had changed for the better encouraged me. It felt as if she were saying "don't be afraid of your feelings, experience them. Try to understand what they're telling you." I took to heart her amazing triumph and transformation and decided to get down to the business of really grieving too.

Job's words seemed to express how I felt. "Therefore I will not keep silent; I will speak out in the anguish of my spirit, I will complain in the bitterness of my soul." (Job 7:11 NIV)

Three months after the screws had broken in my tibia, and the bone came apart, Dr. Norton sanctioned me to drive again. Once he did, I couldn't wait to take myself to a place I'd rarely visited. A place where I hoped I could return to my own little corner of heaven just by entering the door. Church.

Over the next several weeks, of the five churches I attended, one in particular drew me in. It was the church where Leah, my friend from Great Foods Manufacturing was a member, and it was one of the places I felt Jesus' presence the strongest and witnessed His love most clearly reflected in the congregation.

On my first visit, I pulled up in front and crutched to the front door. A young woman opened it, grinned at me, and gave me a hug. "Welcome to our church," she said. An usher guided me to a seat near the front.

I can still see that simple white sanctuary, decorated with its brightly colored handmade wall hangings with a stage in the front. The moment I settled into my seat and the musicians began to play, my eyes welled with tears. With the first murmur of Jesus' name, they spilled in earnest down my cheeks.

My tears surprised me. It had been weeks since I'd cried. I could hear others around me weeping, too. Feeling Jesus' Spirit so strongly, and surrounded by others who felt it too, I could finally let it out.

At the end of his sermon, the pastor invited us. "If you have anything you need to heal, now is the time to come to the front. If it's an injury, an illness, high blood pressure, a relationship, your finances, or depression. Whatever it is, there are people waiting up here to help you."

A few people got up and moved forward. The pastor paused. "Don't worry about what other people think. If you need help, come and get what you need." The musicians kept on playing as singers chanted. "We love you, we need you, Lord."

Get up. It was the voice inside me. I got to my feet in spite of myself and crutched slowly to the front.

A burly man with a shaved head and a kind face approached me. He gave me a gentle smile and placed one hand on my forehead and the other on my shoulder. He leaned in, and began to pray. Quietly, at first, then in a language I'd never heard. Strange, yet soothing.

Speaking in tongues.

At first nothing happened. My grief stuck in my throat. *Jesus, help me release the pain.*

Nothing.

The man continued to pray. "Unloose this fear," he shouted as the music pulsed louder.

Out of the corner of my eye, a muscular man with dark skin threw himself onto the steps that led to the altar. His shoulders shook with sobs. A woman placed a blanket over him, but otherwise left him alone to cry. At the sight of him, a high pitched sound escaped my throat. The armor that held my emotions in check began to crack. Tightness in my chest had become unbearable, the man's voice, louder. "With all you've lost, you aren't sure what you have to offer."

My God, how did he know?

My throat gave a painful wrench as the dam burst. I wept, broken-hearted, for my once athletic body. I cried in anguish for the loss of my nursing career. I wept for how hard I was struggling to make a new life, and because I didn't know if I could.

Wave after wave of sorrow hit me and convulsed my body with sobs. Others around me cried too. It was healing at its messiest. Together we coughed, gagged, sputtered, wailed, sobbed and cried out. But I was far too lost in my own grief to care.

The voice that prayed over me reached a crescendo as the room swirled. I lost my balance and found strong arms waiting to catch me. They eased me down to the floor. Someone tucked a nice, soft blanket around my body. I lay on the carpet, wrapped in my cocoon, trembling, but devoid of pain.

For some time, I lay without moving. Then I opened my eyes. An usher helped me to my feet and handed me my crutches. I made my way slowly back to my seat before crutching out into the sunshine and the car. My body felt weightless.

For a few days, I lay limp on the couch, empty and wrung out, but at peace.

A few weeks after that, I drove back to the church and went through it all over. I wanted to release what was left of the pain.

From then on, I did most of my grieving from my seat near the front of the church. There, I swayed to the music, prayed, wept, and cried out to Jesus. I let myself feel everything, from anger to despair, and as I did, my heart opened. I cried with thankfulness and joy.

Love overflowed my heart as I sent healing energy to all the people who'd gone to the front of the church to be healed. Then I pictured it flowing to Pierce and Dave and all the others I knew that were in need.

As the weeks passed, it was easier to cry. It was also easier to smile. My body felt lighter and lighter as if I'd grabbed each heavy layer of pain and dropped it to the floor like a winter coat I no longer needed. Emotional healing was becoming a reality.

MESSAGES FROM GOD

few weeks later, I drove to a neighboring town and parked in front of the health food store where I'd volunteered regularly. I'd ridden the forty-odd miles to have a session with an "energetic" healer the owner had told me about. "I think he'll really help you release what remains of the emotional pain you took on during your time in the hospital,"

"I've been doing a lot of that lately, but I still have a way to go."

Ready to continue the process, I arrived promptly at the time of my appointment. A slim man with shaggy brown hair greeted me warmly at the door. He led me back to a little room while I followed slowly on crutches.

"Tell me what's been happening," he said.

For the first hour, we just sat and talked.

I told him about the tree falling, and how God had brought me hope in the hospital and done miraculous things to make sure I lived. It excited me to share that part of my story.

"And lately?"

I told him how my employer had taken my job, and about the sadness I'd felt. Without interrupting, he listened, making notes. Every now and then he looked up and commented.

"Tell me about your relationships with Pierce and Dave and how things are going there."

"I guess I've been worrying about my son. He hasn't been well since the accident, and lately he's gotten worse. He never eats until late at night or gets any sleep. He works twelve-hour shifts as a police officer. I try to get him to take better care of himself, but he never does." I could feel the tension rising in my chest. "I'm afraid he's going to get really sick if he doesn't change."

"Advice not solicited is heard as criticism," the healer said. There was a gentle, yet matter of fact tone to his voice.

"You're right about that. Pierce and Dave both tell me they feel like I nag them sometimes when I'm just concerned and trying to help."

"When you have a strong emotional reaction to the people or things around you, consider that those feelings might actually relate to what's going on inside *you*."

That fit with the fear that drove me to encourage Pierce to get more rest.

"Intense feelings can also be messages from God. He may be trying to get your attention for some specific purpose or just to draw you closer. When fear comes up, thank Him for the message. Then try to figure out what your fear is telling you about yourself or your situation. Under no circumstance should you act on it as you usually do. Before you act or speak always ask, what is my motivation?"

"Messages from God? I hadn't really thought of intense emotions that way."

"Just remember. Your only job with your son is to love him," he continued. "He's God's child. In fact, that's your only real purpose with everyone who comes into your life."

Then he said something that grabbed my attention. "Lara, we're not meant to suffer."

That thought comforted me. It resonated with my belief that God loved me and wanted me to be happy.

When I got home that evening, I couldn't wait to tell Dave about my session. "He says unsolicited advice is seen as criticism. He told me not to nag Pierce."

I could see by the look in his eye my husband must have thought the healer was onto something.

"Maybe you ought to write some notes," he said. I could tell he was hoping from now on I would nag him a little less too.

The next day with the healer's remarks about messages from God echoing in my ears, I began to edit the chapters I'd written earlier in the year that spoke of my preparations to return to work. Mentally, I noted all the roadblocks that had thwarted me and the panic I'd felt in trying to push through them.

I sat thinking and a light went on. Had the roadblocks and the panic been messages? Had God been trying to slow my return to work? And once back, had He pulled me out? My chest warmed in confirmation. God's messages had been right in front of me. I just hadn't wanted to see them.

Pretty amazing.

A friend of mine who'd suffered a terrible head injury once said, "I just wish God would speak English."

While God may not have been speaking English, He'd been guiding me all the same.

"If you'd known then what would happen, would you still have gone back to work?" Jenny asked one afternoon.

I thought for a moment. "That's a hard one. I certainly wouldn't have knowingly set myself up to re-break my leg or suffer the worst surgery of all and be stuck at home for another four months on crutches. Yet, neither would I have wanted to jeopardize my job by waiting longer to go back to work. Ultimately, I think God let me return because He knew I needed to say goodbye to my friends at the factories and realize the goal I'd set for myself in the hospital. I think He did it to give me closure."

"Any regrets?" she asked.

"Not really. Going back gave me some peace. It was worth the pain."

She smiled and leaned over the table. "How about this? What if God brought you and me together at Great Foods Manufacturing because He knew you would be needing our friendship to face what was coming?"

"That's a good one," I said, "and not that hard to believe." Three weeks after my first session with the healer, I drove back to see him again. This time he talked more about addressing my fear.

"Pain and fear are not bad. They're messages that make us go within to find our connection with God," he said. "Whatever the question, the answer is love, God's love for us. Everything that happens is a gift. It's His way of reminding us that we're not separate, that we can trust Him. God's actions are often like love in disguise."

"Even the tree falling?"

"Everything."

"I've long thought He used my accident to shape me into a better person and show me He was real. To let me know, He had my back."

He nodded and the corners of his mouth curled into a smile. "God always uses our experiences without exception to teach us out of love."

I couldn't believe what I heard him saying. For months I'd felt God nudging me to focus on the good that would come from the tree falling, and more recently from losing my job. I'd decided Jesus was using both to help me grow into someone more like Him. That thought had made me feel special, privileged. Now I heard confirmation.

As I drove the long way home, I considered all the problems in my life that had sent me into a tailspin. How much easier might it have been if I'd seen them as loving messages from a God who just wanted me to grow wiser and stronger and rely on Him more?

FORGIVENESS

From the time I first opened my eyes in the hospital I understood that healing was about making the right choices. I could hold fast to signs of hope or I could despair. Find new purpose and see meaning in the smallest things I did for others or get depressed. Seek a connection with God or go it alone.

In early November 2010, fourteen months after the tree had fallen and three after losing my job, I turned my attention toward forgiving. I had to if I wanted to move forward. But if forgiving meant letting the ones who'd taken my job off the hook, I wasn't sure I could.

My sister, brother, sister-in-law, nieces, and mother came for a visit. It was the first time I'd seen them in almost a year. All month I'd looked forward to their coming, but by the second day of their stay, I felt down. Still on crutches, I watched them skipping joyfully out the door to take Marley for a walk and bustling in the kitchen to cook our Thanksgiving dinner. Instead of being grateful for all they were doing to help, my heart broke.

I barely noticed eating dinner. What I remembered instead was a few of them talking about what they appreciated most about their jobs.

My eyes burned. *How can they talk about job fulfillment when I've just lost my entire career?*

The next morning, overcome with emotion and too uncomfortable to be around them, I mumbled some excuse and left everyone at home with Dave and Pierce. I cried, my chest heaving, as I drove down the rural highway.

For a while I felt awash in pain, the last vestiges of grief. Then the river of tears stopped flowing and the tightness in my chest eased.

For years the relationship with my family had been a loving but complicated one. Now I'd let their words hurt me. Contemplating my painful reaction, I recognized the need to forgive them, too. I knew they had never intentionally hurt me, but my feelings of loss were still too raw. I couldn't talk myself out of them.

The drive took me back to the health food store where I pulled into a space in front. The owner had given me a key and I crutched in. The place looked dark and deserted. I made my way to the couch in the back and lay down, savoring the quiet and calm of that space. I prayed, offering up all my hurts and resentments to Jesus. "Lord, please, fill me with so much love, that there's no room for envy, anger or fear," I whispered. "Let me see everyone just as you see them."

I was lying there in the silence when I heard the lock click and someone strolled in. It was the healer. His eyes twinkled as he stood over me.

"What are you doing here the day after Thanksgiving?" I asked, sitting up, happy to see him.

"I was about to ask you the same thing. I had to see a client over this way and had the impulse to stop by to see if you were at the shop today. Didn't your family come?"

"Yes," I said. "But when I watched them doing all the things I wanted to do but couldn't, it broke my heart."

His face remained unchanged. "How else did you feel?"

I thought for a moment before I replied. "As if I didn't fit in. Like I'd become invisible and lost everything."

"Did you tell them?"

"No, I just left. By the time I got here, I felt better, so I lay down and talked to Jesus instead."

"And what was Jesus' message?"

"That I wasn't alone or any less valuable. That I was more than my job. That I didn't have to rely on the approval of others. That what I'd lost was nothing in comparison with what I'd found."

He smiled. "You can also think of the ones who hurt you as powerful teachers. Pain pushes you to go within and find your connection with God. I hope that will help you let go of resentment and forgive. Just remember when fear comes up, go straight into trusting God, into your heart. The longest distance is the eighteen inches from your head to your heart," he said, laughing. "Our job in this life is so simple. We just need to love and return to God."

At home, everyone had been cleaning the house, and it sparkled in every corner. My mouth dropped open as I looked around. "This place looks amazing. Thank you so much." I stood motionless, stunned by their love and generosity. I grabbed each one in turn and pulled them firmly into a hug, glad they were with me.

That night I watched a documentary. A man was saying, "If you don't forgive, you are like a dry leaf that is swept away." Just as he suggested, lately I'd felt resentment forcefully sucking the life out of me, leaving me rigid, like that dry leaf.

I'd already seen how often anger and its close cousin, depression, erupted out of fear. I'd also witnessed how quickly those same emotions faded whenever I chose to focus on loving myself and others. Since life was just a series of choices, I should be able to let go of worry and resentment anytime I chose to love. That thought gave me hope.

My family left, and Jenny and I got together for lunch. "Little by little I'm learning to forgive more and worry less," I said.

"All of us face uncertainty every day. If we want an excuse to doubt God, worry, or resent others, there are dozens available." There was no hint of judgment in her voice.

She's right, in these things too I have a choice. Still emotional, my eyes welled with tears. I could choose to trust God and give everyone, myself included, a break or focus on fear and how we'd all fallen short. I knew which I wanted to do. Anyway, if Jesus had been willing to forgive, so would I.

Over the next few weeks, sage words on forgiving kept showing up in the books I read and the emails people sent me. God was pretty clever that way.

One passage encouraged me to look past the words and actions of an individual, no matter how awful they were, to the place inside them where they longed for the same things I did. Another prodded me to see everyone's words and actions as coming from either love or fear.

I thought of my boss and how fear had likely played a role in what she'd done. Maybe she'd taken my job knowing that otherwise she risked losing her own? Wasn't that how it worked in businesses these days? Follow the rules, even the unspoken ones, and above all make certain no one compromised the bottom line. My hospital bills had been exorbitant. No one had to tell me what that must have meant to my employer. Viewing my boss as fearful rather than cruel helped me begin to see her in a new light.

One night I dreamed I went back to Great Foods Manufacturing. As I made my way with careful steps into the older plant, I saw that they'd relocated my clinic to an open area in the middle of the warehouse floor. Dust and dirt covered my once spotless desk and treatment table, and someone had piled file folders on the chairs. *What have they done to the place? Doesn't anyone care? And where is the nurse who's supposed to be working here?*

When I awoke, I replayed the dream until I understood. I didn't belong at my nursing job any more. That chapter had been closed. It was time to move on.

Forgiveness had begun.

With fall in the air, I knew more than ever that God wanted me alive, helping others, and learning to forgive. Beyond that, I hadn't a clue what my new life would look like. I prayed and asked Jesus to guide me and give me strength and courage. What surfaced was the longing to tell my story. Not just to share it one to one, but with a group. My heart raced. Given my history with stage fright, could I? And if I could, would it bring the ones who listened, hope?

After Thanksgiving, I attended a conference at Jenny's church. While my family had often fallen silent when I spoke of the miracles God had given me, it was different at my friend's church. There, the members greeted me with welcoming smiles and, seeing my crutches, asked what had happened.

"A tree fell on me," I replied, not planning to elaborate.

They stopped smiling. "And you survived?" one said. Something in her voice suggested she wanted to hear more.

I recounted how I'd called out in desperation to God, and to my amazement, He'd answered. How in the midst of desolation and pain, Jesus had brought unspeakable hope and joy. How He'd filled me so full of love, I'd had to share it with everyone who showed up in my hospital room.

No one batted an eye. None acted as if they thought I'd suffered delusions, been drugged or naive. Instead, they grinned from ear to ear and grabbed my hand, saying "thank you, Jesus." Elation filled me.

The featured speaker that day turned out to be a young woman who was delivering her testimony only seven months after losing her equally young husband to cancer. She inspired me in her willingness to put herself out there to share something so personal and painful. I vowed to start thinking about my own.

A week later, I met Hope for lunch. We'd been catching up when she changed the subject. "I really don't know how you made it through everything that happened." she said, her eyes brimming with tears.

"I made it because in the hospital in my darkest moment, Jesus showed me that even in the worst situation He was with me. I wasn't alone. Knowing that transformed me. After that, I knew to look for His love, peace, and messages in everything that happened."

I took a sip of my tea. "And I made it because people like you answered God's call. Where would I be if you and Sandi hadn't put your lives on hold to help me? Who else would have carted me hundreds of miles to physical therapy and doctors' appointments? And who would have suited up to give me my first shower in nearly six months?"

"Like I've said, sometimes God whispers in someone's ear. That time, it just happened to be me."

I smiled at her. "I've told my story to so many individuals. But lately I've been thinking I should share it with a larger circle."

Hope looked at me and smiled. "I think you should. I've been in some pretty dark places myself, and the stories that others shared on overcoming their own trials always encouraged me and helped put mine in perspective."

"Hmm, I'd love to hear more when you're ready to tell me."

"You will, but that's for another day."

We sat for a moment in silence before I spoke again. "I know you've said you're not much of a believer, but I think everyone has their own relationship with and understanding of God. I like to think the Holy Spirit is refining mine day by day. Lately I've been thinking more and more that Jesus' Spirit doesn't just visit us when we're going through a rough time. Neither do we have to wait until after we die to be with Him. Rather He's always with us, part of us. That's why we can go within to find Him whenever we want. It's like visiting our own little corner of heaven."

"I admire you for not letting what happened make you bitter or give up."

"I appreciate that, but this has never really been about me, but what God did for me, working through you and all the others. You're the real heroes."

Time with Hope always flew by too fast, and before I knew it, it was time to go.

Days went by and December rolled around and I worried less and less about money. We still had food, a house, and clothing. We still paid our bills. With God's help and that of family and friends we'd made it through the year. Without extra money to spend, I'd had to focus far more on simple pleasures, those like enjoying friends and family, singing, playing my guitar, writing, reading, and talking with God and far less on shopping. Having less turned out to be a blessing of a different kind, what the healer had called "love in disguise."

It was nearly Christmas and time for one last session with him.

"I'm a little uneasy not knowing what my new life is going to look like, or what I should do next," I said. "But on the positive side, the ginkgo, rosemary, bacopa, and other herbs I've been taking have been working their magic. The fog is lifting and my mind is getting clearer. I'm starting to feel more confident in myself again."

"Good. Don't fear change, trust it. The world around us is in a cycle of rapid transformation, and that scares most people. Remember, nothing is permanent. Only God is. But we're all connected with Him. Pain comes when we believe we're separated, but that idea is just an illusion. Until you get that, you'll continue to have experiences to show you. Remember, when you're afraid, leave your thoughts and go straight into your heart. Choose to love. It's the antidote for fear. And don't forget, you don't have to do everything on your own. 'But seek ye first the kingdom of God.'" (Matthew 6:33 KJV)

I nodded.

"Remember when we met after Thanksgiving? That day you thought you'd lost everything." He paused. "You hadn't, had you?"

"No, God has given me more than I ever imagined."

GOD WHISPERS

A few weeks later on a Sunday, my legs and back ached so much from standing, I couldn't drive to Jenny's church. Sad at the thought of missing the service and not seeing my friend, I called someone else who I knew would be missing her service. Ann, my mother in law, answered. The doctor had recently diagnosed her with stage four breast cancer, and she'd been ailing.

"Hi Ann, how're you feeling?"

"Oh, hey darling. It's good to hear from you. I'm trying to do better," she drawled in a weak voice. "I'm in the kitchen making some breakfast." She sounded tired, but determined. I knew how she felt.

"I'm glad to see you're up and able to eat."

We talked about Dave and Pierce and her friends. The more I focused on Ann and forgot myself, the more I felt our spirits join and lift together. Before long we were both laughing and joking as we had so many times before.

"I'm glad you called," she said.

"I am too. I've really missed you."

A few weeks later, making good on my promise to write notes to the people in the hospitals who'd been especially kind to me, I called County Hospital to get Dr. Lassiter's address.

"He's no longer here," the operator said.

Determined to thank him, I googled his name and found a cell number with a Colorado address. I'd forgotten he'd mentioned he was from there. Without hesitation, I dialed the number and left a voice mail.

To my surprise, he rang me right back.

"I'm so glad to hear from you, Lara. I remember you well. You were someone I really admired, because you always seemed so positive and strong."

"Thank you for saying so, and believe me I'd love nothing more than to take credit, but I can't. I honestly believe God gave me the will to keep going, often by bringing me support from good people like you. Otherwise, I'm pretty sure I would have thrown in the towel."

"You think it was God's doing? I was about to say it was your positive attitude that attracted good people to you."

"But who gave me that outlook in the midst of so much misery and pain? The truth is, before I called out to God and felt His Spirit come to me, I had little hope left." I paused, remembering. "But that's not the reason I called you. I had to tell you how much your kindness meant to me in that dark place. There were only a handful of doctors who treated me as if I was still a full-fledged human being and made me feel as good about myself as you did."

"You have no idea how good that makes me feel to know I helped. Are you doing okay?"

"I'm good, recovering from a bone graft and in some pain, but up on crutches. How about you? Are you back in Colorado? The operator at County Hospital told me you weren't there anymore."

"I'm still here in the same city, just not at the hospital." His voice sounded slow, despondent. "I've had a hard two years since I saw you."

"Why? What happened?" There was something wrong.

"I got caught up in the politics at the hospital. I trusted someone who turned out to be unethical and didn't say no when I should have…"

I could hear the pain in his voice. Silently, I asked the Holy Spirit to guide me. *Give me the words to comfort him.*

"I'm a pretty good judge of character. From the first time you came into my room on the Trauma Unit, I knew you were a really good person and a wonderful doctor. Without hearing the particulars, I already know you never meant to harm anyone. I'm so sorry you've been having such a difficult time."

"You can't imagine. You're obviously a believer in God. I pray, but I admit I've been really mad at him lately. I've thought He must be punishing me. Have you ever felt that way?"

"I definitely got a bit mad at God when my boss took my nursing job away. It felt like the end of the road, as if He might have abandoned me. But eventually I've come to see things differently. In fact, now I don't blame Him at all. Quite the contrary, I see how He used even the worst situations to teach me and draw me closer to Him. God doesn't punish us, He loves us, Dr. Lassiter, though I can certainly understand why you might feel otherwise. Don't believe it for a moment. I'm sure He wants you to be happy, despite any mistakes you've made," I paused.

"How did you get over being mad at Him?"

"I reminded myself of all the gifts God had brought me when I saw nothing but despair. Anyway, I knew how much I needed Him. It didn't seem productive to stay mad for long. Over time, I've come to realize that even the loss of my job wasn't by chance, that God's been very busy behind the scenes helping me use what happened for good." I took a breath. "So if you want my advice, it's to identify everything that makes you feel grateful and give credit where it's due. Spend some time talking to God. Ask for His love and guidance. Then wait for a message. Finally, stop blaming yourself. That's difficult for people like us, who're hard on themselves, but you need to try. You made some mistakes, but you're human and worthy of God's love. Adding guilt and shame to the mix will only make matters worse."

"I think I know some of what God's been telling me," Dr. Lassiter said, "but I wish he'd used some other means of communicating."

"What do you think He was saying?"

"That I needed to learn to say no. That I didn't have to worry so much about pleasing other people. Those sorts of things."

"Those sorts of things are no small matters. It sounds like God might have been telling you to trust yourself, to realize that you have tremendous capability and worth. That He's with you and, like me, you're stronger than you think."

"You've helped me a lot today," he said. "I'm feeling more hopeful that I can get through this and that something good will come out of it."

"I'm just giving you back what you gave me. Your kindness got me through some of the darkest days at County Hospital. Now, you deserve some blessings, too, so I'm going to pray that you feel God's peace, Dr. Lassiter."

"Please, call me Adam. There shouldn't be any titles or barriers between us."

"If you ever want to talk just reach out," I said. "I'd love to hear from you for any reason."

"And you can call any time," he said. The despair had left his voice.

When I hung up I knew it wasn't by accident that I'd called Dr. Lassiter. This time, God had whispered in my ear. I had come full circle.

RETURNING TO WHOLENESS

By December 2010 and over three months after the surgery to reconstruct my leg, Dr. Norton declared my shin bone healed well enough for full weight bearing. The graft had taken hold. My leg would be much stronger. I was thrilled beyond words to be back on my feet.

"Thank you, Jesus. I trust whatever plans you have for me now."

This time I would pay attention to my body's pain messages. I never wanted to go through another leg reconstruction surgery again.

In January, Social Security Disability came through after only three months, a New Year's present from the government. Pierce and Dave joined me in thanking God. No doubt, Dr. Bolling's letters of outrage, topping the three inch stack of grisly medical documentation, also had something to do with the government's shockingly prompt reply.

Dave continued to go to work and do more than his fair share of the household chores. Pierce, no longer a rookie, started his second year at the Police Department and bought a motorcycle to ride on his days off.

I had come to think of my life in two parts: the one before the tree fell and what came after. As the days passed, my body and spirit began to relax, and my mind grew clearer. I still viewed every day as a gift, a gift I might not have had if Jesus hadn't made His presence known and brought me the hope, faith, and courage I needed to heal and start over.

I continued to quiet my mind and pray to stay more firmly rooted in the present and connected with that still small voice within that I had come to know as the Holy Spirit. As time passed, emotional wounds slowly healed and despite the pain in my legs, ankle, and back, life went on.

I persevered writing my story and joined a small group of local writers for help on polishing my rough draft. They gave me useful suggestions while providing a diverse and colorful new circle of friends.

Later that year, I started working out in a new rehab facility in town alongside other clients who'd also been badly injured. There, I pedaled, stretched, and lifted weights, shouting encouragement to the others who, still in the early stages of their recovery, winced and cried out in pain. Each day before I left, I stopped to give each of them a hug and offer a prayer.

"Thank you," they said, tearful and clinging to me.

Exercise session over, I grabbed my crutches to cover the distance between the building and my car. Though I could walk short distances without them, using crutches allowed me to cover more ground before the pain in my ankle got to be too much and I had to sit down. My body would never be the same, but thanks to God, it was definitely getting stronger. I made it a point to focus only on what I could still do while ignoring the rest.

As some of our financial pressures were easing, the second anniversary of the tree falling loomed. It brought memories from the two hospitals pouring back, sadness along with them. The memories became such an obsession I drove to Regional Medical to visit Dr. Bolling.

"You know I've never seen anyone else who continued to heal this long after an accident," Dr. Bolling said. "Must be all the exercise you're doing."

"That, God, and the herbs I've been taking. They've worked wonders healing my wounds and giving me the energy to keep moving. God knew what He was doing when He put those special plants on the earth for us."

"You're a testament to what God will do to heal us when we do our part." He beamed at me. "Hey, are you still working on your book?"

"Yes, it's nearly done." Then realizing something, added, "I never told you why I'm writing it, did I?"

"No. I'm not busy now, so tell me."

I told him about the difficult days in the Trauma ICU. About the doctors and nurses who with a few kind words had soothed my fears and given me hope. And about the tired transporter who'd stopped for a moment to comfort me and ended up changing my life.

Dr. Bolling's face lit up. "I had no idea," he said. "I can't wait to read it. You'll be in great demand to give your testimony."

"There's nothing that would make me happier. I'm almost ready." I smiled at him. "My only regret is that I never got to thank that transporter. Now, she'll never know what she did for me." My smile faded.

We hugged goodbye, but instead of crutching out to the parking lot, I headed through the long hall that connected his office building with the hospital. Taking the elevator to the third floor, with trepidation, I crutched into the ICU. I had to see it again.

As I stood inside the cubicle where I'd lain the first five days after the tree hit me, I looked out the opening toward the nursing station and pictured the friends who'd lined up there to visit me. Smiling at the memory of their radiant faces, alone in that dim space my heart expanded as I recalled the incredible love of the friends, family, nurses and doctors who'd cared so well for me there. "Thank you, Jesus," I whispered.

On the drive home, I made a quick detour to stop by our local EMS to thank the paramedic who had done such a remarkable job straightening and immobilizing my crooked leg at the scene of the accident. Not long after coming home from the hospital, I'd written a note to his boss and was surprised when the paramedic himself wrote back:

> …As you know by now, (and probably that day) your injuries were very severe. Knowing that I was able to demonstrate some skill that aided in your recovery is rewarding to hear. Your kind words made my day…

Now, two years later, I couldn't wait to thank him in person. I pulled into a parking space in front of the EMS building and crutched in.

"What can I do for you?" a woman in a uniform asked.

I explained who I was and why I'd come.

"You're right. You were extremely fortunate that our most experienced paramedic was the one who showed up to help you that night. He'd served in the first Gulf War as a medic and has worked with our agency the past sixteen years. They recently promoted him to Captain over all the emergency personnel in our county. You can go down the hall. His office is the first one on the right."

I crutched slowly down the hall and turned into the open doorway. A nice looking man who might have been in his forties sat behind the desk.

"Hi, I'm Lara Easting. You took care of me after a tree fell on me two years ago. I just wanted to stop in and let you see for yourself how well I'm doing, thanks to you and your team."

His face broke into a grin as he jumped up to cover the ground between us. Gathering me up in his muscular arms, he squeezed me before letting me go. "You know, I rarely get to see my patients after I drop them off at the hospital. I'd been wondering what ever happened to you. I could tell that night you were a fighter. Thank you so much for coming by and showing me know you're okay. "

We talked for a while before I thanked him again and hugged him goodbye. On the ride home, I couldn't stop myself from smiling and thanking God for sending such a dedicated man to take care of me.

Later that same week, I went to see a chiropractor who'd been recommended to me.

Crutching inside her clinic door, I met her. She was a tall woman with a knowing expression. She greeted me and escorted me to a small room.

"Have a seat and tell me about your injuries and why you're here." She sat facing me.

Starting at the top of my head, I worked my way down to my feet.

"Oh my goodness." Her voice cracked with grief.

"It's okay," I replied, not wanting to hear her sympathy or feel my own sadness.

"No, it's not, but it will be," she said, her face earnest. "What happened to you was horrific. And not just your legs and back were fractured when the tree hit you. Other parts were, too. Do you know what I'm saying?"

"I'm not sure."

"Right after the accident, you couldn't stand to feel the grief, the panic, or the despair. You were far too busy just trying to survive. Now, those parts that split off are coming back. The first ones to leave will be the last ones back."

"Why now?" I asked, puzzled.

"Because you're strong enough to deal with them." She smiled. "You're becoming whole again."

I was still processing what she'd said when she spoke again.

"You're like an angel, aware of and sensitive to everything around you and with a loving heart. But you often hide your emotions from others. The time for hiding them is over."

She was right. It was time to take off the mask I sometimes wore to let people think I felt okay even when I didn't. But first, I had some unfinished business. I had to face what remained of my demons. I had to go back to County Hospital.

PURGING DEMONS

Despite my resolve to face the demons at County Hospital, it would be a couple years before I did. By that time, it would be three years since I'd last visited Dr. Norton and five since I'd been a patient in the Trauma Units.

Before I could return, two things happened that forced me to dig deeper into my spiritual well for strength. Ann, almost ninety, had been fighting a tough battle against metastatic breast cancer. Every week or so, I drove north to care for her.

Pierce faced a battle of his own. A gastroenterologist diagnosed him with a severe inflammatory bowel disease and prescribed medications that created serious problems of their own. In typical fashion, I went to work researching what changes in his diet and nutritional supplements might reduce his need for the drugs.

Watching them both suffer, while I felt powerless to help, left me feeling anxious, tired, and sad. Ann was old and frail, but Pierce barely twenty-two.

A short time later, Ann passed away leaving a gaping hole in my heart. Pierce, always close to his grandmother, wept. Even Dave, who'd sometimes been at odds with his mother, felt heartbroken. I spoke at Ann's memorial service, wanting to share the deeply comforting and spiritual side of Ann I'd witnessed in the hospital.

After the service, I focused on getting Pierce well, cooking some of his favorite meals to help him gain back the thirty pounds he'd lost.

"Now I see why you couldn't force yourself to eat anything in the hospital," he said, looking over at me. "These last few weeks the thought of food has made me sick."

"And I see why you were always so upset with me when I wouldn't eat," I countered, gently. "Anyway, thank God, you're getting better."

"People keep telling me God has a plan for my life. But with everything that's happened to both of us, I'm not sure I buy it," he said, not bothering to conceal his anger.

I recognized the familiar question. It was the same one I'd asked myself in the hospital. "I don't blame you for being angry. You've worked so hard, and this illness has dashed your hopes for the future you'd planned. I don't have all the answers, but I can give you my opinion."

Pierce nodded.

"I'm not convinced God has a plan for every detail of our lives, and I've never believed He causes bad things to happen. But when they do and we call out to Him for help, He answers. He draws us closer, guides our steps, and puts the right people in our path. Through their love as well as His own, we find comfort and hope. Then God's incredible peace. And once we do, everything, even healing, becomes possible."

We sat in silence for a few minutes before Pierce spoke again. "How do you know it was Jesus who came to you in the hospital?"

"Because in the worst situation of my life when I cried out to God and a tired looking woman pushing my stretcher answered, I felt nothing but joy. For the first time, I knew I wasn't alone, but filled with a powerful presence that loved me beyond all imagining and wanted me to live. And, no matter what happened, I'd be okay."

I shifted my weight. "I believe that presence was Jesus. After all, it was Jesus I'd been talking to for months before the tree fell, asking Him to let me feel His presence and show me He was real."

"I believe in Jesus but I'm not sure I've ever felt His presence."

"I'll bet you have. You just didn't recognize it, in much the same way that people seem to discount the still small voice within as mere intuition."

"You think so?"

I nodded. "I think Jesus' Spirit is with you right now, and if you want to feel His presence, you can. Just close your eyes, go into your heart, and focus on a memory of a person, place or thing that fills you with an overwhelming sense of wonder or love."

"Can you picture one?"

With his eyes closed, Pierce nodded.

"Now come back into the present, bringing that awareness with you..."

"How do you feel?"

"Good, like everything is okay just as it is."

"Well, that sense of being completely at peace is what came to me in the hospital and changed how I felt about my terrible circumstances. It's a feeling I'll never forget. I've experienced it many times since, simply by remembering. When I do, I think Jesus is reminding me He's with me and loves me." I patted the left side of my chest gently with the palm of my hand. "Pierce, He's with you too. You're not alone. All you have to do is go into your heart to find Him."

Pierce smiled. All of my son's frown lines had faded and light shown in his eyes. Healing had begun.

After Ann's service, I had little interest in making the long drive to the big city which had been her home as well as County Hospital's. Little interest, until the still small voice, grew into a yell.

Life in the Trauma ICUs and Hyperbaric had often been dark, terrifying, and surreal. And though I'd already done an enormous amount of healing, sometimes painful memories haunted my dreams. My visit to the Regional Medical ICU had made certain I remembered the wonderful gifts God had given me in the first hospital. Maybe a trip to County Hospital would do the same.

So, in late 2014, I loaded my walker into the back of my car. "It's a twenty-minute walk from the parking deck to the Trauma Unit," Dave had warned. "You'll need the walker to give your legs a rest."

Driving up the highway, finally on my way, my heart fluttered with excitement and a great deal of trepidation. "Jesus, please help me get exactly what I need from this trip," I whispered. The warmth in my chest told me He would.

I turned into the big city and after several miles, crested a hill. I caught sight of the yellow brick behemoth that rose sparkling from the ruins of a neighborhood whose glory days had long since passed. County Hospital.

In the parking deck, I pulled into the last available space in the entire place, lifted my walker out of the car, and took the elevator down to the first floor.

I strolled into the Physicians Center, pushing my walker in front of me, and took another elevator to Dr. Norton's new office.

The receptionist waited only a minute before sending me in. I left my walker in the waiting area and opened the door. There, in a line, smiling at me, stood Dr. Norton, his x-ray technician, and physician's assistant. "Not even a limp," Dr. Norton said.

"Well, it's still early in the day," I said, laughing and hugging each in turn.

We stood visiting for ten minutes before I thanked them for all they'd done and said goodbye. Strolling back to the front and grabbing my walker, I smiled at the receptionist. "Guess I'll be heading over to the hospital Trauma Floor."

"That's a long walk. Why don't you let me call you a transporter?"

"That would be great."

In the time it took to turn around and take a seat, a jovial woman bounded in pushing a wheelchair. "Where to?" she asked.

"The Trauma Floor, please."

"Are you visiting a patient there?"

"No, I *was* a patient there five years ago. I just came for a visit."

The transporter looked puzzled so I added, "I just want to see if the Trauma Unit's still as scary as I remembered."

Propelling me out of the office and through the atrium teeming with visitors, she deftly maneuvered me through a dozen corridors bustling with staff and patients. We finally stopped in front of a bank of elevators.

"How long were you in the hospital?" Her voice broke the silence.

"About six weeks in this one."

"Your injuries must have been pretty bad."

"They were."

Ding. The doors opened and she pushed me onto the elevator.

As we ascended, I took a deep breath and said a prayer to give me strength to face whatever came next. The car came to a stop on the fifth floor and the door opened. I looked up and down the hall for any sign of something I recognized. Nothing. Then, I saw it in the distance. The Trauma Unit nursing station. A huge L-shaped counter opened to the ceiling, just as I remembered. Transporters had pushed my gurney past it dozens of times on my way to Hyperbaric, Radiology, and the Surgery Department.

Today, a stranger stood behind it. Her badge read "Registered Nurse" and she was typing as she talked on the phone.

I stood from the wheelchair and turned to face the transporter. "Thank you for the ride."

"No problem. Do you want me to wait?"

"No, that's okay, I might be awhile."

"My name is Betty. Have them call me when you're done."

"Okay, I will."

I walked slowly, but deliberately up to the counter, my walker in tow.

The nurse glanced up. "May I help you?"

"I'm a registered nurse, and I was a patient here a few years ago. I spent six weeks on this floor. Would it be possible for me to see one of the rooms again?" I motioned to my left. "I'm pretty sure I stayed in one of those."

For a moment, she studied me. "The second one is empty if you want to go in."

Limping, I pushed the walker ten yards down the hall before I stopped in the doorway. The room was so much smaller than I remembered. Smaller and brighter.

My stomach tightened. Taking slow, methodical steps, I walked past the hospital bed, still situated in the middle of the floor, and up to the head. I turned around to face the door, needing to feel what it had been like to be a patient there.

Other than its diminutive size and brightness, everything looked the same. A sink hung on the wall to the right of the foot of the bed. Nurses and techs had washed their hands and filled my water pitcher there. On the opposite side was a corner shelf. When I'd been a patient, packages of protein shakes I couldn't drink had overflowed those shelves and landed unceremoniously onto the floor, upsetting my dietician. To my right and even with the head of the bed, a single shelf perched high on the wall. A hospital phone had been there and later my cell phone, pad of paper, and pen. *No wonder I could never reach them.* IV poles still stood at attention like sentinels watching over the now empty bed from all four corners of its frame.

I stared past the open curtain that divided my room from its alcove, out the door, and into the hallway. Through that portal, I'd entertained myself for hours watching the throngs of visitors, nurses, and injured patients pass by. Some of the lucky ones, guided by physical therapists, had taken their first tentative steps toward freedom. They'd been my lifelines to the outside world, reminders of what might be waiting.

Today, the hall was quiet. Today, it was my turn.

In the earliest days in the Trauma Unit, my room had looked cavernous, dark, and foreboding. Ghosts had lingered in the shadows and strangers' voices reverberated in the hall. Never before had I felt so frightened, alone, or confused. Now, as I peered around the room, I could do something I'd never been able to do as a patient. I could turn to look at what lay behind me. A picture window.

"Lara, we sure wish you could see this," Dave had once said.

Now, I walked over to the window and drank in the view. In the distance, a fast moving river wound its way through the valley. Below, cars and pedestrians bustled their way through the city street. All of a sudden, I felt cheated. *All those weeks lying here and no one found a way to turn me around to see this?*

I turned back around and sat down on a bench under the window. For a good ten minutes, I closed my eyes. Images came flooding back, some disturbing. Silent nurses appeared in the dark, working overhead while I lay scared and helpless below. Tears welled in my eyes and trickled down my face. A small sob bubbled from my throat.

Then out of the shadows came others. Sara, the nurse who'd sat with me charting while I'd slept, Cat, the float pool nurse who'd brought me hot tea to comfort me during withdrawal from hydromorphone, Francesca, the diligent dietician, Dr. Lassiter and Dr. Norton. All of them were smiling down on me.

I opened my eyes. Light streamed in the window and sparkled into every corner. The shadows and ghosts had gone. As suddenly as the memories had come, they retreated into the sunlight. All that was left was peace.

A healing place.

I took a few minutes to soak it all in before I stood, grabbed my walker, and pushed it back out the door. "How do I get to Hyperbaric?" I asked a man in the nurse's station.

"It's at the other end of the hospital. Do you need me to call you a transporter?"

"No, that's okay." I didn't want company on this leg of my journey.

The man gave me directions, and I made a mental note before setting out with my walker. By the time I wound my way down several long corridors, stopped a few times to rest on the walker's seat, and took two elevators to arrive in the basement of the hospital, I was limping like Long John Silver. A sign over a door at the end of the hall read, HYPERBARIC UNIT. It was twelve-thirty when I walked in.

The place appeared to be empty except for a woman who sat behind a small counter. "Hi, can I help you?"

"I'm the nurse who called you a couple weeks ago to see if it would be okay to come visit your department."

"Oh, yes," she replied, jumping up. "I'm so sorry the charge nurse never called you back. She got the message mixed up. But this is a perfect time for you to go in. All our morning patients have gone."

"I remember you. You're the nurse who I asked for some hydromorphone. You told me you couldn't give me anything that strong. I think I may have cried."

"You know I've always felt bad we couldn't do more for patients like you who were in so much pain, but the hospital still won't let us give hydromorphone in here." She looked apologetic. She led me past the counter and into a much larger room. Four enormous transparent torpedo-shaped chambers stood in a line facing me.

"That's it," I said, excited. "It's the one to the right." I walked over to the big unit and stopped.

She pulled a tarp off the chamber and turned to look at me. "Do you need anything else?"

"Can I use that stool?" I motioned toward a medical stool across the room.

"Sure, just make yourself comfortable. Stay as long as you want."

I rolled the stool over and sat down a few feet from the chamber. It looked exactly as I remembered, a clear, tight container with a narrow stretcher inside, and a hatch that slammed shut at one end. A TV still hung from the ceiling near the far end. It was the same one I'd tried watching to distract myself from the devils and demons that had writhed and danced in front of my eyes. "In Jesus' name, devils be gone," I'd shouted at them. The demons had faded. Had Jesus made them go away? My heart told me He had.

I closed my eyes and remembered lying in the chamber, the glass wall just inches from my face. Mr. Layton, the technician, stood just outside giving me a menacing look. Then he'd turned his back and walked away.

My chest tightened. For a moment I came back to the present. "Holy Spirit, help me let go of memories that no longer benefit me," I whispered.

Peace filled me. I saw Mr. Layton fading and in his place a transporter's face appeared. She was a tired looking woman. I began to weep and call out to God.

"You're going to be okay. God is going to heal you," she'd said in a commanding voice.

The weight on my chest had lifted. I was in the biggest mess of my life but all I could feel was peace.

The peace that passes all understanding.

The image of the transporter soon left and was replaced by one of Ann, Pierce, and Dave standing over me, smiling. "Lara," Dave said, "the hyperbaric oxygen's doing a great job. You're starting to look a little more like yourself."

That memory vanished, too, only to be replaced by a revelation. The pressurized oxygen hadn't just saved my legs and face. Along with God's healing herbs, it had restored my brain and given me back my life.

I opened my eyes. I stared hard into the chamber, putting my hand out and laying it on the glass. It felt smooth and soothing to the touch. Someone had covered the mattress pad inside with a fuzzy sheet. It looked soft, inviting, and cozy like a womb.

"Thank you," I whispered, tears starting down my cheeks. "Thank you for healing me. And thank you, Jesus, Holy Spirit for making me come back here to see it."

"Is everything okay?" The nurse stood in the doorway, looking concerned.

"Just fine. I've had a love-hate relationship with this place for years, but not anymore. I'm so glad I came."

I rose slowly, gathered my things, and thought of something else. "By the way, where is the little rectangular hyperbaric chamber that used to be next to this one? The first time I woke up in here, I saw an old man, must have been one of your ambulatory patients, climbing into it carrying his newspaper. There was a chair inside. I remember thinking, 'Lucky man who can come and go as he pleases.'

The nurse raised an eyebrow and gave me a curious look. "I've been here over twenty years, and we've never had a hyperbaric chamber like that. Just these four. It must have been all the medication you were on."

"Or a message," I said, quietly. "Maybe God was trying to show me what was possible to give me hope."

"I never thought of it like that. Can I call you a transporter? It's a long walk back to the parking deck."

In five minutes, Betty bounded in pushing a wheelchair. "Did you get what you came for?"

I smiled and climbed aboard. As Betty pushed, I talked. "I didn't tell you before, but when I was a patient here, I had some pretty rough times. But it was one of your fellow transporters who changed things. She gave me hope. Honestly, she probably saved my life. I only regret I never got her name."

Betty stopped pushing and came around to look at me. Her mouth dropped open, and she stared in amazement. "Wow, what did she look like?"

"She was black, probably in her late thirties, and slim. When she spoke, her voice was full of conviction."

"Tamara. That's Tamara!" she exclaimed. "She's the only slim woman on the transport team and she's full of the spirit." Betty laughed. "Had to be her."

My eyes widened with amazement. Tamara! Yes, of course. Somehow I knew she was the one. Now, I had to thank her and let her know what she'd done.

"Here," I said, reaching in my purse and handing Betty a card. "Would you give Tamara my telephone number? Tell her I would really love to thank her personally."

Betty nodded. Once back inside my car, I grinned, fist-pumped the air, and let out a whoop. "Thank you, Jesus. Thank you, Holy Spirit. Thank you for helping me find Tamara."

ANOTHER MIRACLE

A week later, after my trip to County Hospital, I still hadn't heard from Tamara. Did she get my message? Was she reluctant to call?

Frustrated, I called the hospital. "The supervisor in the Transporter Office, please."

"They have a new one," the operator said. "I'll connect you."

It rang and rang and then went to voice mail. A young man's voice came on. I left a message.

Several days went by. I dialed him again. This time the call went straight to voice mail.

Would he ever return my call?

A few days later, he did.

"You're right; Tamara was a wonderful employee, but she no longer works here. She's been promoted off-site under a different supervisor."

"Please help me," I said, feeling a door closing. "I really want to tell Tamara and her boss how much I appreciate what she did." I told him the story.

"I'll call her supervisor and give her your number."

Three more days passed. Had I gotten this close only to be let down? Surely, God hadn't dangled the carrot only to jerk it away.

"Lord, please have Tamara call."

That night, I was sitting in my writer's group when my cell phone rang.

"Hello, Lara? It's Tamara."

I jumped up, almost dropping the phone, and rushed from the room. My heart was pounding through my chest and my hands trembled. Hurrying into a quiet room next door, I collapsed into an easy chair. "Oh my God, is it really you? This is an answer to my prayer."

I couldn't believe it. The woman who'd given me so much hope with only a few short sentences was actually speaking to me.

"No, I should thank you. It was wonderful that you called to let me know how much I'd helped."

"Tamara, you didn't just help me. Despite how exhausted you looked, you led me to Jesus and He saved my life. Because of you, I'm still alive and enjoying myself. I've gotten to see my son grow into a man and spend more time with my husband."

"Thank you, so much." Her voice cracked with emotion.

"I know it's been five years, and you've transported hundreds of patients since, so you probably don't remember me."

"No, I'm pretty sure I do."

"You do? Well, I'm not sure how much you remember, but the day you came to pick me up from Hyperbaric, I was at the end of my rope. For the first time, I could see what a mess I was in and how little control I had. To make matters worse, a few of my nurses and techs were treating me badly. I thought they cared so little they might even let me die."

"That's awful."

"It was, but I'm only telling you this so you'll understand just how low I was feeling that day. Despite my depressed state, I remember noticing how tired and worn down you looked. It was as if you had the weight of the world on your shoulders. But when I wept and cried out to God, your appearance changed. There was power in your voice and light shone in your eyes. You looked like a completely different person. 'You're going to be okay,' you said, 'God is going to heal you.' I'd never really had that much faith, but in that moment, I believed you. All pain left my body, and a peace like nothing I'd ever experienced filled my heart. That's when I knew. Jesus had spoken through you and awakened His Spirit within me. I was no longer afraid. God wanted me to live. I was going to be okay."

"Thank you so much for telling me," she said, her voice quavering with emotion. "It means the world to know I made such a difference...

I guess we never really know how what we say or do is going to affect another person, do we?"

"No, we don't. If you hadn't stopped that day to encourage me and allow God to use you in that way, I don't know if I'd be here today. One thing for sure, what you said changed me and gave me the strength and faith to face another day." I paused... But that's enough about me. I want to know more about you and how you've been doing these past five years."

"To be honest, I've had my ups and downs." She sounded weary.

"I kind of guessed that from how tired you looked that day. You know, Tamara, we really don't know much about each other, but I'd love to hear more."

"Well, I'm a single parent with three kids. I was very young when I had them. My husband left and never paid any child support, so I had to work two jobs. I had to accept that I was a single parent and try to make the best of it. I didn't want to go around pissed off all the time so I told myself 'Tamara, be positive and speak positively to others.' Sometimes, that wasn't easy."

"You made the choice to be happy, rather than bitter. I know your children benefited from that decision. I certainly did."

"I had to lean a lot on God. That's how I learned that God would help even the smallest person, so I felt it was important to pass it on."

Tamara wasted few words and those she uttered were honest, measured, and impeccable just like the transporter's I remembered.

"I think God wants us to ask Him for help," she continued. "Why, I believe he's hearing us right now. We're speaking Him into existence by talking about Him in this way. He's right here within us. You know, we're really just here to praise Him and help each other."

"I love how you put things. I've probably told the story about what you did for me and how it changed my life a hundred times. People tell me it inspires them and gives them hope. And look at me. I had little faith and now I have a lot. That's all because of you, Tamara."

"Wow. I can't believe this. You have no idea what it means to hear how much I helped you. But wouldn't it be funny, if I wasn't the right person?" She laughed.

"Oh, you're definitely the one."

When I hung up the phone, I settled back into the chair and thought about everything Tamara had said before returning to my writers' group. I pondered the setbacks I'd encountered trying to reach her. After the tree fell, God had given me more than my share of miracles. He'd carefully put the people in place to make sure I survived and walked again. He brought others to encourage and assist me financially. He'd even sent an angel in the form of a tired transporter to give me hope. Everything He'd done, He did by working through others. There'd been so much evidence of His loving touch everywhere I looked.

Then, very slowly, my life had returned to normal. Not the old normal but a new one. And as I fell into the routine of my new life, memories of what happened in the hospitals had faded, and I sometimes forgot to look for God's magic in the world.

But God wasn't finished with me yet. Even after I'd stopped looking for a miracle, God had been busy working on a new one. What He had done once again to arrange the pieces of my life into a complete and positive whole was nothing short of amazing. I'd gone back to County Hospital hoping to purge a few demons and come back blessed beyond measure. I'd returned with a pearl of a friend named Tamara, a shining gem amidst so much pain. It was a clear testimony to how God worked. My life had once again come full circle.

In the days after my conversation with Tamara, other thoughts came to me. I knew Jesus, working through Tamara, had changed me. He'd given me hope and calmed my fears. What I'd never anticipated was how He would also end up helping Tamara. But hearing the joy in her voice, I knew He had.

I pondered something else. I'd come to believe Jesus' Spirit was not just with me but part of me. If that were true, it suggested I was powerful beyond measure. So was Tamera. So were we all. It was a truth I'd considered as a small child but somehow forgotten.

Now, I considered it again and felt ready to give my testimony. Maybe if I asked her, Tamara would come with me and share hers, too.

A few weeks later, Dave and I were driving up our hill when he stopped the car and stared out his window. "Look over there." He pointed to the place where the dead tree had collapsed on me. New saplings now stood in its place. The old, dead pine had crumbled, providing fertile ground for new trees to grow, just as pieces of my old life had fallen away making room for my spirit to blossom.

"Maybe it's a sign," I said, feeling happy.

"Maybe," Dave agreed.

Up at the house, I'd just stepped inside and sat down on the love seat when my husband shouted from the front door. "Lara, you need to come out here and see this."

I knew it must be important, so I got up, grabbed my cane, and ambled toward the open door where he stood. To my surprise, he took my hand and led me slowly, carefully out into the yard to get a closer look. He pointed at the snowball bush in Marley's pen.

I peered across the fence and saw what had him so excited. The entire surface of the bush was covered in white blossoms while dozens of butterflies were dancing on them. There were yellow and black Viceroys and Swallowtails with iridescent blue and black wings fluttering over the flowers.

"I've never seen anything like it," he said.

"Me neither. Maybe it's another sign," I whispered, smiling. "Maybe God's telling us to have hope, to never give up."

Dave, who'd always seen God most clearly in the natural world, smiled back. "Now, that's the kind of message even I can relate to."

He put his arm around my shoulder and pulled me close. I felt a tingle pass through my body. We watched in silent delight as the butterflies played on the white flowery bush. A warm breeze rustled the leaves on the trees overhead. It would take time, but we would get through this new chapter together.

The End

UPDATES

Lara's back and legs continue to grow stronger. She bikes most weeks with her husband and works out. She also teaches people how to heal by eating the right foods and supplementing with God's healing plants (herbs). In her spare time, she volunteers in Pastoral Care at her church, plays guitar and sings, and shares her story with anyone who has suffered loss and needs to find hope.

In 2016, Dave retired, taking up bike riding, bird watching, and photography to spend more time in nature. He also likes to accompany Lara on his bass guitar. Dave and Lara just celebrated their thirty second anniversaries.

Pierce's health continues to improve. He works at the local police department, now as a Sergeant. In 2015, he was baptized and married a beautiful and compassionate woman, a registered nurse and accomplished photographer. The two of them live in a house with their three cats not far from Dave and Lara.

Printed in the United States
By Bookmasters